TREDEGAR IRON WORKS

TREDEGAR IRON WORKS

RICHMOND'S FOUNDRY ON THE JAMES

NATHAN VERNON MADISON

Published by The History Press
Charleston, SC
www.historypress.net

Copyright © 2015 by Nathan Vernon Madison
All rights reserved

Front cover, top: Tredegar Ironworks, Wales, circa 1860. *Blaenau Gwent Heritage Forum*; *bottom*: Tredegar Iron Works, Richmond, Virginia, 1992. *Virginia Commonwealth University Libraries.*

First published 2015

Manufactured in the United States

ISBN 978.1.46711.894.1

Library of Congress Control Number: 2015952222

Notice: The information in this book is true and complete to the best of our knowledge. It is offered without guarantee on the part of the author or The History Press. The author and The History Press disclaim all liability in connection with the use of this book.

All rights reserved. No part of this book may be reproduced or transmitted in any form whatsoever without prior written permission from the publisher except in the case of brief quotations embodied in critical articles and reviews.

But man has become the miner and the artificer far more so than in Biblical days, and from one end of the Earth to the other he has burrowed, and by persistent labor and skill brought all the metals into the domestic, scientific, or trading uses of the world...Instinctively, man knows that there are incalculable treasures to be won without the aid of genii or of lamp, and this thought-legacy has been handed down the ages, and each age has labored, and each age has won.
—*Charles Wilkins,* The History of the Iron, Steel, Tinplate and Other Trades of Wales, *1903*

Our family felt that the Tredegar was the "Papa" of all who worked there. It was home, the place you went when you had problems. Everyone knew each other.
—*Elwood O. Harris, 1985*

CONTENTS

Foreword, by Peter Morgan Jones   9
Acknowledgements   13
Introduction   15

1. Origins to 1849   19
2. 1849–1865   47
3. 1865–1892   78
4. 1892–1918   104
5. 1918–1957   131

Epilogue   161
Notes   169
Index   189
About the Author   192

Foreword

A TALE OF TWO TREDEGARS

The name "Tredegar" is rare even in Wales, where it originated, being found only at Tredegar House—a seventeenth-century gentry mansion near Newport and the sea—together with Tredegar and New Tredegar, nineteenth-century industrial settlements that developed on its upland estate. Such rarity made the existence of similarly named ironworks some three thousand transatlantic miles apart—one in Wales, the other at Richmond, Virginia—appear more than mere coincidence. Clearly, there had to be some underlying reason they shared this name, but any relationship between the two sites seemed to have been forgotten, overlooked or even ignored.

Over the years, some living in the Welsh town of Tredegar, named for its eponymous ironworks, had been intrigued by the matter, especially in light of Tredegar's established U.S. associations. In the nineteenth century, individuals and even entire families had migrated from the town to various parts of the United States, seeking work and prosperity in its coalfields or as settlers on the country's expanding western frontier. Yet apart from miners or farmers, there were others whose impact on their adopted country was even more marked. One example was Allan Pinkerton, of U.S. detective agency fame, who claimed to have marched with local men in the 1839 Chartist attack on Newport. Another was Tredegar-born James Davies, "Puddler Jim," who became a U.S. senator, presidential candidate, initiator of the world's first legislated minimum wage and founder of Moose International, of which, incidentally, Tredegar has its "Number One Lodge." These and

Foreword

other local contributions to U.S. development were known and appreciated, but any Richmond association remained a mystery.

Intrigued by this matter, in 1957, a teacher in the town of Tredegar, David Perry, wrote to both London's U.S. Embassy and Richmond's still-extant Tredegar Company querying whether some link might exist between the two similarly named works. Responses, though courteous, were disappointing, with Richmond's Tredegar stating that, although its early works had certainly employed Welsh migrant ironworkers, it had not been founded by anyone from that country, and no record existed of any other connection. Frustrated, Perry then abandoned his search, believing that this reply from what he considered a prime source had to be taken as established fact.

There the matter rested for over forty years until the *Hereford Times* newspaper of November 24, 1838, was found to contain a short obituary entitled "From a Richmond Paper" that not only established a link between the two Tredegars but also named the man responsible: "Rhys Davies. Died at Richmond Virginia early Sunday morning in consequence of having been stabbed a fortnight ago."

Rhys Davies—a brilliant engineer—had received his training in a town and works sited one thousand feet above sea level at the South Wales Coalfield's northern edge. Furnaces and towns had sprung up along a narrow strip of land where rich mineral seams outcropped, the fiery glow on night skies attracting rural dwellers to this new "Iron El Dorado." Small-scale ironworking had taken place here for millennia, but by the early nineteenth century, when Rhys Davies arrived, these remote uplands were known more for their grouse and pheasant shooting than charcoal-fired furnace or forge. From this region, dotted with prehistoric cairns and burials, wooded valleys ran some twenty miles southward to the Severn Sea, their rapidly flowing streams often serving as boundaries for largely undeveloped and low-income estates. With little more than rough tracks for communication, much of this area would remain isolated and primitive until industry's sudden arrival, when farms and woodlands would be swept away by iron furnaces, settlements, tramroads and turnpikes. Even though they despoiled landscape, these new industries bestowed prosperity on their workers while providing vast wealth for estate owners and ironmasters. Within very few years, Tredegar Iron Works would make the Morgan family of Tredegar House millionaires.

The speed of change was dramatic. Tredegar Iron Works was pouring white-hot metal twelve months after being proposed. National needs were the spur: by the late eighteenth century, Britain's Continental wars and burgeoning Industrial Revolution were demanding ever more iron, the raw

Foreword

```
                    ESTABLISHED 1836
            TREDEGAR  COMPANY
         PROJECTILES · IRON CASTINGS · BARS
           JOINT BARS · SPIKES · HORSE SHOES
                RICHMOND  (T)  VIRGINIA
                                       April 18, 1957

Mr. David R. Perry,
Crown Cottage
Nantybwch
Tredegar
Monmouthshire, Great Britain

Dear Mr. Perry:

            It was interesting to receive your letter and
I will try to answer your questions.

            (I) Our company was founded in 1836, not by
emigrants from Wales. I understand there were employees
who came from Wales but mostly they were iron workers and
I don't believe had much to do with management.

            (II) I do not know whether there are any of
their descendants still living here, but doubtless there are.

            (III) We pronounce Tredegar incorrectly and
do not accent the "dee" as you do.

            Our company has made most products of iron in
the olden days and steel in more recent years. We operate
re-rolling mills only and do not make steel.

            During the War between the States the company
was known as the "Arsenal of the Confederacy" and produced
much cannon and shot. It also rolled iron 8" x 2" for
The Merrimac, the first ironclad vessel of the Confederacy.

            In recent months we have merged with a paper
company and will no longer continue operation at the old
location. However, the Tredegar Timber Company, Inc. has
been formed and chartered for manufacture of many items of
iron and steel which we formerly made.

            There is a small town, now almost a siding,
called Tredegar, Alabama, but I do not know anything of the
history of this little town.
```

An April 18, 1957 letter from E.H. Trigg of the Tredegar Division of Albemarle Paper Manufacturing Company, replying to David Perry's inquiry regarding the Welsh origins of Tredegar. *Image courtesy of Peter Morgan-Jones.*

materials of which were known to lie in abundance along the coalfield's northern edge. Along this narrow belt little more than two miles wide, iron towns had rapidly developed, attracting thousands from rural districts to seek employment and prosperity, among them a young Rhys Davies, whose story might never have been known had it not been for a Herefordshire newspaper paragraph.

Foreword

The mystery had been solved and connection between the two Tredegars explained. But why use the same name? In 1890, Richmond general Joseph R. Anderson solved the problem by stating that Mr. F.R. Deane, the U.S. works' former proprietor, had named it Tredegar Iron Works "in compliment to Mr. Davis [sic] who was educated at the celebrated Welsh establishment"—permission to use the title, having been granted, incidentally, by Sam Homfray Jr., ironmaster of Tredegar, Wales.

It would be difficult to overemphasize the historical and social significance of either town. Among its other achievements, Tredegar, Wales, produced Daniel Gooch, the engineer whose transatlantic and other oceanic telegraph cables changed international communication from weeks and months to minutes, while the Richmond works led to that city becoming the Confederate capital and a Civil War arsenal. The world's first steam locomotive to run on rails was initiated by the Welsh Tredegar's ironmaster, and the Virginia works supplied equipment for the United States' expanding railways and rolled armour plating for the first ironclads. Both Tredegars had national and world influence, but ironically, that of Richmond would lay the foundation for the U.S. competition that helped end iron making in Wales. However, each of these great works bestowed a legacy of national and world development of which both nations should be proud.

For these, and many other reasons, it is a privilege to provide the foreword for this important book and help strengthen the relationship between these two remarkable Tredegars.

—Peter Morgan Jones
Former University of Wales extra-mural lecturer,
current vice-chairman of the Blaeneu Gwent Heritage Forum and
editor of the *Blaenau Gwent Heritage Forum Journal*

ACKNOWLEDGEMENTS

I have a good number of friends and co-workers to thank regarding this work, all of whom I simply lack the room to cite sufficiently. My co-workers at Historic Tredegar, including Emma Bishop, Katrina Mantooth Hitt, Candace Hart, Ben Anderson, Eric and Scott Slaughter, Brian Musselwhite, Gail Anderson, Rachel Harper and Jason Spellman, each in their own way, helped allow for the time and opportunity to research and write this story. Kristen Gray was instrumental in helping to establish contacts between myself and the descendants of several Tredegar workmen from all over the United States—contacts that I cannot imagine would have been possible otherwise. I owe thanks to Michael Gorman for his work on a National Park Service source file of Tredegar-related newspaper articles that has proved immensely helpful to this project; I am also indebted to Mike for many hours' worth of discussion that contributed a great deal to formulating the narrative to tell the history of Tredegar. I thank Joshua LeHuray for his help in my attempts to make sense of some of the Tredegar Archives' oft-confusing account ledgers. My appreciation also belongs to the Virginia Historical Society; the Botetourt County Historical Society; the staffs of the Library of Virginia, particularly Kristen Allen and Dave Grabareck, as well as the staff of the Manuscripts department; Nicole Kappatos, archivist at the *Richmond Times-Dispatch*; and Kelly Kerney at the Valentine Museum for the aid I received in perusing its expansive (and at times daunting) collections and archives. My gratitude to Christy Coleman, co-president of the American Civil War Museum, for her support and advice concerning my delving into

Acknowledgements

Tredegar's past, even before this project was conceived. For personal and familial remembrances, I sincerely thank Bruce Gottwald, Anne Hosbon Freeman, Charles Miller, Viola Baecher, Howard Templin and Don Browne.

And thank you to Peter Morgan-Jones of the Blaenau Gwent Heritage Forum and Kevin Phillips of Made in Tredegar for the information they generously and enthusiastically provided regarding "our" works' Welsh namesake and for friendships that have renewed ties between the "two Tredegars."

Of course, with this and all endeavors, my greatest appreciation is to my family: my parents, James and Sylvia Madison, and my sister, Natalie Casper, who indulged me enough to accompany me through the thick of Botetourt County forests in search of long-forgotten and crumbling blast furnaces.

August 2015
Richmond, Virginia

INTRODUCTION

The Tredegar Iron Works of Richmond, Virginia, has for the last 150 years existed as an inextricable facet of historiographical explorations into the American Civil War, and with good reason—as the largest cannonmaker within the confines of the Confederacy, Tredegar was a leading factor behind the relocation of the Confederate capital from Montgomery to Richmond, as well as one of several firms that composed the backbone of Southern industry in the years immediately preceding and following 1861. There exists a wealth of information and annals of historical research regarding Tredegar's service during the Civil War, the most notable examples being Kathleen Bruce's *Virginia Iron Manufacture in the Slave Era* (1930) and Charles Dew's *Ironmaker to the Confederacy—Joseph Reid Anderson and the Tredegar Iron Works* (1966), expertly researched and masterfully written accounts of Tredegar's operations before and during the Civil War. Numerous other journal, magazine and online articles over the years have only further contributed to a better understanding of this Richmond institution's role during the war.

On the other hand, the Civil War encompasses only 4 years of Tredegar's 120-year history—a minute percentage of a much longer and varied story. The only significant work to chronicle Tredegar's postwar existence is Dennis Maher Hallerman's 1978 master's thesis, "The Tredegar Iron Works: 1865–1875"; outside of that endeavor, very little exists. What little has been written regarding Tredegar beyond the Civil War portrays the company as something of a fading giant, an enterprise long past its prime that never

Introduction

fully recovered from the ravages of war; a relic of the Old South that had receded to the point of near obscurity by the turn of the twentieth century. This understanding has persisted throughout the last several decades of scholarship; Brady Banta's contention, in *Iron and Steel in the Nineteenth Century* (1989), that Tredegar, by the late 1890s, had become a "profitable, but parochial, iron foundry," while certainly correct in ascribing much of the firm's decline to its unwillingness to adopt steel, ignores, on some level, Tredegar's significant role throughout the railroad, horseshoe and ordnance industries well into the early 1920s.

Tredegar's role as a "minor player in the iron industry" just before the turn of the century, as described by Diane Telgen, again does not make note of a company that, at that time, was recording millions of dollars in sales from across the country, and whose principal shareholders were among the wealthiest of Virginia's citizens.[1]

For many decades, Tredegar was the chief employer in the city of Richmond, and before Fort Sumter, it was already the largest ironworks in the southern states. Tredegar successfully competed with larger and more established firms in the North for highly coveted U.S. government contracts, both before and after the Civil War, producing everything from cannons to steamships to shells. Tredegar was a major supplier to the railroad industry, not just in the South but across the nation, particularly during the postwar railroad boom of the late 1860s and early 1870s. Throughout its history, it served as employer to and, to a large degree, an engine of assimilation for a significant portion of Richmond's immigrant population; many of these workers either remained at Tredegar for the entirety of their working lives or moved on and served other companies and municipalities with abilities learned and honed on the banks of the James River. In a boast that can be held by only a few select firms, the Tredegar weathered no fewer than ten nationwide economic downturns throughout its history. Even after its closure in the mid-twentieth century, Tredegar remained a part of Richmond; its fires long extinguished, its storied history and importance would not allow it to be razed and something else, something invariably lesser, erected in its stead.

From 1847 to the mid-1940s, General Joseph Reid Anderson and his descendants owned and operated the works and, in the process, became just as much of a Richmond institution as the ironworks itself. Writers past have written of J.R. Anderson in a number of lights, mostly fairly positive. Fritz Redlich, in his *History of American Business Leaders* (1940), wrote that he was "one of the greatest organizers of his generation" and that "Anderson was the organizational genius of this group of coevals," a cadre of industrial

Introduction

leaders, including Henry Frick and Leland Stanford.² Clay Bailey, in his article "Joseph R. Anderson of Tredegar," referred to Anderson as the "Carnegie of the Confederacy."³ While Redlich's assessment of Anderson's organizational abilities are, to a large degree, supportable, Anderson cannot accurately be described as being in the same arena as Carnegie, J. Pierpont Morgan and other luminaries of America's Gilded Age. The keeping of the company in the family was not dissimilar from the Vanderbilts' hereditary ownership of the New York Central railway, yet the size and scope of the operation is the divergence. While no small operation, Tredegar's failure to adapt to an economy increasingly built on steel created invisible barriers to growth beyond a certain point; as Bessemer convertors at Andrew Carnegie's steel plant in Braddock, Pennsylvania, were going into blast for the first time, Tredegar continued to produce the same iron implements as it had three decades prior. Anderson did not manage Tredegar as a modern corporation, along the lines of U.S. Steel, Standard Oil, Ford or other companies present at the end of the nineteenth century and the dawn of the twentieth—rather, Tredegar was, in many ways, operated more along the lines of a small, antebellum southern enterprise. The survival of this enterprise and its continued profitability were, to be sure, of grave concern to the owners, but certain factors—particularly the keeping of the company (and most of its stock) within the family and an apprehension toward expansion and experimentation demonstrated at several instances—amalgamate with one another to produce an operation very much at home in the antebellum South and somewhat antiquated by the time of the pecuniary empires helmed by Carnegie, Morgan, Munsey, Pullman and the like.

The Andersons were a constant presence in everyday Richmond life, lauded and praised by the press, their fellow Richmonders and even their employees as businessmen of the highest order and stalwarts of the community. If a central theme of this work is to explain the history of the Tredegar Iron Works, a second point is to demonstrate this difference between Tredegar and many of its contemporaries—it was not a modern-style corporate entity, nor was it simply a small-time local business. Rather, it was an interesting halfway point between the two, an amalgamation of the antebellum family enterprise and the nationwide business model of the Gilded Age, with a corporate and social identity all its own.

If judged solely by the monolithic standards of a J. Pierpont Morgan or an Andrew Carnegie, Joseph Reid Anderson would be considered a minor success, but it is my contention that Anderson harbored no ambition toward being a Morgan or a Carnegie, nor were there any such aspirations on the

Introduction

part of his descendants. Actions that would have been required in order to reach such national prominence would have clashed with the paternalistic nature through which he managed Tredegar. Anderson wished to be a First Citizen of Richmond rather than of the entire United States.

I have endeavored to provide an overall history of the company, making use of the Tredegar Business Records held at the Library of Virginia and even reaching back to the firm's namesake in the Welsh countryside just west of Monmouthshire, founded at the turn of the nineteenth century. The Tredegar Business Records are, in a word, immense—thousands upon thousands of boxes, folders and ledgers that constitute arguably one of the most complete records of any antebellum (or post-bellum) business, all in one location, and within a five-minute drive from that business's remnants, no less. The history of the site on the James River that would eventually hold the works is covered—a history that does not end in 1957 with the cessation of manufacturing operations at Tredegar. In a manner of speaking, that was the beginning of an entirely new chapter that is still unfolding to this day.

This work is intended to provide what has been lacking in years past: an overall, concise history of the Tredegar Iron Works. There is no intention on my part, however, to record the "end all" composition of Tredegar historiography—the sheer volume of information regarding the company and the myriad facets of social, economic and industrial history into which it reaches require far more pages than what is found here. There are many facts, stories and incidents that I have decided to omit for no other reason than that, at some point, work on this particular history of Tredegar had to come to a conclusion. It is hoped that this is only the first of many inquiries into the history of Tredegar and that, in time, many aspects of its story will be explored further.

I approached this work as I would approach a biography, in this case not of a person but of a company—its forebears, its birth, the trials and tribulations experienced over the course of its life, its waning years and, ultimately, its end and its legacy.

Chapter 1

ORIGINS TO 1849

Beginnings

The history of Richmond's Tredegar Iron Works actually begins decades before its founding, and not in Richmond or even in the United States. This history has its origins in the United Kingdom. Before there was a Tredegar Iron Works in Richmond, there was the *original* Tredegar Ironworks in Wales.

Just outside Monmouthshire in southeastern Wales lies the town of Tredegar, in the county of Blaenau Gwent. The town was named after Tredegar House, the estate and ancestral home of the Morgans, one of the most influential families in the region. The possible origins and meanings of the name "Tredegar," as well as the history of the land itself, are myriad and span the centuries. One of the earliest claimants to the lands in question was Bledri ap Cadivor Vawr, a Welsh nobleman who inherited his late father's properties around the turn of the twelfth century.[4] Legends trace the Morgans to Bledri and even as far back to the Trojan War. Just as the refugee Aeneas is credited with conquering Italy and laying the groundwork for Rome, similarly did Geoffrey of Monmouth ascribe to Aeneas's grandson (and mythical progenitor of the Morgan family) Brutus the honor of being the first king of the Britons; familial claims extend even further to a descent from Ham, one of the sons of Noah who survived the destruction of the antediluvian Earth.[5] The earliest connection between Tredegar and the Morgans that can be historically verified appears in the form of a poem dated 1460 by the Welsh bard Gwilym Tew (or William the Fat), wherein praise is hoisted on both Sir

Tredegar Iron Works

John Morgan, a knight belonging to the Roman Catholic Church's Order of the Holy Sepulchre, and his property, known by the name of *Tre-Degyr*.[6] Numerous spellings, each with their own meaning, abound throughout the centuries: some accounts speak of *Tre-Deg-Erw*, or "mansion of the ten acres"; others refer to *Tref-Deigr*, the home of Teigr ap Tegonwy, a mythical Welsh prince "of King Arthur's time." The modern "Tredegar" came into common usage no earlier than the seventeenth century.[7]

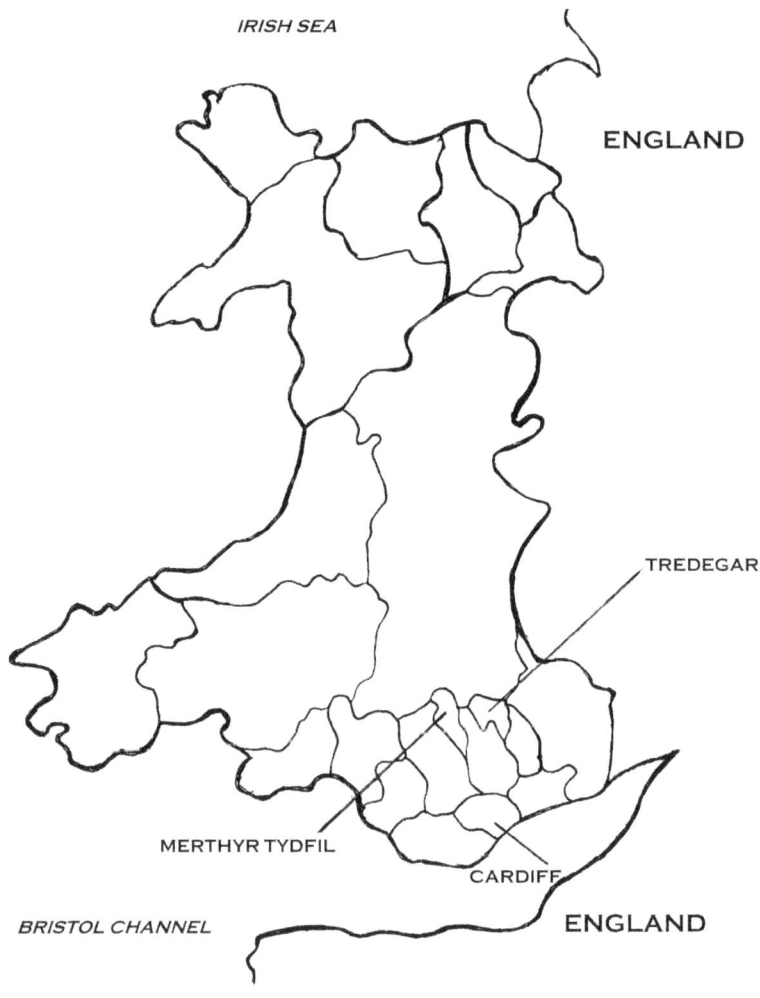

Southern Wales was one of the most important regions during the Industrial Revolution, and ironworks in Merthyr Tydfil and throughout the greater Sirhowy River valley—Tredegar included—provided much of the iron and machinery that fueled that revolution. *Nathan Madison.*

Origins to 1849

Regardless of its etymology, the town of Tredegar is situated one thousand feet above sea level at the very head of the Sirhowy River (*Afon Sirhywi*), a body of water with as many legends regarding its name as those attributed to Tredegar. It is a tributary of the Ebbw River, which is itself an offshoot of the longest river in Britain, the Severn. For most of its history, large and small farms dotted the countryside alongside the Sirhowy, with large-scale industrialization of the area, particularly the mining of coal and iron ore to be used in furnaces at nearby Pontggwaith-yr-hairan, beginning around the turn of the nineteenth century.[8]

As early as the Middle Ages, small-scale mining of coal, limestone and some iron ore were the primary industrial endeavors to be found in both northern and southern Wales. Following the Acts of Union in 1536 under the reign of the Tudor king Henry VIII (who was, incidentally, of Welsh ancestry himself), which united the kingdoms of England and Wales into a single state, there was a substantial expansion of industry throughout the country, as Englishmen now found it easier to make use of Wales's natural deposits.[9] The mining of coal increased significantly, and small ironworking establishments appeared for the first time in large numbers over the course of the sixteenth century, predominantly in southern Wales along the coast of the Bristol Channel.[10] The area was particularly well suited to support ironworks, due to both the numerous coalfields and ferrous ore veins that covered the countryside, as well as the extensive deposits of limestone nearby, as limestone was needed as a purifying agent (or flux) in the smelting process.[11] In 1788, there were 8 blast furnaces in South Wales, producing over 8,000 tons of pig iron annually; within sixty years, that number had jumped to over 630,000 tons per year, with 192 furnaces in operation.[12]

Pig iron is the name given to the most rudimentary form of man-made iron. Iron ore was deposited into a blast furnace, along with fuel (primarily charcoal and, later, coal or coke) and fluxing agents, resulting in the formation of molten iron and slag, a byproduct that contained impurities expelled from the iron. The resultant iron when cooled was relatively brittle, typically being composed of between 2 and 4 percent carbon. Owing to this high carbon content, cooled pig iron could not be hammered or formed without cracking, so, while still molten, it was usually cast into simple tools and implements, or run into ingot patterns dug into the ground (called pigs, due to the pattern's likeness to a sow suckling her piglets). For sturdier products, wrought iron, with its lower carbon levels and ability to be molded into a wider variety of shapes without breaking, was necessary. For centuries, wrought iron had been produced in bloomeries, wherein iron ore was melted to a near-molten state containing both iron and slag (called a bloom) and then removed and thereafter literally beaten (worked, or "wrought") until as much of the impurities as possible were removed—this process was inefficient and time-consuming and consumed even larger amounts of charcoal fuel, which in the United Kingdom was rapidly becoming a scarcity.[13]

In the middle of the eighteenth century, the British reliance on charcoal was proving to be a detriment to its iron-makers; an island nation, the United Kingdom did not have an abundance of forests from which to draw timber for producing charcoal, and what timber was available was sought by others for home building, ship construction and additional industries. An alternative to charcoal was desperately needed.[14] In 1780, Henry Cort, working at the Fontley Iron Works in southern England, invented a process through which wrought iron could be produced in larger quantities and on a consistent basis while using coal in place of charcoal.[15] This stronger iron was created using reverberatory furnaces, which kept fuel and pig iron separate. Heat from the fuel was transmitted through the furnaces' bricks to the pig iron, melting it without introducing impurities, creating a composition more abundant in pure iron. A workman then stirred, or "puddled," the iron to ensure that there was uniformity in both temperature and composition throughout. This process did not allow the iron to reach its melting point; the iron instead formed a thick, semi-viscous substance more solid than liquid. Finally, the iron was removed from the furnace in large balls and squeezed or rolled to remove any remaining slag, although some trace amounts always remained—the iron was then ready to be hammered or rolled into the sturdier, final product.[16] This method was known as "dry puddling"; a later development, called "wet puddling" (due to the boiling affect it produced in the slag), involved adding iron scale (essentially rust) to the iron while still in the furnace, resulting in the further expulsion of carbon.[17] In time, the puddler became one of the most skilled workmen in the industry; much of his knowledge could be acquired only through years of apprenticeship and accumulated experience. More dependent on intuition and a "feel" for when the iron (sometimes referred to as the "charge") was ready, experienced puddlers were a prized commodity.

Throughout southern Wales, particularly in the area of Merthyr Tydfil, several ironworks appeared in the latter years of the eighteenth century, and the success of one in particular, the Sirhowy Iron Works, encouraged its proprietors to expand. In 1799, Sir Charles Morgan, Second Baronet (whose son would serve in the House of Lords and take the title of Baron Tredegar), granted a portion of his holdings, roughly three thousand acres,

Origins to 1849

Sirhowy Iron Works. *Blaenau Gwent Heritage Forum.*

to several interested entrepreneurs for the purposes of mining the region's coal and iron ore deposits. A year later, Richard Fothergill and Reverend Matthew Monkhouse (veterans of the Sirhowy Works and recognized ironmasters), along with Sam Homfray, a brother-in-law of Morgan's and proprietor of the nearby Penydarren Iron Works; William Forman (a partner at Penydarren); and William Thompson, of the nearby Tintern Abbey Works, with an initial capital of £30,000, founded the Tredegar Ironworks.[18] The eponymous town, primarily constructed for the housing of workmen and their families, was founded the following year.

Tredegar benefited early on from the expertise of one of the realm's greatest mechanical engineers. Richard Trevithick, a native of Cornwall, designed and constructed a high-pressure steam engine used to power rolls, hammers and other tools in the works' emerging puddling mill in 1801. Trevithick, among other innovations, is best remembered for constructing the world's first successful high-pressure steam road locomotive, the "Puffing Devil," that same year. Trevithick's engine at Tredegar was so well constructed that it remained in operation for over half a century, finally shutting down in 1856.[19]

Shortly after they began operations, Tredegar's blast furnaces were producing up to fifty tons of pig iron on a weekly basis.[20] By 1806, four furnaces were operating at Tredegar, and a year later, the puddling mills were complete and in full operation, allowing the company to produce wrought iron on a much larger scale. Within another decade, the town had grown alongside its namesake ironworks, and with roads fully completed, materials from farther away than Sirhowy were entering Tredegar, which, of course, allowed for an even larger increase in production. Each furnace was now producing weekly what the entire works had produced annually only several years before, with more efficient transportation of raw materials, goods and workers realized with the completion of the Sirhowy Tramroad around 1812.[21] Within fifty years of its founding, the Tredegar Ironworks had become one of the most important iron establishments of the so-called Iron-Making Centre of the World, Methyr Tydfil at its epicenter, providing a large amount of the iron that at first propelled and then further fueled Britain's booming Industrial Revolution. From simple bars to rails to engines, if the Revolution required something, odds were Tredegar could, and did, produce it.

Tredegar, however, did not only produce iron. The talents and abilities of several highly respected ironworkers and engineers were honed at the works. The construction of the steam engine by Trevithick, overseen by Tredegar's Homfray, is laudable enough; Daniel Gooch, born in Northumberland and trained in Tredegar's pattern shop, was a first-class railway innovator and engineer who went on to serve in Parliament's House of Commons and later oversaw, under the auspices of the Telegraph Construction and Maintenance Company, the laying of the first transatlantic telegraph cable.[22] One of Tredegar's sons in particular, however, figures more prominently than others for our purposes—his work would leave lasting repercussions throughout the history of the southern United States and Virginia more than a century after his death.

Rhys Davies, born sometime between 1795 and 1800, was a native of Breconshire (in present-day Powys County), roughly thirty miles north of Tredegar. At the age of eleven, Davies came to Tredegar and became an apprentice in several shops at its namesake ironworks, mastering the skills of patternmaker and millwright, specifically. An account of Tredegar's history from the turn of the twentieth century mentions briefly that a "Mr. Rees Davies, a native of Llangynider [Llangynidr], Breconshire" was responsible for the construction of the first three furnaces used at Tredegar; this may be an allusion to Davies's father of the same name, who is known to have worked at Tredegar as well and whose presence at the works may have allowed for his son to attain his apprenticeships.[23]

Rhys Davies left Tredegar, presumably by the mid-1820s, for military service, enlisting in the British army and joining the Royal Corps of Engineers, helping to forge the tools and machines needed for the regiment's myriad construction projects. Much of Davies's travels can be discerned not from Davies himself but from records left by one of his fellow workmen. Born on December 16, 1802, James Hunter, son of Samuel Thomas Hunter and his wife, Susannah, grew up on his father's farm on the banks of the Sirhowy River before beginning work at Tredegar alongside Davies.[24] Following his time in the army, Davies, along with Hunter and several other Tredegar men, traveled to France. The French government had sent several delegations of ironmasters to the Merthyr Tydfill area in the late 1700s in order to absorb Welsh prowess regarding the construction of ironworks, and this know-how was obviously valued several decades later, following the Napoleonic Wars and the reestablishment of civil communications across the English Channel.[25] It is known that Davies constructed rolling mills under the direction of Auguste de Marmont, a former marshal of France appointed by Napoleon who betrayed the emperor during the restoration of the Bourbon dynasty in 1815, following Napoleon's defeat at Waterloo. After the July Revolution of 1830, which ousted the Bourbons in favor of the house of Orleans (which remained in power until the Revolutions of 1848), Davies aided in the construction of a rolling mill ordered by the former duke of Orleans, the newly crowned King Louis Philippe I.[26] It was after several years working in France that Davies and his workmen then journeyed to the United States.

VIRGINIA

The mining of iron in Virginia reaches back to its colonial foundations, with the first seventeen tons of bog iron sent back to England shortly after the colony's establishment.[27] For many British ironmasters, the Virginia colony promised untapped veins of ore but, even more importantly, held a solution to a mounting dilemma: the lack of long-term, substantial resources of wood (i.e. charcoal) for Britain's blast furnaces.[28] In 1619, engineers from across Europe were called to Falling Creek, a few miles south of what would one day become Richmond, to the first ironworks in America, erected under the guidance of English ironmaster John Berkeley. The site, however, was destroyed in 1622 by a Powhatan assault on Jamestown and surrounding settlements, during which a quarter of the colony's population, including Berkeley and two dozen of his workmen, were killed.[29] In 1714, nearly seven decades after the establishment of America's first successful integrated ironworks, the Saugus Iron Works of Massachusetts in 1645, approximately forty German immigrants (men, women and children) arrived in Virginia at the behest and personal expense of Lieutenant Governor Alexander Spotswood. Spotswood had originally intended for the immigrants, whom he settled in the new village of Germanna along the Rappahannock, to continue their vocation from the Old World: silver mining. However, unable to attain the royal approval needed to begin mining that precious metal, Spotswood decided to set his German settlers to iron making, jumpstarting the Virginia iron industry that had laid essentially abandoned since the disaster at Falling Creek.[30] The works at Germanna, known as the Tubal Furnace, were soon joined by other works throughout the colony. Several years before the birth of his son George in 1732, Augustine Washington Sr. permitted the Principio Company of Maryland to operate the Accokeek Furnace on property he held in Stafford County.[31] Saugus, Germanna, Accokeek and other early colonial sites cleared a path, and small forges and furnaces began to appear throughout the expanding colonies, to the point that on the eve of the American Revolution, the colonies collectively had become the third-largest producer of iron on earth, a majority of which was the product of Virginia furnaces.[32]

Aside from small farming tools and other implements, the output of these establishments was limited to pig iron. Due to several factors, including the practice of British mercantilism (in which the colonies were expected to only produce raw materials for further refinement in the mother country) and the strictness with which British ironmasters kept their secrets closely guarded, finishing enterprises such as rolling mills and large-scale foundries were extremely limited in number. For the most part, anything more complicated than a shovel, knife or other domestic tool was expected to come from England, and England alone. During heated meetings at St. John's Church in Richmond, American revolutionaries emphasized the need for increased iron production if the colonies were to have any hope of success against the British; consequently, the number of small furnaces grew to meet the demand for American-made iron weapons. Many of these, such as David Ross's Oxford Iron Works about one hundred miles east of Richmond in Campbell County, continued service well into peacetime and provided the foundations for the burgeoning American iron industry.

As turnpikes, roadways and canals made Richmond more accessible to the rest of the state, and because of its abundant natural resources, the city quickly began to grow into an economic and industrial hub. Flour mills, tobacco and cotton plantations and many newly erected ironworks either received supplies or sold their products along the trading veins that passed through the city, courtesy of both newly built roads and the winding course of the James River itself. In 1809, the Virginia Manufactory of Arms began operations on the banks of the James, the following year yielding some thirty cannons. The Bellona Foundry (complete with its own eponymous coal mine), constructed in 1814 under the guidance of Major John Clarke along the James's banks in Chesterfield County, within three years had become a supplier of government ordnance and even hosted a federal arsenal on site.[33]

A Foundry on the James

Francis Brown Deane Jr., the son of Francis Sr. and Ann Hughes Deane, was born in 1796 in Cartersville, a small village in Cumberland County, Virginia.[34] The son of a merchant, Deane worked under his father in the family business as a young man and served briefly in the Virginia Militia during the War of 1812.[35] In 1827, Deane married Arianna Cunningham of Richmond, and, in doing so, secured a place among the city's leading business leaders; his father-in-law, Edward Cunningham, owned several of the city's most productive flour mills.[36] Even though flour-milling was quite lucrative at the time, with Richmond's Gallego Mills known as the largest establishment of its kind in the world, Deane's interests were instead swayed toward the potential profits to be gained from operating a large ironworks in the South, where such ventures were far less common than in the more industrialized North. Virginia's long-standing presence among America's leading iron-producing regions, when paired with a swiftly evolving infrastructure and transportation system, nearly guaranteed success for an entrepreneur willing to undertake such a task.

Innovations in the larger American iron industry also allowed for the existence of ironworks in Richmond and other areas outside of their traditional settings; these innovations, in turn, spurred the growth of further industries that made an urban ironworks not only possible but increasingly necessary. As the domestic iron industry developed, the practices of the tradesmen changed in accordance with regional and technological needs. Charcoal was the predominant form of fuel for early furnaces, which resulted in many works residing in isolated, wooded areas, which provided a steady supply of timber for making charcoal but also strained the ability to import ore (if no veins happened to exist nearby) and hampered attempts to export finished product. The growth of coal as a fuel allowed for and encouraged works to be built closer to major commercial and transportation hubs, such as cities and canal ways.[37]

Richmond was an early beneficiary of the increase in coal use, as one of the highest-quality deposits of bituminous coal in the region existed just outside the city, in a basin that was estimated to span approximately ninety-six thousand acres throughout Goochland, Amelia, Powhatan, Henrico, Hanover and Chesterfield Counties, where commercial coal mining first began in the United States in the mid-1700s.[38] Before the onset of extensive mining of Pennsylvania anthracite, it was Richmond coal that supplied homes and industries with warmth and energy in New York, Boston and other northern markets. During its years of highest productivity, 1822–77, the Richmond Coal Basin produced an average of 102,000 tons of coal per annum.[39] The first commercial railroad in Virginia, a thirteen-mile-long wooden gravity rail assisted by mules, was completed in 1831, for the expressed purpose of conveying coal from mines in Midlothian to ports in Manchester on the James.[40]

On January 5, 1785, the James River Company was chartered by the Virginia General Assembly. The primary goal of the new company was to construct a canal that connected the James with the Ohio River, creating a commercial tie between the center of the eastern states to the farthest reaches of what was then America's frontier.[41] Following several years of initial hindrances and leadership changes, the reorganized James River and Kanawha Company succeeded in connecting Richmond to towns and cities throughout the western part of the state. Although never reaching its intended connection to the Ohio, the canal did help establish Richmond's clout as an industrial and manufacturing powerhouse in the South in later years. Among other benefits, it allowed for easier transportation of coal and ores from the more mineral-rich western sections of the state.[42] Locally, transporting coal from the Chesterfield mines to Richmond via roadways could cost up to nine cents, per bushel; this cost dropped to only three cents if shipped on the canal.[43] A second byproduct of the canal running through Richmond was the power it could generate for any mills, foundries and factories located along its route; it was channels, or raceways, from the canal that provided power to dozens of small industries along the riverbanks.

In 1832, Francis Deane purchased the Bear Garden Furnace, a charcoal-fueled furnace just outside the town of New Canton in Buckingham County, about sixty miles west of Richmond. Bear Garden was adjacent to an extensive tract of land Deane inherited from a recently deceased uncle and

Origins to 1849

Above: Five-dollar note issued by the James River and Kanawha Company, circa 1850. *Nathan Madison.*

Right: A preserved blast furnace at Roaring Run, Botetourt County, Virginia, and now a part of the Jefferson National Forest. *Nathan Madison.*

close to a considerable vein of iron ore known as the Ballendine Seam.[44] With Deane acting as superintendent, Bear Garden produced an estimated thirty to forty tons of pig iron per week, which, as canal construction progressed, could easily be shipped eastward to Richmond.[45]

What Would Become Tredegar

The land that would later hold Virginia's most important ironworks had been the property of Englishmen (at least, in their minds) since May 24, 1607, when a band of colonists led by Christopher Newport claimed the area near the falls for King James of England, land that was within the domain of the powerful Powhatan chiefdom.[46] Numerous battles with Native Americans left the land's ownership in some measure of questionability, although the English were still laying claim to the area in deeds, inheritances and sales. In 1661, a prosperous trader, Thomas Stegg Jr., purchased three hundred acres along the James River, and upon his death in 1671, with no heirs to his properties, Stegg left his landholdings along the James to his nephew William Byrd.[47] The land then passed to William Byrd II in 1705, following his parents' death and composing a small portion of the tens of thousands of acres that made up his inheritance. It was William Byrd II who, in 1737 while surveying his extensive holdings, founded the city of Richmond upon Shacco (later Shockoe) Hill.

In 1768, William Byrd III inaugurated a lottery, the purpose of which was to divide his extensive hereditary properties into parcels of land expanding the overall size of the city his father had founded; it was one of these parcels, Lot 741 on the river's north side across from Broad Rock Island (later Belle Isle), that Samuel Overton, a veteran of the French and Indian and Revolutionary Wars, purchased at the cost of £700.[48] Years later, Overton, in turn, parceled out portions of this land to various interests.[49] One of Overton's parcels went to Colonel John Harvie, a childhood friend of Thomas Jefferson who served in the Second Continental Congress as well as in the Continental army. After the war, Harvie was appointed the fourth mayor of Richmond in 1785 and later represented the city in the Virginia House of Delegates, beginning in 1793.[50]

In June 1801, Colonel Harvie signed an agreement with the James River Company (of which Harvie was also a director), allowing him to "tap" the water from the canal to power flour mills on his property, mills that operated

Origins to 1849

Richmond, overlooking the James River and Kanawha Canal, just west of the future site of the Tredegar Iron Works, 1834, by W.J. Bennett. *Library of Congress.*

under the name of the Virginia Company. While the agreement for water power was between Colonel Harvie and the James River Company, the actual operator of the mills was Thomas Rutherfoord, a Scottish immigrant who had amassed quite the fortune in the Virginia tobacco and grain industries. In January 1801, Rutherfoord had agreed to purchase the mills on Harvie's property for $50,000, paid in five yearly installments of $10,000.[51] A fire struck the mills shortly after the purchase, but Rutherfoord oversaw the reconstruction efforts personally, and by 1805, the mills were again working at full capacity. Soon, Rutherfoord's mills were second only to those of Gallego in terms of sales and production volume.[52] Rutherfoord sold his land (roughly four acres) and milling operations in the summer of 1812 to Edward Cunningham, who reaped quite the windfall; around 40 percent of the grain produced in Richmond came from Cunningham's mills between the years 1818 and 1825, when Cunningham finally retired from the milling business.[53]

In late January 1829, Edward Cunningham sold for $15,000 his land and mills to his son Richard and his associate Richard Anderson, jointly operating under the name of the Richmond Manufacturing Company, for the purpose of building a cotton mill.[54] In June 1832, the nearby holdings of Thomas Green, a businessman who had acquired one hundred cubic inches worth of canal raceway for a proposed iron foundry, transferred all of his interests

Tredegar Iron Works

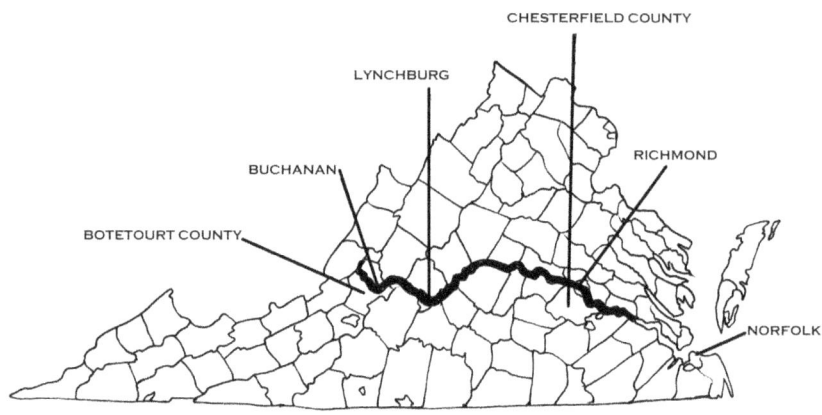

The James River and Kanawha Canal followed the course of the James River, traversing nearly two hundred miles from Richmond in the east, westward to the town of Buchanan in Botetourt County. *Nathan Madison.*

at the site to Colonel Harvie's son, J.B. Harvie, who in turn transferred those interests to Cunningham and his Richmond Manufacturing Company.[55]

Following this rapid exchange of land, mills and interests, the next large-scale change occurred in 1835, with the incorporation of the Virginia Foundry Company. Composed of Richard Anderson, Richmond bankers Joseph Marx and Beverly Blair and several others, the Virginia Foundry Company was recognized by the General Assembly as "a body politic and corporate, for the purpose of manufacturing iron and steel" along the banks of the James.[56] Shortly after its formation, Francis Deane was appointed president of the Virginia Foundry Company and entered into contracts with the Richmond Manufacturing Company to use land owned by the Cunninghams.

The Tredegar Iron Works, Established 1837

Although the exact channels through which contact was initiated are now lost, at some point prior to 1836, Rhys Davies's expertise was requested at the behest of Deane, who with his brother-in-law had formed a separate concern for the purposes of rolling finished iron. Davies had immigrated to the United States in the early 1830s, overseeing the construction of rolling

Origins to 1849

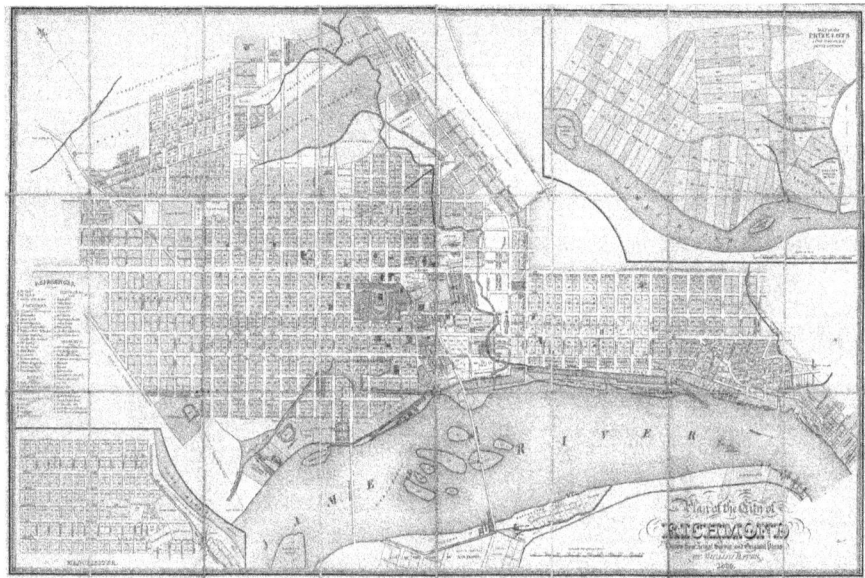

Map of Richmond, 1835, including much of the land included in William Byrd III's lottery, by Micajah Bates. *Albert and Shirley Small Special Collections Library, University of Virginia.*

mills for the Samsondale Iron Works in Haverstraw, New York, beginning in 1832, before accepting Deane's offer and moving south with his wife and five children.

Under the guidance of Davies, Hunter and several other workmen from the Sirhowy Valley (including Davies's father), the first mill for rolling iron on the site was constructed. Wishing to honor Davies's efforts, and perhaps to capitalize on a name already well known in the European iron industry, Deane wrote to the mayor of Tredegar, requesting permission be granted to name the new works in the town's honor; the mayor soon returned his gracious approval.[57] Thus, Richmond's Tredegar Forge and Rolling Mill began operation in May 1837 on land adjacent to the Virginia Foundry Company.

Shortly after work began on the Tredegar Rolling Mill, as was the likely intention all along, Deane, the Cunninghams and their investors sought to enlarge the scope of their operations by merging the Tredegar mill with the Virginia Foundry Company and proposed such a consolidation to Virginia's General Assembly, which allowed the merger on February 27, 1837.[58] The two firms did not operate under the single Tredegar Iron Company title until after January 2, 1838, and the merger was not legally finalized until that following March.[59] The Virginia Foundry Company had already been in operation for some time prior to the proposed merger, producing over 1,105 tons of bar iron between May and December 1837, equaling roughly 7 tons per day. In the charter proposal, Rutherfoord himself (writing as a stockholder of the Virginia Foundry Company) estimated that the works, as then constructed, would be capable of producing up to 2,500 tons of finished iron per annum.[60] While an admirable goal, Richmond's Tredegar had some work ahead of itself if it was to ascend to its namesake's efficiency. In 1840, Wales' Tredegar Ironworks was turning out 15,000 tons of pig iron per year.[61] Deane was named the first president of the Tredegar Iron Company, and Rhys Davies was appointed first superintendent of the firm's rolling mills. Shortly after Tredegar's consolidation with the Virginia Foundry Company, it began to receive glowing praise from Richmond's newspapers:

> *Richmond is destined ere long to become a place of great importance in the line of manufactures, especially in operations in Iron. Every article in that metal, from the heaviest ordnance to the smallest wire, can, I confidently believe, be made here cheaper than in any other of the Atlantic States, and yet it is owing to the zeal and enterprise of a single individual, (Mr. F.B. Deane,) that a mere beginning has been made! He has erected large works for the purpose of manufacturing Bar Iron in various forms. His works are admirably constructed under a most skillful engineer, (Mr. Reese [sic] Davies,) and are now in full and profitable operation. The iron is of excellent quality, and is in demand in different markets in the United States.*[62]

In the northeastern states, blast furnaces and foundries were normally detached enterprises from rolling mills and other "finishing" shops. One reason for this was the legacy of British rule and mercantilism, wherein the colonies were expected to furnish raw materials, and raw materials alone, to Britain; this legacy resulted in a relative dearth of refineries in the earliest years of the republic. Growth of capital among ironmasters over the course of several decades, as well as the obvious benefits to a proprietor in maintaining greater control over both the influx of raw materials as well as the quality of this material, spurred the trend in combining furnaces and mills into singular, commercial entities. Deane was following a growing trend at the time: an integrated ironworks that produced much of its raw materials and furnished its finished products all under one "roof." Deane's connections to the mines and furnaces of Botetourt made such an integrated ironworks possible in Richmond, where no large-scale iron ore deposits existed.

PROPOSALS

FOR UNITING THE

VIRGINIA FOUNDRY COMPANY

WITH THE PROPERTY OWNED BY

Messrs. DEANE & CUNNINGHAMS,

UNDER THE

FOLLOWING CHARTER,

AND FOR THE SALE OF

FIFTY THOUSAND DOLLARS

OF

STOCK IN SAID COMPANY.

RICHMOND:
SHEPHERD & COLIN, *Printers.*
1837.

Proposals for Uniting the Virginia Foundry Company with the Property Owned by Messrs. Deane & Cunninghams, 1837. *Library of Virginia.*

Tredegar Iron Works

"The Tredegar" (as it soon came to be called) began its nascent years with about fifty employees, six puddling furnaces and two additional furnaces for purposes of further refinement. The new works were powered entirely by the James River and Kanawha Canal, its raceways driving the enterprise's primary source of motive power—a twenty-two-foot-diameter, twelve-inch-wide overshot water wheel, utilizing a solid cast-iron flywheel over fifteen feet in diameter and weighing six tons.[63] Deane's initial offerings included bar iron; rolled, flat, hoop and band iron of varying dimensions; car and railroad axles; tobacco screws; axes; adzes; and components for cotton, saw- and gristmills.[64] Shifts were operated around the clock, day and night, and Deane took great pride in publicizing the fact that all of the materials—both the Tredegar's machinery and the iron that machinery refined—were products of Virginia. The Tuckahoe Coal Pits, about a dozen miles west of Richmond, supplied Tredegar with much of its bituminous coal; when a new and potentially significant vein of natural bituminous coke was discovered in the Black Heth Mines of nearby Chesterfield County, Deane's furnaces were the first to test its offerings.[65] The early site also boasted a two-story structure that served as a small locomotive engine and machine shop, which utilized its own twenty-foot-diameter water wheel that powered hammers and other machinery and also supplied air to adjacent furnaces.[66]

Unfortunately, Rhys Davies did not survive long following the establishment of this second Tredegar. In the fall of 1838, Davies began work on a new rolling mill, this time for the Belle Isle Manufacturing Company, located on the eponymous island south of Tredegar, across the James River. In September, an altercation occurred at the construction site on Belle Isle. In what the Richmond newspapers at the time only described as "an evil hour, [during which] he gave way to his passion, and fell its victim," Davies was stabbed to death by a member of his own work party.[67] The fact that the newspapers make clear the unnamed worker was "examined and discharged" lends some credence to the notion that Davies may have been killed in an act of self-defense on the part of the workman or perhaps even during an illicit duel; this, however, will likely never be determined. The newspapers lavished praise on Davies in their notices concerning his death, following his burial on Belle Isle: "To a warm and generous temperament Mr. Davies added an uncommonly plain practical and clear understanding and had so much mechanical genius that improvements continued suggesting themselves to his mind."[68] James Hunter, as well as the elder Davies and a majority of the other Welshmen who had come with Rhys to Richmond, remained in the city and constituted the nucleus of Tredegar's embryonic, skilled workforce.

Origins to 1849

Richmond's Tredegar faced a number of obstacles during its formative years. Francis Deane, for all of his good intentions and obvious enthusiasm for the enterprise, was sorely lacking in terms of actual business experience, at least on the level of an operation the Tredegar's size. In what was in many instances a common practice of the time, Deane, in his testimonials to Tredegar's stockholders, often counted unsold iron (which was beginning to accumulate) as a (potential) profit, thus augmenting the company's reported income to inaccurate and increasingly unreliable levels. He was also failing to acquire orders on a consistent basis, necessitating the hiring of a sales agent, David Anderson, who assumed a portion of Deane's duties—Deane's yearly salary was reduced to $2,000 from an initial $2,500.[69]

Beyond Virginia's borders, loans and other sources of capital from England, which were in many ways the backbone of the emerging American industries, began to dry up as a result of a severe economic depression sweeping the United Kingdom. From January 1834 to January 1837, $43 million worth of gold was brought into the United States, while only $11 million left it. A large portion of this European investment underwrote not only private industries but also state and federally funded infrastructure projects—a sudden drop in this cash flow, which had been depended on for years without even the slightest preparation for a potential withdrawal, was sure to threaten economic stability across the country.[70] A poor showing in America's wheat harvests in 1836 further impacted the national economy and resulted in lower than expected exports, leading to cutbacks on spending in both the private and public sectors.[71] The resulting Panic of 1837 crippled industries across the country, including the iron and nascent railroad industries.

Tredegar was dually afflicted with increasing debts on the one hand and an inability to sell off stores of finished products on the other.[72] As if to further compound the situation, in March 1838, the company's operations were nearly halted entirely as the portion of the James River and Kanawha Canal behind Tredegar was completely drained and the canal widened to allow for greater traffic. Consequently, no pig iron was shipped from Botetourt, on-site furnaces were shut down and Deane was forced to purchase cast- and wrought-iron stock from other firms to fulfill orders.[73]

Tredegar's stockholders realized that the company needed a new direction if it was going to survive beyond the 1830s, and they found that direction in a young man from western Virginia named Joseph Reid Anderson.

JOSEPH REID ANDERSON

Anderson was born on February 6, 1813, at his father's estate of Walnut Hill in Botetourt County to parents Colonel William and Anna Thomas Anderson.[74] Joseph was a third-generation Virginian of Scotch-Irish descent whose father was a veteran of both the American Revolution and the War of 1812; his mother was from a family related to future governor of Maryland Francis Thomas.[75] While holding a prominent place in early American military history, the family was not wealthy by any stretch, and William instilled in Joseph a strong work ethic and acute attention to pecuniary matters.[76] The family history of military service was a constant in Joseph's early life, so it is no great surprise that he, in 1832, began studies at the United States Military Academy at West Point.

Shortly after enrolling at West Point, Anderson decided against making the military a lifelong career (later lamenting to his brother that his tenure at West Point was "four years of valuable time lost") but nonetheless remained and graduated in 1836 with the rank of cadet captain. In August 1836, after a brief stint in Washington, he was sent under the auspices of the Army Corps of Engineers to Fortress Monroe, just outside Norfolk, Virginia.[77] At Fort Monroe, Anderson befriended an army surgeon also stationed there, Dr. Robert Archer, as well as Archer's seventeen-year-old daughter, Sarah Eliza. Courtship soon followed, and after a brief separation that winter, during which he was stationed in Savannah, Anderson returned to Fort Monroe in May 1837 and married Sarah.

Joseph resigned his commission in the United States Army following an offer from Colonel Claude Crozet: Anderson became an assistant engineer on the Valley Turnpike, a project under Crozet's supervision intended to link Shenandoah Valley towns, such as Staunton and Winchester, to northern markets.[78] At several industrial and political events between 1838 and 1840, Anderson met representatives of the Tredegar Iron Company and actively sought any possible openings within the firm. Francis Deane hired Anderson as purchasing agent for the company on March 26, 1841, following David Anderson's (no relation) resigning the position two months prior.[79] As purchasing agent, Anderson not only was responsible for acquiring sales and contracts (for which he received a commission) but also oversaw much of the company's financial administration.

Hiring Anderson made good business sense on a number of levels. While the discipline learned at West Point was likely taken into account, it was more so his background as an engineer that was among the most attractive aspects of Anderson's résumé. Perhaps just as importantly, Anderson's short military service had allowed for contacts to be made, both in ordnance and engineering circles, which could aid in Tredegar's pursuit of lucrative government contracts.

Anderson's familiarity with the Shenandoah Valley itself was also an asset. The valley region contained some of the richest mineral deposits in the state, including veins of minable iron ore, forests (for charcoal) and limestone for flux that had been mined since the late eighteenth century, particularly in Anderson's home of Botetourt County, just at the foot of the Appalachian mountain range. Further, Anderson's elder brother, Francis T. Anderson, was a partner in the Cloverdale furnace properties in Botetourt; Cloverdale Furnace #2, a cold-blast charcoal furnace built in 1841, would become an invaluable source of pig iron throughout the next several decades.[80]

The year 1841, when Anderson assumed duties, was relatively productive given the dire financial and operational straits the company was facing at the time. The Tredegar foundry and mills filled several large orders, most notably a four-ton, twenty-three-foot-long water wheel shaft cast that summer for the Manchester Cotton Manufacturing Company, located opposite Tredegar on the southern bank of the James. While it was acknowledged that the casting of the shaft was actually a loss for the company on a dollar-for-dollar basis, the Tredegar was praised for demonstrating that, even during those uncertain economic times, such large orders could be accepted and successfully filled.[81]

Anderson was quite cognizant of the fact that Tredegar's future could be better secured by moving beyond solely domestic and industrial goods and quickly began making use of his connections within the military in order to obtain federal contracts for shot and shell (about $90,000 worth in 1842 alone) and convinced the company's stockholders to invest in needed upgrades and equipment to allow for the casting of large cannons. By late 1841, Tredegar was fulfilling orders for small cannons and siege howitzers, successfully competing against well-established and respected northern foundries such as West Point and Columbia.[82] Over the course of the following year, Tredegar's workmen were honing their abilities and casting cannons of ever-increasing proportions.[83] In 1847, Tredegar's boring mill was capable of boring five cannons at once; five lathes, each with their own crews, pushed cannon production ever higher.[84]

Anderson was better equipped than most for overseeing the production of ordnance, thanks to his education. As a West Point graduate, he benefited from an education that modeled itself on European military standards that blended an appreciation of technology and the sciences with an

Certificate of stock, four shares to Joseph Reid Anderson, in the Tredegar Iron Company, July 1842. *Library of Virginia.*

understanding of what would be demanded from a modern army.[85] Owing almost entirely to his military-minded discipline and engineering acumen, Tredegar's reputation began to rise almost as soon as Joseph Reid Anderson arrived on site. Northern visitors to the works lauded the quality of products produced, and local newspapers gladly reprinted any praise Tredegar received that compared Richmond's ironmasters with the respected manufacturers to the North:

> During a recent visit to Richmond, I examined, among other things very worthy the notice of the American traveler, the extensive Iron Works owned by the Tredegar Iron Company, and was particularly struck with the admirable arrangement and permanent character of everything about this establishment; so much so that I instituted an inquiry in my mind, to see how this work would compare with others of a similar character which I had seen in the Northern States, and I cannot bring to my recollection any works equal to those at Richmond, in their general arrangement, or in the complete and workman-like manner in which all of their machinery has been gotten up…To see such a display of enterprise, directed by evident knowledge of the important branch of industry to which it has been applied at the Tredegar Iron works, inspired me with great hopes that the Old

Origins to 1849

Dominion may yet be made to know her true interest and proper destiny in the Republic.[86]

Just as Anderson assumed his duties in Richmond, Francis Deane's salary had been further reduced, as he was now (demoted to) superintendent of the works. As of June 1842, Nicholas Mills assumed the presidency. Mills was already president of the Richmond and Manchester Coal Working Company, as well as several other local coal mines. Virginia's first railroad, the aforementioned gravity rail, was built to connect Mill's Railey Mines in Chesterfield to docks along the James River.[87] An early success on Anderson's part was his handling of potentially devastating financial crisis, a dilemma born years earlier on the part of Tredegar's founders. In 1835, Deane and the Cunninghams had taken out a sizable loan (to the tune of $25,000), with the Tredegar land itself as collateral, from Littleton Waller Tazewell, a former U.S. senator and (in 1835) governor of Virginia. As the first $15,000 installment of the loan repayment came due on October 1, 1842, Tredegar lacked the funds to meet it, and soon advertisements appeared in local newspapers announcing an impending auction of the firm's assets and holdings. Quickly, Anderson organized a committee composed of the leadership of both the Tredegar company and several local banks. Thanks to connections with several of Richmond's prominent lenders and other moneyed interests, particularly the Virginia Bank (which granted the works a sizable advance and was already a primary stockholder in the venture), Anderson helped arrange for the payments to be met, and Tredegar was saved from default.[88]

Owing largely to several meetings between Anderson and President John Tyler, in December 1844 Tredegar began work on an iron steamer, the revenue cutter *Polk*; revenue cutters were vessels generally employed in the enforcement of tariffs and other maritime regulations, but also often appropriated for anti-piracy efforts.[89] All iron needed for the vessel was manufactured and rolled by Tredegar and then transported down to the docks at Rocketts, where Anderson had arranged for the use of facilities needed for the ship's actual construction.[90] After President Tyler left office in 1845, the hold Anderson and other Richmond businesses had exerted on the former "Virginian-in-chief" mattered little with a new administration, and attempts at many more new shipbuilding agreements met with disappointment. A lack of further steamer contracts, however, may not have been due entirely to the lack of a fellow Virginian in the White House; although certainly a financial boon to Tredegar, the *Polk* was not one of the better-constructed ships in the revenue cutter fleet. It sprang several leaks during one of its early assignments in 1847, and following several other accidents, it was converted into a masted barque, with its engines and paddle wheels removed for use on other vessels.[91] Despite the *Polk*'s shortcomings, government contracts for ordnance continued to come Tredegar's way and became an increasingly vital contribution to the company's yearly income.

It was shortly before construction began on the *Polk* that Tredegar experienced its largest managerial shake-up since its inception. Despite the owners and stockholders of the company acquiescing to his demands for the tools and equipment needed to cast such large projects as cannons and steamers, Anderson found his having to answer to them, and what he perceived to be their meddling in his work, detrimental to his efforts at making the Tredegar a name among southern industries. Further, it seemed that president Nicholas Mills still lacked faith in the company's ability to meet all of its obligations and actually recommended in the fall of 1843 that operations cease after all current contractual commitments were met. Concurrently, the board of directors had made quite clear its desire "to discontinue business" within the year.[92]

On November 6, 1843, the board of directors accepted an offer on Anderson's part to lease the entire operation for the price of $8,000 per annum for the succeeding five years; the agreement covered all of the Tredegar property—"the landed premises conveyed to [Tredegar] by John A. Cunningham, Edward Cunningham and Francis B. Deane and the Virginia Foundry Company," which, by this point included not only the foundry and rolling mills but also several smith, machine and pattern shops. Nicholas Mills remained president of Tredegar for several more years, but Anderson now held greater sway in the overall management of the company's undertakings and finances. The firm's founder, Francis Deane, had resigned his position as superintendent in November 1842.

As much has been made of Francis Deane's inability to adequately manage Tredegar, it is important to briefly make note of his later life and success, if for no other reason than to demonstrate that perhaps his performance at Tredegar was largely the result of inexperience and that he undoubtedly learned from his mistakes if his life after Tredegar is any indication. In fact, he would enjoy a prosperous career that in many ways would mirror that followed by his most famous successor at Tredegar. After his resignation from Tredegar, Deane remained in Richmond for some time, forming an ill-fortuned concern with Charles Dimmock to create iron steamers for use on the James River and Kanawha Canal. After the failure of this venture,

Origins to 1849

he moved westward to Lynchburg, where, in 1847, he and several other area businessmen formed the Lynchburg and Botetourt Iron Company, later renamed F.B. Deane Jr. & Son.[93] Deane's new enterprise utilized several Botetourt blast furnaces, primarily Etna, Roaring Run and the Grace furnace, which ironically also provided Tredegar with much of its pig iron. Similarly to Anderson in his later years, Deane held several titles outside that of ironmaker. He was director of the James River and Kanawha Company for several years, served as the Lynchburg commissioner for the Richmond and Ohio Railroad and, beginning in 1848, was the vice-president of the Lynchburg and Tennessee Railroad, renamed the Virginia and Tennessee in 1849. In 1854, Deane was elected as Lynchburg's representative to the Virginia House of Delegates. Deane's foundry merged with the newly formed Lynchburg Arms and Engine Manufacturing Company shortly after the onset of the Civil War and began producing munitions for the Confederate army and navy, not least of which included forty twelve-pounder howitzer cannons and several thousand tons of ordnance.[94] Deane was named assistant marshal of Stonewall Jackson's funeral procession as it made its way through Lynchburg to Lexington and served as an advisor on industrial matters in Jefferson Davis's privy council shortly before war's end; he later served another term in the House of Delegates and devoted the remainder of his life to running his foundry before dying on November 26, 1868.[95] Commercial and personal contacts between Lynchburg and Richmond were never severed. Deane's foundry would often send Tredegar scrap or pig iron in exchange for finished products, and Tredegar's founder acted as the namesake for several Anderson descendants. During the Civil War, Anderson and Deane consulted regularly regarding the fluctuating price of iron throughout the Confederacy.[96]

Back in Richmond, Anderson's newly elevated status among Tredegar's administrators began on a high note, as demonstrated in late 1844 with contracts for 60 and 112 cannons for the Ordnance Bureau and the U.S. Navy, respectively—two significant orders that attested not only to Anderson's leadership but also the interest he took in making sure the best ore and foundry practices went into any and all Tredegar products. Following an unsuccessful cannon testing in 1843 that resulted in a number of his cannons being rejected by the government, Anderson placed even greater emphasis on the quality of everything from the coal used in the blast furnaces in Botetourt to the pig iron puddled in Richmond.[97] Tredegar also began to fill more orders for structural and decorative iron; in 1845, Tredegar aided in the construction of St. Paul's Church, just a short walk away from the state capitol. Between February and September 1845, Tredegar produced for the church 216 leaves, 49 ornamental flowers, 9 ornamental honeysuckles and other items, including the church's 140-pound spire.[98]

In 1845, a small boring operation commenced in the basement of the nearby and by then largely unused Virginia Manufactory of Arms, under the supervision of captain of the Public Guard Charles Dimmock. Within a year, the Armory Iron Company had been incorporated, with Dimmock as superintendent. Joseph Reid Anderson was encouraged to take stock in the firm himself, and later, as the armory mills began to make a profit, Anderson was appointed president, in addition to his duties at Tredegar.[99] Relations between armory personnel and workmen of the Armory Iron Co. were, at first, on a tense footing, leading at one point to Joseph R. Anderson requesting the governor deploy the public guard at the armory to ensure that his men could work unmolested.[100] Initial animosities were eventually smoothed out, and under first the superintendence and later, beginning in January 1848, the presidency of Dr. Robert S. Archer (J.R. Anderson's father-in-law, recently resigned from the army), the newly rechristened R. Archer & Company's fortunes prospered alongside those of Tredegar.[101] Dr. Archer, while likely owing his position chiefly to his son-in-law's influence, possessed an engineering acumen that quickly demonstrated itself; within a few years

Certificate of Stock, Eleven Shares to Joseph Reid Anderson, in the Armory Iron Company, June, 1849. *Library of Virginia.*

of taking over the Armory Iron Company, Dr. Archer had two patents to his name: one for improvements to railroad chairs (which helped fasten iron rails to wooden railroad ties) and another for percussion fuses.[102]

During the latter years of the decade, Anderson, ever the skilled West Point engineer, experimented with a rather new innovation that was making inroads throughout American manufacturing: the water-powered turbine. Up until this point, all canal water that Tredegar harnessed for power was captured in the form of overshot waterwheels. When the works were leased to Anderson in 1843, four overshot wheels were active on site—one for powering the rolls that turned recently puddled iron into bars, one that powered a blacksmith's hammer and two for use in boring cannons and in the machine shop.[103] Tredegar's designers followed the course taken by many northern industrial powerhouses, such as Francis Cabot Lowell's Boston Manufacturing Company, recognized birthplace of the American factory system, in using overshot wheels. Tredegar, however, was different in that water dropped directly from the canal to its intended destination, as opposed to running into a secondary, lower canal for further distribution, as was the case at Lowell.[104] In 1847 and 1848, Anderson arranged for the installation of two turbines designed by Pennsylvanian William Dripp, not at Tredegar itself but rather at the neighboring R. Archer & Company. Following the turbines' installation, Anderson apparently found much to be lacking in the new machinery, believing it to be far inferior to the overshot wheel in terms of both water wasted and the amount of power actually generated. Anderson soon removed the turbines and reinstalled overshots, writing to a friend in the summer of 1848, "I would not use it [the turbine] for any purpose [even] if the patentee would make a present of it and put it up and attach it gratis."[105] The failure of the Dripp turbines ostensibly produced some weariness on Anderson's part in relying on anything other than overshot wheels as the prime motive force behind his ironworks, with more than a decade passing before this apprehension would be reconsidered.

With orders rising and his name gaining in prominence throughout Richmond's industrial circles, Anderson, with some financial assistance from his brothers, sought to gain ownership of the ironworks outright just as the Board of Directors once again displayed a desire to relinquish control of the operation by forming a "Committee for Disposing of the Tredegar Iron Works."[106] In addition to leasing the works several years prior, Anderson had, between July 1843 and April 1849 augmented his holdings in the company by purchasing (at least) an additional 178 shares, increasing both his stake in the enterprise as well as his influence among the board of directors.[107]

Tredegar Iron Works

Anderson and the stockholders agreed to a price of $125,000 for the entire operation, beginning on the first of the year (1849) with a down payment of $25,000 and $20,000 per annum for another five years.[108] The stockholders could offer no real argument against Anderson's evident ability to turn the struggling company around. In the six-month period between January and June 1845, a year and a half after the works were leased to Anderson, the Tredegar noted roughly 1,620 products in its castings ledger, around 230 of those being railroad tools such as car wheels, braces and pinions; from July to December 1848, six months before Anderson assumed ownership of the Tredegar, the number of cast products sold more than doubled to 3,300.[109]

Anderson's full proprietorship of the works came at an auspicious time and coincided with a growth toward industrialization across the city, the commonwealth and the nation. The interstate economy, "the world's largest geographic free-trade zone," that the Constitution encouraged, despite occasional fiscal setbacks, continued to grow at an astounding rate.[110] The span bridging the 1830s and the 1850s has been called a "breathless generation," during which American innovations and industry thrived and rapidly pushed the nation's economy far beyond the post-colonial status it had held the past several decades. The specter of 1837 was passed, and in the years since his arrival, Anderson had built the Tredegar from a relatively small iron-making establishment on the banks of the James to what was quickly becoming the premier ironworks in the region. The South in general and Virginia in particular were racing to lessen a long-standing dependence on northern goods and manufacturers, just as America had instigated its own manufacturing revolution in order to lower its reliance on British machinery and wares decades earlier. Across the nation, industrial hubs sprang up as transportation via railways and canals continued to improve and as the shipping commerce that had cradled the early Republic gave way to domestic industries, particularly after the discovery of large gold deposits in California in the 1840s.[111] In competition with northern interests, a significant number of Virginia railroad companies were incorporated in the 1840s and 1850s, and they all needed iron. Whether it was in the form of rails, spikes, railway chairs or even engines, Tredegar was there to meet their requests.

CHAPTER 2

1849–1865

Following Richmond's emergence from the economic depression of 1837, the city began to rise in prominence, infrastructure and wealth, with the decade immediately preceding the Civil War witnessing the apex of Richmond's ascension. The arts and education were beginning to prosper; following the ratification of the new state constitution in 1851, public primary schools began to appear in Richmond, and private institutions of higher learning, including Richmond College (founded in 1840, the modern-day University of Richmond) continued to grow. New schools, such as the Richmond Female Institute (1854), began to appear as well. The *Southern Literary Messenger*, under the masterful hand of editor Edgar Allen Poe from 1835 to 1837, continued to flourish into the 1850s as one of the leading literary periodicals in the country. Richmond's theaters and musical venues were fast becoming required stops for many of the most popular touring artists of the day, such as "the Swedish nightingale," Jenny Lind; Shakespearean actor Junius Brutus Booth; and later, his sons, Edwin, Junius Brutus Jr. and John Wilkes. Foreign luminaries who called on Richmond in the antebellum years included British novelist Charles Dickens in 1842 and the future king Edward VII, then Prince of Wales, in 1860.[112] The erecting of the massive stone base of Thomas Crawford's equestrian statue of George Washington in Capitol Square drew large crowds in 1851; the grounds of Capitol Square itself were actually a work in progress throughout the following years, with the centerpiece of the monument, the figure of Washington himself, finally placed on the enormous pedestal in 1858.[113]

Tredegar Iron Works

Perhaps the most important aspect of Richmond's ascent, per its later importance to the Confederate economy, was the city's industrial growth, which developed at a rapid pace. Richmond's booming industries were complemented by a jolt to the city's population, which rose from 27,570 in 1850 to 37,910 just prior to the events at Fort Sumter.[114] By 1850, Richmond had been Virginia's most active commercial port for thirty years, a status it would enjoy for another two decades.[115] Thousands of workers filled hours at Richmond's numerous tobacco warehouses, as Richmond was the world's chief exporter of Virginia's most ubiquitous cash crop. Richmond was also the largest distribution point in the United States for Brazilian coffee beans. The city's hurried growth in industrial concerns also affected population in terms of foreign immigrants; many Germans, Irish and other foreigners (36.2 percent of the city's total population in 1850) made their homes in the city during the 1840s and 1850s, a large percentage working as laborers on the James River and Kanawha Canal.[116]

This period also witnessed the rising fortunes of Joseph Reid Anderson, newly christened proprietor of the Tredegar Iron Works. As Tredegar expanded, so, too, did the Anderson family. Following the 1838 birth of Archer Anderson while the family was still stationed at Fort Monroe, the Andersons welcomed six more children between 1840 and 1851. In 1847, the family moved into a new house at 113 West Franklin Street, several blocks north of Tredegar—a far cry from the small tent the small family had occupied for several weeks upon their initial arrival to Richmond.[117] Anderson also began to dabble in first local and later statewide politics. Following a stint on Richmond's city council beginning in 1847, in 1852 (and, following reelection in 1853) Anderson served in the Virginia House of Delegates as a member of the Whig party; Anderson was once again elected to that body in 1856 following his abandonment of the Whigs in favor of the Democrats as sectional tensions continued to rise.[118] Anderson served among the directors of the Farmers' Bank of Virginia and the rectors of St. Paul's Episcopal Church, and also helped fund several missionary endeavors on behalf of Richmond's historic Monumental Church. In the mid-1840s, in an unused gun house turned chapel on the grounds of the Virginia Manufactory of Arms, Reverend William Duval established and ran a school for the city's children known as the Tredegar Free School. A joint effort subsidized by the commonwealth, the city of Richmond and parents, the school (of which Anderson was a trustee) offered education in, among other topics, "reading, geography, mental and practical arithmetic, grammar, history and astronomy," and was lauded alongside the city's famous Lancastrian School as a bastion of educational greatness.[119]

The iron-making workforce along the James grew to 250 workmen (100 of whom were slaves) in 1850 at Tredegar and the Armory Mill combined; within two years, this number had grown by an additional 100.[120] By 1850, Archer's Armory Mill, capable of producing railroad spikes, axles and even rails themselves, consisted of rolling machines, three heating furnaces and eight furnaces used in puddling. Archer even boasted a small subsidiary division, the Hecla Iron Works, located on an upper floor of the state armory, which specialized in small edged tools, such as axes.[121] Under Anderson's direction, the physical presence of Tredegar grew by several structures—from 1850 to 1861, at least six new buildings appeared on the site. Among the new additions were new boiler and locomotive shops, along with new furnaces for the spike mill, all constructed in 1852.[122] The locomotive shop occupied a parcel that was formerly the site of Cunningham's cotton factory, which had been destroyed completely by fire in February 1851, with the remaining grounds, water rights and machinery subsequently purchased by Anderson.[123] With the growth of Tredegar's operations (and particularly his role in local political circles), Anderson was able to make and secure the necessary business and financial connections that would allow him to further augment Tredegar, acquiring new partners, engineers, machinery and, perhaps most importantly, access to credit and capital that were desperately needed if Tredegar was to become the premier ironworks of the south. The product diversification that necessitated these new structures, as well as Anderson's emphasis on the casting of guns, cannons and other items outside of the railway industry years earlier, allowed Tredegar to survive at a time when many other ironmasters failed.

In the late 1840s, England's railway boom was coming to an end, and as a result, cheaper British rails, the bane of American railmakers, began to flood into the U.S. market. In 1848, 48 percent of all British railroad iron exported went to the United States; by 1853, this number had risen to 63 percent. For years, American railroad iron producers suffered in competition with the inexpensive, imported rails—until 1858, when American railmakers rebounded and the number of imported rails dropped to nearly half the number of those domestically produced.[124]

The years between 1840 and 1860, while certainly a period of radical growth and innovation, were also largely defined by constant fluctuations throughout the American economy and its industries. By 1845, the damage to the national economy inflicted by the Panic of 1837 had largely healed.

TREDEGAR IRON WORKS,
Foundry and Machine Shops,
RICHMOND, VIRGINIA.

JOSEPH R. ANDERSON, Proprietor.

This Old Establishment is prepared to Execute Orders for

Marine, Locomotive and Stationary
STEAM ENGINES,
And all kinds of
Railroad and Bridge Work,

CHAIRS AND FASTENINGS, BOLTS AND NUTS, &c.

We invite the especial attention of those in want of *HEAVY CASTINGS*, as our experience and success in casting heavy Ordnance, Shafts, Cylinders, &c., gives us great advantage in that line—both in our knowledge and command of the strongest iron, and in the treatment of it in our furnaces.

RAILROAD WHEELS.—Having fitted up a Foundry for this business exclusively, we are making Wheels equal to any others, in every respect; and we are prepared to furnish them, with or without axles, on as good terms as any other establishment for an equal article.

IRON TRUCKS FOR CARS.—We would also invite the attention of Railroad Companies to our *IRON TRUCKS*, which we think they will find worthy of their approval and adoption.

THE ROLLING MILLS AND SPIKE FACTORY, formerly connected with this establishment, are now worked by the Proprietor in connection with other parties, under the firm of MORRISS TANNER & Co.; but we will be happy to take orders for *AXLES, BRIDGE BOLTS*, or any other kind of Iron made in that Branch of the Establishment, and when desired fit up the same to order.

We beg leave to refer for the quality of our work, to various Railroad Companies throughout the Southern States, and Sugar Planters in Louisiana;, to the Officers of the United States Navy who superintended the construction of the Roanoke and Colorado—two of the largest class Steam Frigates—the machinery for which was constructed at these works, and to the Ordnance Departments of the Army and Navy.

Apply to the Proprietor, or to the Subscriber,

F. T. GLASGOW, Superintendent.

Advertisement for the Tredegar Iron Works, 1857. *Library of Virginia.*

1849–1865

While painful to the iron industry, the permeation of cheaper British rails into the market resulted in more and more lines being laid across the country, and when the dominance of domestically produced rails returned to the industry in the late 1850s, total mileage further increased, from a little more than nine thousand miles in 1850 to twenty-two thousand within six years.[125] Uncertainty in Europe as a result of the socialist revolutions sweeping the continent in 1848 led to a rise in grain exportations from the United States, as well as increased foreign investment in American industries and infrastructure. The 1848 discovery of and subsequent nationwide rush to substantial gold deposits in the West further buoyed the American economy and the observed stability of its markets. One year before the gold rush, gold production in the United States totaled 43,000 troy ounces (2,948 pounds)—by 1856, the yearly production was 2,661,000 troy ounces a year, or 182,468 pounds.[126] Conflicts in Europe, a general boom in production as 1837 receded into the past and dreams of striking the mother lode: several factors coalesced to entice an increasing number of immigrants to the United States, which allowed for even greater levels of manufacture and production than the domestic workforce could have ever produced. A demand for the type of products Tredegar was producing is evident in the rise of pig iron shipments from furnaces throughout the nation between 1850 and 1856, from 63,000 tons to nearly 900,000 tons. As was the case in 1837, however, situations in Europe (namely the return of peace following the end of the revolutions and the conclusion of the Crimean War) in 1857 precipitated uncertainty on Wall Street, and this uncertainty, joined by rampant speculation and overexpansion on the part of many industries, resulted in another economic panic in America. While the worst of the Panic of 1857 was relatively short-lived, it was not until after several years, and the conclusion of a Civil War, that a recovery truly began. Anderson's business (or businesses, as will be explained momentarily) was impacted negatively by the panic, as were many other industries, but nowhere near to the dire straits he found the company in when he first arrived, and Tredegar continued to grow and diversify its product line.

The Workforce

Diversification into boiler and locomotive fabrication resulted in an ever-increasing number of both skilled and unskilled workers finding employment at the Tredegar. Anderson's were among the higher wages in the city for largely two reasons—first, high wages were needed to first attract skilled workers, such as iron puddlers, from often higher-paying jobs in the more industrialized northern states; secondly, a competitive salary was a necessity if Anderson hoped to actually retain any of these workers for the long run. The workforce at Tredegar was quite diverse; some were natives of Richmond, Henrico County or surrounding areas, while many were immigrants lured to Richmond by either Tredegar directly or other projects, such as the construction of the James River and Kanawha Canal. Various workers were migratory, staying at Tredegar so long as there was decent-paying work and then moving on once they learned of brighter prospects elsewhere. Slaves—both those owned by Anderson and those "rented" from local slave owners—represented a growing segment of the Tredegar workforce during the early to mid-1840s. Immigrant workers fluctuated between temporary and permanent work. Anton Osterbind, a German immigrant whose family will feature prominently throughout the entirety of Tredegar's history, came to work for Anderson as early as the 1840s and remained there for the rest of his life. Others were transitory and sought only temporary employment, as demonstrated by the mention in an early payroll ledger of an "Old Frenchman" and a "Young Frenchman," who only worked for half a day and a full day, respectively, in July 1852.[127] Employee records were not as meticulously kept as they are today, with the two aforementioned Frenchmen as examples. Sometimes only last names were recorded or, in the case of slaves, only first names—Randolph, Jeff, Ezekiel, Little Matt and others.[128]

During Anderson's first years as proprietor, workers were paid on a monthly basis, a particular amount per day worked, to be tallied at month's end with any fees (cash advances, rent at Tredegar housing, coal used for heat in said housing, etc.) deducted before final payment. Wages varied depending on the occupation—a worker in the rolling mill could earn between thirty-five and forty-five dollars a month, based on a daily wage of around one dollar, which could slide either higher or lower depending on several factors, namely, their position and level of expertise. Workers with more desirable skills received higher wages—upward of two dollars, if not more—and likewise, laborers with no sought-after skill set were among the lower paid of employees.[129]

1849–1865

Slavery at Tredegar

One of the most significant tests of Anderson's leadership came shortly before he became outright owner of the works. As a southern industrialist, Anderson was a proponent of rented slave labor, which was both far cheaper than hiring white workers (in 1850, it cost Anderson roughly $100 a year to employ a slave at the works) and could be counted on for much longer periods of time than someone who was free to leave at his discretion—contracts were negotiated not with the slave but rather with the slave owner.[130] If the slaves happened to be purchased personally by Anderson or by the company itself, that was a one-time fee (aside from clothing, food and other necessities) that still amounted to less than the cost of paying the wage of a free white worker.

In utilizing slave labor in the manufacture of iron, Anderson had more than a century of precedent behind him. In the eighteenth century, iron plantations defined the colony's iron industry. These were not stand-alone enterprises, "iron companies" in the familiar sense, but rather just one component of larger commercial and agricultural endeavors. The Neabsco Iron Works, founded in the late 1730s and owned and managed by three generations of the Tayloe family of Prince William County, was one such iron plantation. Annual production levels reached 300 tons of pig iron by the 1750s, but Neabsco's blast furnace was not the only operation on site. Water wheels also powered a gristmill, and corn, wheat and beans were grown and sold, along with livestock, all carried on the same barges that transported iron down the Potomac River.[131] Timber was needed to make charcoal for the furnace but could also be an industry in and of itself as evidenced by Neabsco's sawmill. As was the case with any other plantation, slaves carried out most of the work on site, with a handful of white workers acting as overseers. All of the blacksmiths at Neabsco were slaves, with slaves occupying an increasing number of skilled positions as the years progressed.[132] This was a trend mirrored at nearly all Virginia iron plantations.

Anderson's likeliest inspiration was one ironworks in particular, the furnaces of which had gone out of blast in 1837, just as Tredegar was starting operations—David Ross's Oxford Iron Works.[133] Ross, a Scottish immigrant who came to America in 1750, had, within thirty years, become one of the wealthiest merchants and landowners in Virginia, eventually claiming upward of 100,000 acres across the state.[134] Despite facing accusations of continued loyalty to the Crown, Ross invested heavily in the Revolutionary cause, by both lending much-needed funds to the Continental army and accepting the position of state commercial agent, charged with obtaining much-needed supplies for the war effort; it was during the initial stages of the war that Ross came into possession of the Oxford Iron Works in Campbell County, several miles east of the city of Lynchburg. Oxford, which provided cannonry and ordnance in wartime and easily transitioned to domestic items during peacetime, was a massive complex at its height, boasting several forges, bloomeries and blast furnaces. Much of the property, spanning twenty-four thousand acres at its apex in the early 1800s, was forest, which proved instrumental in providing charcoal for the furnaces.[135] Save for a minuscule handful of white supervisors (at times numbering no more than three), the entirety of Oxford's workforce was in bondage, some hired out from other slave owners but the majority owned by Ross or Oxford itself. Every hand at the site (well over two hundred by 1812)—the colliers producing charcoal, the miners who extricated the ore from the earth, the foundry men at the furnaces, the women and children at the farm and gristmill that helped feed the complex—was a slave. Ross's founder, or chief of all operations, at the works was a slave named Abram, who had spent his entire life at the Oxford estate and in whose skills and judgment Ross placed pronounced confidence. The use of slaves at Oxford saved Ross from having to pay the high wages expected by many skilled white artisans. Ross obviously took great pride in the quality of implements produced by his slaves: "Take again and again one of my most faith[ful] servants, give him some encouragement or a fourth part of what you must give a white lad," Ross wrote to an associate. "You'll find him ten times better than any you can hire."[136]

These bondsmen, among the most experienced and capable ironworkers in the region, helped Oxford become far more profitable than it could have been with a predominantly white working population, and there can be no doubt that this success imprinted itself on Anderson's own designs regarding industrial slavery. While there is no evidence that Anderson intended to replace all of his workmen with slaves to the extent seen at Oxford (it simply would not have been possible if Anderson was to compete in locomotive, ordnance and other rapidly evolving industries), the use of slave labor in many skilled and unskilled positions would have absolutely negated the high wages Anderson needed to pay to northern or foreign transplants to the works.

Anderson had shown a preference for slave labor on particular projects during his tenure on the Shenandoah Valley turnpike and, like many southern industrialists prior, moreover saw slaves as a manner of (to quote historians David Roediger and Elizabeth Esch) "strike insurance," as opposed to free workers who could simply walk away from their job if they so desired.[137] The blast furnace and coal mine properties that Anderson and his family owned operated similarly to previous iron plantations—iron ore was made into pig iron, and coal was mined from the earth, while the surrounding area was farmed in order to feed workers, slaves or otherwise. During the latter years of the 1840s, the railroad boom in Britain came to an abrupt halt, resulting in the flood of cheap, surplus British rails and other iron products into the American market, further necessitating the cutting of costs on Anderson's part at the time and making slave labor, from a profit standpoint, all the more attractive.[138]

Anderson, like many slaveowners, seemed on the one hand to tolerate and engage in an abhorrent institution such as slavery while also, concurrently and paradoxically, showing warmth and even respect to those held in bondage by his own hand. One slave in particular seems to have not only met Anderson's expectations of what a bondsman was capable of at an ironworks but also to have become a respected employee and perhaps even a personal friend. Born a slave in May 1814, Emmanuel Quivers came to be associated with Tredegar when his owner hired him out to Anderson for a term of six months. Quivers apparently impressed Anderson to such an extent that, at Quivers's personal request, the ironmaster purchased him for $1,100 in January 1846 and kept him in the skilled positions he had already held for several months, promising to allow him to work off his purchase price (with no interest) and attain his freedom.[139] Quivers continued to work at Tredegar, likely attaining the position of foreman of the enslaved African Americans employed in the rail mill, all the while investing in his own emancipation, which was finally achieved in the early 1850s, with Anderson having loaned Quivers over $1,300 toward the purchase and emancipation of his wife and children. Soon after freedom was attained, Quivers relocated his family, including his young son by the name of Joseph Reid Quivers, to the West, establishing himself as a respected engineer and organizer and advocate of several civil rights initiatives in Stockton, California.[140]

Anderson's goal in utilizing slave labor was largely to transfer the skills retained by white (often European) workmen to his slaves at both Tredegar and the Armory Iron Company, of which he was president at the time. Slaves had been growing in numbers at Tredegar for several years (rising from eighteen in 1838 to forty-one in 1847) in relatively lower-skilled positions; however, when Anderson attempted to force puddlers to take slaves as apprentices at the Armory Mill, the workers rebelled, demanding that all slaves be removed from the puddling furnaces and any other skilled positions at both Tredegar and the Armory Mill, along with an increase in the amount paid for finished products.¹⁴¹ It should be remembered that, in addition to simple prejudice (which was likely the case for many workers), a significant amount of these workmen were Irish and Welsh immigrants, dedicated to the guild system practiced for generations in their home countries. In their minds, not only did Anderson's actions seem to weaken their trade by passing along well-guarded secrets to the uninitiated, but also his forcing of apprentices on the ironsmiths was perceived as an insult to their time-honored trade and to the workers themselves. In an open letter published in the city's papers, Anderson skipped any sort of ultimatum and rendered sentence on the workmen:

> *To my late workmen at The Tredegar Iron Works…I regretted that you had given up constant employment at good wages, always promptly paid in cash, but that I fully recognised the right of any individual to leave my employment at any time. At the same time I had no idea of relinquishing my right to discharge or employ any one at my pleasure. That I had not designed to put Negroes to puddling at the Tredegar Works but that now I should be compelled by your quitting my employment to do so, and that I had never intended to discharge any of my hands who did their duty…You will bear in mind that you have discharged yourselves…I would never discharge one of you who continued to do his duty to me and now having endeavored to do my duty as your Employer, I wish that you may, one and all of you, never regret that you have given up the Employment you had from me.*¹⁴²

Although the presence of slaves employed at Tredegar and the nearby Armory works (117 in 1848, collectively) did increase as the overall workforce grew in succeeding years, there was never again an attempt on Anderson's part to force slave apprenticeships on puddlers and other white workmen.¹⁴³ In regard to his views on organized labor, it is interesting to note that in a lawsuit subsequently brought by Anderson against his "late workmen," the most egregious crime the strikers were charged with was not racial intolerance or even the disruption of operations but rather the threat of forming an "organization"—a union. Not surprisingly, it would not be until after Anderson's death that a nationally recognized union would have a significant presence at Tredegar. Such sentiment was echoed in newspaper editorials:

> *The right of employers to select such kinds of labor as they may prefer, is one of which the law itself cannot deprive them—much less combinations of individuals, formed either for the purpose of intimidation, or with*

the less criminal, though unworthy design of inducing, for other reasons, acquiescence in their demands. The sympathies of all communities are naturally and properly most generally in favor of the hard working-man [sic], *whose toils ought to be fairly requited; but in* this *community, no combination, formed for the* purpose *avowed by the authors of the recent strike, can receive the slightest toleration.*[144]

ANDERSON AND FOREIGN WORKERS

The importance of foreign workers at Tredegar began with its founding under Deane and the Cunninghams and certainly continued after Anderson gained control of the works. Rhys Davies was only the first of many Europeans to leave their mark on Tredegar, their skills and dedication to their trade ensuring longevity to Deane's venture. As demonstrated by the mostly foreign-born workers' strike of 1847, however, the presence of such employees could, ironically, prove beneficial as well as crippling.

Following his death, Rhys Davies's father and a number of the other Welsh workmen who had journeyed to Richmond with him stayed on at the works, including his longtime collaborator James Hunter. Hunter actually replaced Davies as superintendent briefly before leaving, the position transferring first to Francis Deane and then to bookkeeper John F. Tanner in the early 1850s. James Hunter founded his own business, the Richmond Iron and Steel Works (alternatively known as the Richmond Steel and Iron Works), soon after concluding his tenure at Tredegar. Hunter's establishment was located fairly close to Tredegar, on the banks of the James River, just short of the Richmond & Petersburg Railroad Bridge, which ran from the south side of the James River, in the city of Manchester, to the Richmond side, along what was (and still is) Eighth Street. Due to the proximity of the two establishments and the increased use of Tredegar iron in various smaller firms across the city, it is highly likely that Hunter continued to have some working relationship with Anderson and company.[145]

In some cases, several members of the same family came to work for Anderson, with a select few remaining through successive generations. One such family of Scottish immigrants appears to have started working for Tredegar in the 1840s, the patriarch of which, in recollections decades later, Anderson regarded fondly as "an accomplished mechanic and honest man."[146] Matthew Delaney was born in 1815 in the town of Dalbeattie, located on a peninsula jutting out into the Irish Sea.[147] Young Matthew's engineering acumen was likely honed there, as Dalbeattie was home to some of Scotland's most productive granite mines. Matthew, along with his nephew Alexander, traveled to America at some point in the late 1830s or early 1840s, arriving first in New England, where he married before relocating to Richmond. Anderson, in later years, spoke of Delaney as being at Tredegar when he first became purchasing agent in 1841 and of the Scotsman supervising the construction of the *Polk* in 1844.[148] By 1853, Delaney was a significant enough presence at Tredegar to be made a partner in one of the site's largest operations.

On July 1, 1854, Joseph R. Anderson, Matthew Delaney, Francis T. Glasgow (a nephew of Anderson's) and William Steptoe entered into a partnership that reorganized a portion of the Tredegar operation into Anderson, Delaney & Co. The new organization, alternatively known as the Tredegar Engine Works, was created primarily for the purposes of producing locomotive engines, although naval and stationary engines were also offered. The central locomotive shop, built in 1852, was three stories high and covered an area roughly 150 by 50 feet and utilized tools and machinery produced in Tredegar's other shops.[149] Under the new partnership, Anderson remained the senior partner, while Delaney and Glasgow received one-fifth share in the company; Steptoe received one-tenth. Also per the agreement, Delaney received a salary of $1,500 a year and was also eligible for bonuses, depending on the company's end-of-year profits; today (2015), Delaney's salary would equal the purchasing power of roughly $40,000, an impressive amount for a relatively recent arrival to the States and a testimony perhaps to the technical and supervisory abilities Delaney undoubtedly exhibited.[150] Among Delaney's largest projects was an 1854 contract to manufacture two steam engines for the navy steamer USS *Roanoke*, followed by a February 1855 contract to produce fifty-nine-inch-caliber guns ("cast solid, bored according to the plan proposed by the late Captain Walbach"), also for the United States Navy.[151]

In 1856, Anderson, Delaney & Co. was dissolved; Glasgow stayed on with Anderson at Tredegar, as did Delaney and his nephew Alexander: "And the said parties [Anderson, Delaney, Glasgow, and Steptoe] having each for himself decided that it was desirable to terminate the said association or concern so to cancel it as that it should be treated and regarded as it had never been formed or commenced."[152] Despite the rather cryptic wording of the dissolution, its reasons were far from nefarious. The concern had been formed largely to support Tredegar's locomotive division, which had suffered heavily following the explosion of two locomotive boilers—once losses, and reputation, were recouped, the concern was abolished.[153] Matthew Delaney died on August 6, 1858, at the age of fifty-three. In his will, Matthew provided for his only son, the toddler Chester Alexander, naming Alexander as executor and legal guardian of the boy, to whom Matthew bequeathed his estate.[154]

The arrival of one immigrant in particular laid the foundations for a familial connection with Tredegar that would span well over one hundred years and four generations. Anton Guenther Bernhard Osterbind was born on June 10, 1820, in Atens, in the Grand Duchy of Oldenburg, a small kingdom that later became a city in what is now the state of Lower Saxony in modern-day Germany.[155] Anton was the son of a Lutheran sexton, or church keeper, who acted essentially as groundskeeper, town schoolmaster and lay representative of the church to the community. Anton was enrolled in a seminary after his father's death in 1825, likely for the purposes of following in the family vocation, but did not finish his studies before leaving for America with elder brother Berend and sister Anna Margaretha in 1839.

The majority of German immigrants coming to America in the nineteenth century first arrived in the North and then migrated southward later, if ever at all. For a variety of reasons, ranging from the higher wages paid in the North to an unwillingness on the part of many immigrants to work alongside African Americans, slaves or otherwise, it was difficult for southern industrialists such as Anderson to procure foreign workers who had settled in the North, let alone entice any into relocating to Richmond directly. Taking into account the fact that Anton came directly to Richmond and was immediately employed at an ironworks with no evidence whatsoever that he had any experience in the industry previously, there is the possibility that the family had some contacts in the area, possibly with Tredegar itself. It seems almost from the start that he made an impression, as Archer Anderson related to one of Anton's grandchildren in 1914: "My earliest recollection of the Tredegar Works as a boy 5 years old accompanying my father is associated with your dear old grandfather [Anton]—an image all his life of German probity and fidelity."[156]

Many immigrants to the United States in the nineteenth century were working class and relatively poor; Richmond's German population, however, was an exception, with 90 percent of all Germans arriving in Richmond the decade before the Civil War belonging to the middle classes.[157] Whereas a majority of these immigrants retained their Old World professions (butchers, clothiers, etc.) and sought the company of fellow Teutonic émigrés in the ranks of the many German aid groups that dotted the city—such as the *Deutsche Krankengesellschaft* (German Society for the Relief of the Sick), founded in 1841, or the *Unterstützungs-Verein*, a fund for poor or displaced immigrants, founded in the 1850s—Anton relied instead on Tredegar and religion for his and his family's integration into Richmond society.[158] The Osterbinds became stalwarts in a burgeoning Methodist mission in the Tredegar workman's neighborhood of Oregon Hill, with Anton eventually becoming a trustee, Sunday school superintendent and board of stewards chairman of the Laurel Street Methodist Episcopal Church. Anton's earliest recorded work at Tredegar was as a member of a small collective known as "Osterbind & Co.," which produced cast items for the company at per-piece rates; in time, he was promoted to the position of foreman.[159] As Anton's ever-growing expertise allowed him to assume greater positions of responsibility at Tredegar, his family's personal fortunes advanced; he purchased two lots in Oregon Hill, on which he built two houses, and by 1850, he could even afford to hire live-in servants.[160]

Joseph R. Anderson, & Co.

The aforementioned Anderson, Delaney & Co. was but one of several short-lived firms that Anderson formed shortly after taking control of Tredegar. In order to create multiple ventures through which Anderson could generate profits while sharing operating costs with others, the interests in various divisions of Tredegar's operations were sold over the course of the 1850s, creating several firms that, in time, would be reconstituted once again under the banner of a single unified Tredegar. The formation of these companies and the recruiting of important partners and investors that made them possible allowed for Anderson to simultaneously survive downturns in the American iron industry, primarily the influx of cheap British iron during the late 1840s, as well as garner the funds needed to complete his payments to Tredegar's stockholders.

In 1852, the company of Anderson, Souther, & Pickering was formed. John Souther and D.A. Pickering were veterans of the Boston Locomotive Works (later the Hinkley Locomotive Works), and their presence in Richmond attests to Anderson's ability to attract highly skilled engineers and recognized leaders in their respective fields from all over the country. Souther actually owned his own eponymous locomotive works in Boston by this point and

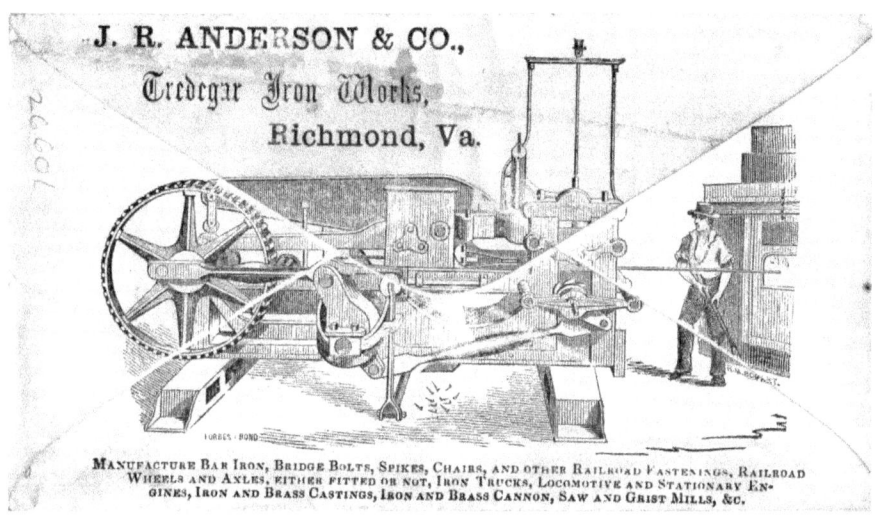

Envelope of the Tredegar Iron Works (Joseph R. Anderson & Co.), displaying the operations of a spike-making machine, 1859. *Library of Virginia.*

brought a fair number of his experienced workmen to Richmond for use at the new establishment. He traveled frequently back and forth between Massachusetts and Virginia overseeing the progress at both firms.[161] Souther brought to Tredegar not only his and Pickering's expertise but also the talents of his assistant at the time, Zerah Colburn. Recognized by historians of the locomotive industry as "a leading authority…and one of the most gifted technical writers of the nineteenth century," Colburn, a native of Saratoga Springs, New York, worked at Tredegar under Souther for some time before moving on and, among other accomplishments, assuming editorship of the *American Railroad Journal* and then the *Engineer*, two leading railway publications of the day.[162] Souther and Pickering's share in the company was purchased by Anderson two years after its founding, the buildings and tools (and possibly some workmen) from which were integrated into Anderson, Delaney & Co., which was formed several months following the dissolution of the partnership with Souther. Forty-one locomotives were produced at Tredegar between 1850 and 1855, a majority of those under the Souther and Delaney partnerships.[163] Souther and Pickering returned to Boston and founded the Globe Locomotive Works, a highly successful venture most remembered for manufacturing the first steam-powered excavator, or steam-shovel, the company's most successful product.[164]

The Tredegar rolling mill was the center of another such firm. A Richmond businessman named Charles Y. Morris and former bookkeeper

Tredegar Iron Works

John F. Tanner (as superintendent) partnered with Anderson to create the firm of Morris, Tanner and Company in December 1853. The price for which Morris bought into the venture, a total of $115,000, was instrumental in helping Anderson to successfully meet his financial obligations to the Tredegar stockholders, thus ensuring his complete ownership of the works.[165] Among Morris, Tanner & Co.'s most notable accomplishments was the 1856 forging of giant iron braces for the dome of the United States Capitol Building, undergoing reconstruction at the time; the government apparently so valued the quality of Tredegar iron that the company was allowed a six-week extension in order to create the massive rolls needed for the project.[166]

In 1859, a major reorganization took place, one that brought all of the various operations on site under Anderson's management. Dr. Robert Archer's armory works, which produced mainly basic merchant bar at the time and had enlarged its operation following the leasing of additional property adjacent to the Virginia Manufactory of Arms in 1850, merged its operations with that of Anderson's Tredegar Iron Works, effective January 1, 1859; with Anderson providing Tredegar as well as $60,000 in capital and Archer, along with son Robert S. Archer, contributing their rolling mill, furnaces and capital equaling $10,000, the firm Joseph R. Anderson, & Company was formed.[167] All previous responsibilities held by the smaller concerns were now assumed by the new, amalgamated firm; Anderson, Delaney & Co. had already been dissolved, and the partnership of Morris, Tanner and Company was concluded as well, finalized with the $60,250 sale of Morris's remaining stake in the rolling mill back to Anderson, effective the same day as the formation of J.R. Anderson & Co.[168] Anderson had created and held partial (and senior) ownership of the various companies involved, so the creation of J.R. Anderson & Co. cannot be thought of as a merger of separate entities in the traditional business sense, although the addition of R. Archer & Company's armory operations arguably constitute one of the few examples of horizontal integration in Tredegar's history.

J.R. Anderson & Co. wasted no time securing lucrative contracts following its consolidation; as the Tredegar name grew, various railroad companies across the South soon dominated its order books with sales small and large. In March 1859, 1,500 eight-inch railroad chairs were ordered for the sum of $480 for use on a section of the Western Railroad Company's line across through North Carolina, and in April, enough car wheels to equip fifty-five freight cars for the Mississippi Central Railroad Company were purchased for over $4,000. On May 23, a contract was signed between Tredegar and the suppliers to the Roanoke Valley Railroad that contained, among other items,

1849–1865

130,000 pounds of railroad spikes, at a cost of nearly $5,200; the contract also called for Tredegar to produce enough wrought-iron railroad chairs to cover thirty-two miles of track.[169] In July, the Jefferson Railroad Company of Tennessee, based in Rogersville, placed a particularly large order with Anderson: two complete locomotive engines at $7,750 each, along with two box cars and two flat cars at $685 and $585 for each set, respectively; the combined price of $9,020 does not include a passenger car Jefferson also ordered, the price of which was to be determined based on the going rate for such cars in the North. A September 3, 1859 contract worth $4,400 called for twenty freight cars to be fabricated at Tredegar for use on the Virginia Central Railroad, and in November, the Richmond & York River Railroad ordered a second-class baggage and mail car at a cost of $1,500.[170] The railroads were not Tredegar's only customers; small portable and stationary engines continued to sell—a sawmill engine was sold for $2150 in the summer—and orders for all manner of machinery from sugar mills to rolling mills continued to pour in. The upswing in business that coincided with the formation of J.R. Anderson & Co. was certainly welcomed and helped to boost the company's name recognition. However, the fact that it was rare for companies to pay in full upon delivery (and Tredegar offered discounts to those firms that could) meant that, while orders came in, Anderson's firm was often in a precarious situation financially speaking, taking out loans to cover production costs and paying for some of their own supplies on credit.

From 1859 to 1861, the company's personnel also expanded by several hundred workmen (free and enslaved) and included the hiring of several

Tredegar Iron Works, circa 1863. *Library of Congress.*

highly skilled individuals needed to keep the various departments running smoothly, efficiently and profitably. On April 13, 1859, Thatcher Perkins was hired, at $2,000 a year (if he stayed on, this was to be increased by $500 upon completion of his first year of service), to be superintendent of the Tredegar Foundry and Machine Shops.[171] Perkins's high pay was justified given his past experience and accomplishments. Born in Maine in 1810, Thatcher, from 1851 to 1858, was a partner in his own locomotive firm, Smith & Perkins (also known as the Virginia Locomotive Works), based in Alexandria; before that, from 1847 to 1851, he had served at the Baltimore & Ohio Railroad, as master of machinery, a tenure during which he produced a number of patents and inventions, including a revolutionary system that redirected excess steam back into the locomotive's engine, providing for the further generation of heat and motive power.[172] Anderson, however, did not benefit from Perkins's expertise for very long. Less than a year after he began work, in December 1859, Perkins left Tredegar and returned to the Baltimore & Ohio and his previous post of master of machinery. There he remained until May 1865, when he was appointed superintendent of the Pittsburgh Locomotive and Car Works, founded by Andrew Carnegie that same year.[173] William T. Francis was hired as the chief blacksmith in the rolling mill and spike factory in October 1859 at a pay of $100 per month—more than double what many workers in the same shops could expect to earn.[174]

Also in October, Anderson signed an agreement with Uri Haskins, an immigrant recently arrived from Canada. For $2.75 a day, Haskins was hired to "keep up the old and construct any new machinery and also to superintend the manufacture of all chairs and other articles made at either mill."[175] Haskins was also provided with three rooms in the office, as well as coal, free of charge. It was also outlined specifically in his contract that, in the event there was a problem at the works and his supervision was required, Haskins would report immediately and without qualms, no matter the hour of day or night. A year later, in August 1860, Haskins signed another contract with Anderson, guaranteeing a yearly salary of $1,000 (in addition to the previously mentioned rooms and coal usage), as well as the right to a furlough from Richmond, for a period not to exceed three months, during which Haskins was expected to "employ [his] time for the benefit of J.R. Anderson & Co., in obtaining information that may be interesting to them"—presumably industry news and expected price fluctuations. Haskins paid his own traveling expenses but was compensated for his time, as well as for whatever information he happened to provide.[176]

1849–1865

In July 1860, Henry McCarty was hired at a pay of $650 a year (later amended to $1,300 in 1861) to serve as the manager of the rolling mills, a position he had held several years prior, before taking a leave of absence in 1853 on account of illness. Per his 1861 contract, McCarty's pay was to be increased to $1,500 per year, provided he was successful in keeping the rolling mill's production costs below a certain percentage of final sales.[177]

The most significant new hire of the period was that of J.R. Anderson's son, Archer Anderson. Archer Anderson was born at Old Point Comfort, Fort Monroe, in the home of his maternal grandfather, naval surgeon Dr. Robert Archer, on October 15, 1838. The first child of Joseph Reid Anderson and his wife, Sarah, at the age of four Archer traveled with his parents to Richmond following his father's assumption of duties at Tredegar.[178] In Richmond, Archer was educated privately, first by a friend of the family (actually the aunt of future major E.T.D. Myers, veteran of the Army of Northern Virginia and later president of the Richmond, Fredericksburg and Potomac Railroad) and then at Richmond's Turner Classical School.[179] In his youth, Archer was an acknowledged intellectual and polyglot; by the age of fifteen, he was completely fluent in German, French and Italian and could write in both Greek and Latin. A voracious reader, Archer was familiar with both the popular works of the day, as well as the classical literature of antiquity. At sixteen, Archer began coursework at the University of Virginia (UVA) in Charlottesville, and by his eighteenth birthday, had earned a master of arts degree; he followed this with a two-year travel-study throughout Europe, at the conclusion of which he returned to UVA and earned another degree from the university's school of law. On August 9, 1859, in Paris, France, Archer married Mary Anne Mason, the daughter of former secretary of the navy and former attorney general (and then ambassador to France) John Y. Mason. While he had toyed with the idea of pursuing a career in science, astronomy in particular, and had worked in a law office for a brief time following his graduation from UVA's school of law, Archer quickly recognized his own talent for business and came to work at his father's firm.[180] Archer's arrival coincided with the departure of Charles Campbell, a Scottish immigrant who had served as Anderson's first foundry superintendent, whose duties Archer assumed; Anderson's firstborn was named as a junior partner in the firm as of January 1, 1861.[181]

Civil War

As the nation inched dangerously toward civil war during the spring of 1861, Anderson (a lifelong Whig until that party's collapse and his switch to the Democrats in the mid-1850s) increasingly grew supportive of the secessionist movement. Due partly to his refusal to adopt cannon-making techniques approved by the federal government, United States contracts had lessened, and Anderson gradually began to offer his services to Southern militias and governments. This growing Southern nationalism, however, did not affect sales to the North whenever they were possible, as Tredegar was still producing for Northern customers well into 1861; the United States government was the recipient of 881 Tredegar cannons in the years between 1844 and 1860, the year South Carolina seceded from the Union.[182] While Anderson grew increasingly restless regarding what he saw as an inevitable conflict between the North and the South and at times called for a boycott of Northern goods, his dependence on both Northern-produced raw materials (particularly anthracite coal) and modern machinery ensured that nothing short of war itself would cut Tredegar completely off from dealings with the North.[183]

In November 1859, Anderson allowed his growing disillusionment with the federal government to affect the fortunes of the company when he refused to adopt a new method for casting cannons, a method the Ordnance Department required all founders to follow. Some fifteen years earlier, in 1844, the deaths of both the secretary of state and secretary of the navy following the explosion of a defective cannon during testing prompted the government to seek a new technique for casting sturdier cannons; the Ordnance Department eventually decided on a process perfected by Captain Thomas Rodman, which cast cannons, not solid to be bored out later (as was the method at Tredegar), but rather hollow—a method that allowed for the manufacture of larger cannons and a cooling period that allowed for consistency throughout the piece, lowering the chances of cracks, fractures and other imperfections that could prove disastrous.[184] Anderson, hoping to avoid costly alterations to his cannon foundry and also partly due to the fact that royalties for the process were being collected by a northern competitor, refused to adopt the Rodman method and, over the course of the next several months, wrote to the secretary of war requesting that he still be allowed to cast cannon solid. Anderson offered as evidence in his defense Tredegar's proven record of quality-tested cannon under his guidance, the failure rate of many Rodman guns and the written support of other ironmasters, from both the North and South. The secretary, however, was unconvinced, and a November 1859 $20,000 contract for columbiads was cancelled, not only costing Tredegar valuable income but also depriving the works, and later the Confederacy, of one of the most advanced methods of munitions production available at the time.[185]

After the assault on Fort Sumter by Confederate artillery (an attack using Tredegar-made weaponry, no less) and the convening of Virginia's secession convention, Anderson led a procession of enthusiastic Richmonders through the streets of the city down to Tredegar, where, as speeches were given by notables in favor of secession and with *"La Marseillaise"* performed by the State Armory Band, Anderson's workers raised a Confederate flag high above the Tredegar spike mill.[186] Fearful that the April 17, 1861 convention called to decide Virginia's possible secession would fail to make a final break with Washington, Anderson was a delegate to an ancillary convention, the purpose of which was to push for secession, if the first convention failed to do so; this was rendered null when secession was indeed sanctioned.[187] Immediately after secession was announced, Anderson's son Archer traveled to Montgomery, Alabama, provisional capital of the Confederate government, to offer Tredegar to the Southern cause, even to the extent of selling or leasing the works to the government outright, with the Anderson family retaining operational control. The Confederate government, however, proved ambivalent concerning the nationalization of Tredegar, and it remained a family affair.[188] Not only did Tredegar's Richmond facility operate in service of the Confederacy, but the many blast furnaces the firm owned in Botetourt County, in addition to supplying Tredegar, also sold pig iron to the Confederate States Nitrate and Mining Bureau to be used in ironworks across the South. Tredegar did not make rifles and other small arms for the Confederacy, although the Virginia government, nearly a year before secession, had contracted the works to construct such machinery as needed for that purpose (later complimenting those that would be taken from Harper's Ferry) at the former Virginia Manufactory of Arms, the Confederacy's Richmond Arsenal as of June 1861.[189]

Early in the war, Anderson realized that conscription threatened Tredegar with a loss of some of its most vital workers, shown quite clearly when John McDonald, the worker in charge of cannon rifling, was conscripted and only returned to the works after much pleading on his employer's part.[190] Anderson entreated the government for a solution. On June 3, 1861, Governor John Letcher commissioned the formation of the Tredegar Battalion (Sixth Infantry, Local Defense Troop), a home unit, three hundred

Tredegar Iron Works

Brigadier General Joseph Reid Anderson, CSA. *Courtesy of Anne Hobson Freeman.*

strong at the time of its creation, composed entirely of Tredegar workers and based at the works; the nearby Confederate arsenal followed suit and formed its own Fifth Infantry Battalion, Local Defense Troops. The formation of the Tredegar Battalion allowed Anderson to maintain prominence in Southern iron manufacture by keeping his most skilled workmen on site while also allowing them to answer the Confederate call for service and to defend the city, which they did on several occasions.[191]

Joseph Reid Anderson wrote to Secretary of War Leroy Pope Walker later that summer in the hopes that he might leave Tredegar temporarily and secure an active field command of his own. While reaffirming his commitment that the Tredegar would meet all expectations held by the Confederate government, he explained that since "I have been educated a soldier and see that the Government finds it necessary to confer military command on citizens who have not had the advantage of military education, I think it is time now for me to claim some exemption from purely business occupations and to ask for a command in the field."[192]

Despite questions from many in the Confederate leadership, including General Lee himself, about whether Anderson could best serve the Confederacy at the head of the ironworks rather than in the field, Anderson was appointed a brigadier general in the Confederate army in September 1861. Anderson assured any remaining doubters that Tredegar would continue just as smoothly as it had up until then by placing its day-to-day operations in the hands of Tanner and Archer Sr.[193] By all accounts, Joseph served with distinction; almost fifty years after the fact, one of Anderson's lieutenants during the war, Dr. William S. Christian of Middlesex County, recounted his short tenure under Anderson's command:

1849–1865

General Anderson's manner always impressed me. There was something in his courage and superb coolness under fire that was an inspiration. He showed himself brave and gallant without ostentation, cool, deliberate, and careful in placing his men, and bore upon his face the marks of unyielding stubbornness when stubbornness was required. But that stubbornness never amounted to rashness. We subordinate officers love to see a General Officer of those characteristics, a man who seemed to know what he was about while he was doing it; who would willingly and cheerfully take the same risks which he required others to take.[194]

Anderson served until 1862, when he was wounded during the Seven Days Battles (at Frayser's Farm, specifically). During his recovery, Anderson acquiesced to those who were adamant that he resign his military commission, and he soon returned to the helm of Tredegar.[195] Archer Anderson also served in the Confederate army during the Civil War. Early on, Archer was made a private in Company F of the First Virginia Infantry, under the command of Captain R.M. Cary. The younger Anderson served in Fredericksburg and Aquia Creek and was soon transferred with the rest of his company to the Twenty-first Virginia Regiment. In September 1861, Archer was promoted to assistant adjutant general and, in February 1862, was promoted again to the rank of major assistant adjutant general under Major General T.H. Holmes. In regard to Archer's actions during the Peninsula Campaign, Holmes recalled "the greatest zeal and intelligence in the performance of his duty and for his bravery on the field."[196] During an October 1862 skirmish near White's Ford, overlooking the Potomac River, Archer's horse was shot out from under him, and the resulting fall knocked him unconscious for over ten hours. In March 1863, Archer traveled with Major General D.H. Hill (who by then had replaced Holmes as his superior officer) to North Carolina, before finally being ordered back to Richmond by General Robert E. Lee. Now a lieutenant colonel, Archer fought in the Battle of Chickamauga, where once again his horse was shot from under him; following the battle, Archer was removed from the field temporarily and served as an advisor to President Jefferson Davis under the command of General Braxton Bragg. Near the end of the war, he was transferred to the command (and at the personal request of) General Joseph E. Johnston to act as adjutant general in the Army of Tennessee, a position he held until the final days of the war.

Tredegar Iron Works

Business During the War

With Richmond's naming as the capitol of the Confederacy in May 1861, the city quickly became a hub of politics and commerce, and contracts with the Confederate government came pouring into Tredegar, necessitating an increase in its workforce, which swelled to nearly eight hundred workers—white, foreign-born and free and enslaved African Americans—by the end of 1862.[197] Anderson continued to purchase slaves for work at Tredegar before hostilities had commenced, spending at least $49,045 between 1842 and 1860, nearly 40 percent of that ($19,510) in the preceding twelve years since the 1847 puddlers' strike.[198] The ever-increasing demands placed on the Tredegar's shoulders emphasized the importance of recruiting and especially retaining skilled (and even unskilled) workmen and slaves, the numbers of both rising significantly by war's end. Despite the formation of the Tredegar Battalion, Anderson was still losing a significant portion of his workforce for a variety of reasons. Many workers were either conscripted into the army or were taken from work in order to help build and fortify defenses around the city; in the case of many of Anderson's foreign workers, some simply went north following Virginia's secession.

In 1861, Tredegar's foreign-born workers once again went on strike, although this time Anderson had less room for maneuverability as he was now, to some degree, answering directly to government authorities. In September of that year, Irish foundry workers went on strike, demanding higher wages; the former Virginia Manufactory of Arms was set to reopen shortly as the new Confederate Armory, and with comparatively higher wages than what Anderson offered at the time.[199] As opposed to the autonomy Anderson demonstrated in 1847 by simply dismissing his striking workers, he now had to take into account Tredegar's role as a central ordnance supplier to the Confederate States. He appealed to Lieutenant Colonel James Burton, commandant at the Confederate Arsenal, but to no avail, and he eventually agreed to the workers' demands for an increase in pay to three dollars a day.[200] Grievances were voiced a second time, in March 1863, concerning the disparity of pay between government operations such as the arsenal and private enterprise such as Tredegar, and once again Anderson was left with little option but to raise wages at the demand of striking workers.[201]

William Brackens, born in 1813, was a free African American who had worked at the Cloverdale furnaces in the 1840s and 1850s before being transferred to Tredegar prior to the outbreak of war. Boatmen, regardless of race, held positions of authority equal to that of many other high-level artisans, and Anderson recognized Brackens for his ability to navigate the canal waters, both in Botetourt and in Richmond, and named him chief of Tredegar's bateau boat fleet on the James. When the Confederate government conscripted Brackens into service in June 1864 to help construct earthen fortifications around the city, Anderson pleaded with the government, reaching out to the secretary of the navy himself for support, to allow Brackens to return to the bateau fleet. Otherwise, Anderson argued, Tredegar's ability to power the war effort would be severely hindered. Brackens was returned to Tredegar within a month.[202]

The war years witnessed augmentations to the Tredegar site, expansions and innovations required in the face of increasing demand brought on by secession. Nearly fifteen years after Anderson's last experiment with turbines, a fifty-four-inch Baird turbine was installed at Archer's Armory works in 1861 alongside similar turbines already operating in the adjacent Confederate Arsenal. Also, in April 1861, Chesterfield's Bellona Foundry was leased by Anderson to supplement Tredegar's output, but the lease was soon relinquished so that focus could be placed on improving the production capacity of the central Tredegar and armory sites.[203] While working under the auspices of, and largely thanks to loans from, the Confederate government, Anderson added new buildings to Tredegar in order to better fulfill its new responsibilities to the Southern Confederacy; the expansion of the Tredegar was just one aspect of a larger Confederate effort, bordering on actual nationalization of the industry, to funnel as much of the South's iron-making resources as possible to the war effort.[204] Between 1861 and 1863, a number of new structures appeared on site, including a new furnace house and a new gun-boring mill. Most importantly, in 1861, work began on a massive new foundry, dedicated solely to the production of cannonry, situated to the lower right of the original foundry, which itself remained in operation and continued to produce cannons and other items needed for both the war effort and Confederate industry.[205] By war's end, both foundries collectively had contributed 473 siege cannons and 626 iron and bronze field artillery to the Confederate cause.[206]

Tredegar produced ordnance ranging in size from six-pounder mountain howitzers to enormous forty-two-pounders, used largely as naval weaponry or coastal defenses. While such cannons were normally bronze in composition, a scarcity of copper resulted in a majority of Tredegar cannonry from May 1861 onward being cast in iron, which itself became an increasing rarity as access to the western blast furnaces in Botetourt County were cut off from Richmond by Union advances.[207] Despite not following the Rodman method of ordnance casting years earlier, Anderson attempted to emulate many aspects of Union cannon-making. In the summer of 1862, Tredegar began producing Napoleon and Parrot guns, based on Northern blueprints and captured Union ordnance from First Manassas, respectively.[208]

Infernal Machines

During Tredegar's time as the "Krupp of the Confederacy," Anderson's works provided more than half of the Southern states' domestically produced cannonry and large guns. Tredegar's military output was supervised by the Confederate government in the form of two men in particular, Chief of Ordnance Major Josiah Gorgas and Lieutenant John Mercer Brooke of the Confederate navy. Gorgas was instrumental in many of the updates that improved Tredegar's manufacturing capacity and in ensuring that the needed amount of ordnance came from the works, whereas Brooke, in addition to overseeing the initial designs for the CSS *Virginia*, was also the inventor of rifled naval and coastal defense cannons that bear his name and that were manufactured first only at Tredegar and later at the Confederate Naval Ordnance Works in Selma, Alabama. Brooke, an officer in the United States Navy until he resigned immediately following Virginia's secession, had also helped design and construct a series of batteries lining the banks of the James River, working directly under General Robert E. Lee, before assisting Confederate secretary of the navy Stephen R. Mallory on the *Merrimack* project.[209]

Northern newspapers, shortly after Virginia's secession, began featuring stories concerning secretive and mysterious machines of war supposedly being constructed at the Confederacy's premier ironworks:

> *There was in process of formation at the Tredegar Works in Richmond a machine intended to act against the blockading vessels. It was constructed of sheet iron, in the form of a segar, and was about from forty to fifty feet in length and six feet beam. It was to be propelled by air, manned by six persons, and would work under the water. It was considered by the people of Richmond to be a very formidable apparatus, and great things were expected of it.*[210]

Designed by Confederate explosives expert William Cheeney, the vessel carried a three-man compliment, two of which would be situated in the cockpit, while the third would be aft in a separate compartment. When a target was determined, the third member of the crew would leave the ship in rudimentary "diving armor" in order to affix an explosive to the enemy ship. After successful attachment, the diver returned to the ship, which then moved to a safe distance before detonation, instigated either by timing or the use of a lanyard.[211] A prototype was completed in the fall of 1861, when a "Mrs. E.H. Baker," an operative under the direction of Allan Pinkerton himself, witnessed the ship's launching and successful "attack" on a practice target in the James River. By early October 1861, the submarine had purportedly been used in an attack on the USS *Minnesota*, the flagship of the North Atlantic Blockading Squadron, the Union fleet tasked with blocking trade and shipments to and from Virginia and the Carolinas. The "infernal machine," as many Northern accounts referred to the submarine, failed, however, and was reportedly severely damaged in its attack but not before inadvertently alerting Federal forces as to the danger posed by Confederate submersibles and hastening the Union's construction of similar vessels.[212] The ultimate fate of the Tredegar submarine is uncertain, as no records or news reports attest to any subsequent sorties. Whether it was sunk during this or a successive attack or removed to Richmond for repairs and eventually cannibalized for other uses as the war caused shortages of iron is unknown, as is the fate of a second submarine, supposedly constructed at Tredegar, the existence of which is known only from brief mentions in several notes and journals.

The First Ironclads

The American government had first investigated the possibility of manufacturing armor-clad vessels following observers' reports from the 1853–56 Crimean War, which noted that the European powers' armaments had advanced rapidly and that the creation of a fleet of steam-propelled, ironclad vessels was but one avenue through which the United States could evenly compete with the navies of the Old World. By 1861, no such American vessel had been satisfactorily completed—this, however, did not prevent the Confederacy from realizing the need for such ships, for both combat and in the breaking of the Union blockade, which was composed entirely of wooden vessels. The Confederate Congress approved $2 million to be used by agents sent abroad to purchase ironclads in Britain and France; these agents were also ordered to investigate the possibility of having ships

Tredegar Iron Works

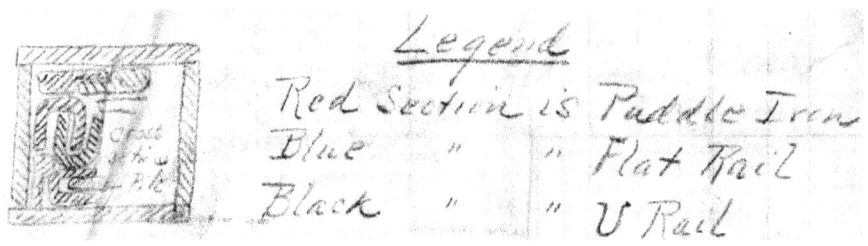

In 1925, Tredegar president Archer Anderson Jr. began collecting documents, records and firsthand accounts regarding the history of the Tredegar Iron Works. In October of that year, Anderson obtained a statement from former employee Charles E. Wade, concerning his memories helping his father, Edward Wade, roll the armor-plating of the CSS *Virginia* during the Civil War: "When the order was started to roll the Merrimac Plate Mr. Edward Wade brought his boy Charles E. Wade, then thirteen years, to work on the Bar Mill [later the site of the Tredegar Spike Mill] and to operate the housing screws to roll this particular Merrimac Plate…Mr. Charles Wade states that the pile for rolling these places was made with puddle iron sides, the interior of the pile being fitted up with U rail and flat rail cut to the length, as shown on the detail cross section shown below…The Mill was a 3 Stand 2 High Mill, one roughing stand, one Bull Head stand and one finishing stand. The pile was so large that the furnace doors had to be rebuilt so as to take this large pile. After heating, the pile was given two or three passes in the roughing rolls. It was then put back in the furnace and given a wash heat, then worked into a finished plate." *Library of Virginia*.

constructed in French and British stockyards if no finished specimens could be procured.[213] While ships were being searched for abroad, Secretary Mallory had already begun to prepare for the construction of ironclads domestically, and the Tredegar Iron Works was the only establishment in the South capable of rolling the iron plating called for, according to ship designs drafted by Lieutenant John Mercer Brooke.[214] After conferring with General Anderson regarding the prospective timeline for constructing such a ship from scratch (at least a year), Mallory decided, on Brooke's urging, to use as a base for the Confederacy's first ironclad the hull of the USS *Merrimack*, a Union vessel scuttled and burned by American sailors as they evacuated the Norfolk Naval Yard on April 20, 1861.[215] Salvaging and retooling the *Merrimack*, Brooke estimated, would run about one-third of the projected cost of building an entirely new vessel.[216]

Canadian-born Tredegar engineer Uri Haskins was one of the chief engineers on the *Merrimack* project, aided by, among others, fellow workmen Anton Osterbind, Charles Wade and German immigrant Jacob Ehbets. The son of an architect employed by the government of Hamburg, Jacob Otto Ehbets was born on September 26, 1836, and was a graduate of what is today the Karlsruhe Institute of Technology in Baden, Germany, one of the oldest research institutions in the country.[217] As soon as he arrived in Richmond in 1857, Jacob found work at the Tredegar Iron Works and aided in the site's cannon production shortly before the Civil War. Another engineer tasked with constructing the vessel's iron-plating was a fairly new hire: Peter Derbyshire, an immigrant from England who would go on to work at Tredegar for another three decades, eventually attaining the post of foundry foreman.[218] When tests demonstrated that one-inch-thick plating was inadequate for protecting the ship from enemy fire, Anderson ordered that adjustments be made in regard to equipment and staff, hiring more workmen and redesigning several of Tredegar's rolling mills in order to produce two-inch-thick plating—723 tons worth by the time the newly christened CSS *Virginia* was completed, shortly before its March 8, 1862 encounter with the USS *Monitor*.[219] The Confederate government placed orders with Tredegar for further ironclad components, including a set of Brooke rifles and the central propeller shaft for the CSS *Mississippi*, an ironclad scuttled and destroyed before completion ahead of the Union capture of New Orleans (the vessel's construction site) in April 1862.[220]

Natural and Man-made Disasters

In May 1863, a fire swept through the Tredegar complex, severely damaging several buildings, including the boring mill, which necessitated the removal of many cannons to the nearby Richmond Naval Ordnance Works, near Rockett's for the purposes of boring and finishing. Also largely destroyed by fire was the Crenshaw Woolen Mill; located between the central Tredegar foundry and the former site of Richard Cunningham and Richard Anderson's cotton mill (an area then housing the Tredegar locomotive shop), the Crenshaw mill was built in 1854 and operated as a flour mill, built on a parcel of land originally sold to Lewis Crenshaw two years prior. With waterpower granted to the mill as part of the original purchase, Crenshaw purchased further water power grants from the James River and Kanawha Canal in May 1854 to power his milling stones and other equipment, which by July was producing 300 barrels of flour per day. In 1862, the building was repurposed once again for textile purposes, supplying the Confederate army with materials for blankets and uniforms until the fire put an end to that venture.[221] The building remained unrepaired and unused for the remainder of the war. The same May 15, 1863 fire also destroyed Tredegar's locomotive shop, a blacksmith shop and several other adjacent machine shops and small foundry-support buildings.[222]

Tredegar Iron Works

Two months prior, an explosion had rocked Brown's Island, a small island in the James River, just south of the Richmond Arsenal and at the time the site of a Confederates States laboratory producing cartridges, percussion caps and other incendiary items. The facility, consisting of several buildings agglomerated on the eastern portion of the island, was vital to the Confederate cause, as it provided over the course of the war more than 1 million friction primers and 74 million rifle cartridges to the Army of Northern Virginia.[223] Due to the constraints of conscription at the time, as well as the nimbleness of fingers required to work on the munitions lines, young girls (mostly immigrants) were the most numerous (84 percent) of laboratory employees and earned relatively high wages for the time that fluctuated with inflation—an unmarried girl who earned roughly $1.60 a day in 1863 was being paid at least $12.00 a day by war's end.[224] On March 13, a collection of friction primers (small brass tubes containing gunpowder, used in the firing of cannons) exploded in the hands of an eighteen-year-old Irish immigrant named Mary Ryan as a result of her attempts to dislodge

Tredegar Iron Works, looking westward, April 1865. Photograph by Alexander Gardner. *Library of Congress.*

a primer that had become stuck to a varnishing board by hammering the entire board against a table. The initial explosion ignited stores of powder in the facility, and soon the entire complex was an inferno. While Ryan was known by the other workers to handle the primer boards in such a manner fairly often, and responsibility for the first blast was justifiably attributable to her, official investigations later concluded that the severity of the blast was more likely the result of unsafe practices and storage methods at the facility than any one worker's actions.[225] Workers from Tredegar and surrounding buildings, including Mary's father, rushed to the scene in an attempt to aid the survivors, many of whom were running about, engulfed in flames and attempting to douse themselves in the river's waters. Approximately fifty women, ranging in age from preteens to seniors, were killed in the explosion.

Fires and accidental explosions took their toll on Tredegar productivity, but the largest obstacle in Anderson's path was a lack of raw materials, which only worsened as the prospects of Confederate victory slowly dwindled. As Union advances first encroached on and then completely severed Richmond's access to coal and iron ore deposits in the western portion of the state, production levels at Tredegar ebbed to nearly a trickle, with operations ceasing completely in March 1865.[226] Six months before the end of the war, one cannon was cast using a variation of the Rodman method and another in February 1865, but the lack of proper tools for finishing and the end of the Confederacy prevented these two "Tredegar Rodmans" from ever reaching the battlefield.[227]

CHAPTER 3

1865–1892

On April 2, 1865, Confederate president Jefferson Davis sat quietly in a reserved pew at St. Paul's Church, attending services with, among others, Brigadier General Joseph Reid Anderson. As services commenced, an usher quickly rushed up the aisle and passed a note to President Davis, who abruptly withdrew. Several moments later, General Anderson was also alerted to the news that soon began to circulate throughout the congregation: General Robert E. Lee had sent word that Petersburg was lost and that Richmond must be evacuated immediately.[228] As Davis hurried to the Presidential Mansion and a general panic spread across the city's populace, General Anderson raced back to the Tredegar to advise his workmen of the situation.

As citizens rushed to banks to withdraw whatever funds they could before fleeing the city and the military prepared to relocate the Confederate government to Danville, Anderson looked to the men of the Tredegar Battalion to help him preserve their collective livelihoods: the Tredegar Iron Works.

Fears of a possible Federal invasion of the Confederate capital had been spreading among Richmond's military and industrial leadership for several months. As the city's situation grew more precarious, Anderson became increasingly fearful of what would become of the Tredegar in the event of an evacuation and the need to burn any and all items that could possibly be of use to an occupying force.[229] As the Confederacy's largest single ironworks, the Tredegar could provide the Union army with readily available materials and weapons. Anderson sent several missives to high-ranking Confederate officials, imploring that the Tredegar be spared in any evacuation contingencies; despite opposition from the Secretary of the Navy Stephen Mallory, both Chief of Ordnance Josiah Gorgas and Secretary of War John C. Breckinridge agreed with Anderson, as the ironworks was never marked for destruction.

Up until the very end, President Davis intended to do whatever necessary to keep Tredegar in operation as long as humanly and materially possible. As late as April 1, one day before the evacuation, Davis wrote to General Robert E. Lee in the field, citing his hopes that the Tredegar could maintain its ordnance production:

> *To-day the Secretary of War presents propositions from the proprietors of the Tredegar Works which impress me very unfavorably. We will endeavor to keep them at work, though it must be on a reduced scale. There is also a difficulty in getting iron, even for shot and shell, but hope this may, for the present be overcome by taking some from the navy, which, under the altered circumstances, may be spared.*[230]

Such hopes were dashed, however, with the advance of the Union army toward Richmond, when even the assurances of those in the highest ranks of the Confederate government were subordinate to the whims and frenzies of a terrified populace. To prevent valuable tobacco stores from falling into Federal hands, several warehouses were set ablaze by order of General Richard S. Ewell, and due to shifting winds, fire quickly spread across a large portion of the city's industrial and economic sectors. The fires stretched from Capitol Square eastward to Fifteenth Street and down along the banks of the James River, sweeping back westward literally to the doors of Tredegar itself. Thousands of citizens and military personnel fled across the James River to Manchester on bridges that were subsequently destroyed in the hope of hindering the impending Union advance across the city. The Confederacy's Richmond Arsenal, to the immediate east of Tredegar, was set ablaze by arsonists and its remaining inventory exploded, completely destroying the building itself and blowing out windows across the Tredegar property. While it is unknown if General Anderson actually stayed at Tredegar as the fires raged across the city, the survival of the ironworks, which emerged from the conflagration relatively unscathed, was credited to the efforts of the Tredegar Battalion in fending off any would-be arsonists and looters.

During President Abraham Lincoln's visit to Richmond following the evacuation of the Confederate capital and the suppression of the fire by Federal

TREDEGAR IRON WORKS

Tredegar Iron Works, as viewed from among the ruins of the Confederate Arsenal, April 1865. Photograph by Alexander Gardner. *Library of Congress*.

forces, the president met with several Richmond leaders to discuss options for a speedy resolution to Virginia's involvement in the rebellion. As a result of this meeting, and following a suggestion of Lincoln himself, a committee was formed, composed of several prominent Richmonders, including Anderson (who was later named chairman), which was tasked with the possibility of pressuring the Virginia legislature to disavow the Confederacy of its own volition, as opposed to being forced to do so by the Federal government. Such an endeavor was rendered rather meaningless, however, following Lee's surrender and the effective end of Virginia's role in the rebellion.[231]

Removed from Anderson's control by Federal forces, the Tredegar remained largely silent in the days immediately following the capture of

1865–1892

Archer Anderson, circa 1870. *Library of Virginia.*

Richmond, restarting operations only briefly under Union supervision in order to produce equipment and materials needed to repair a bridge across the James River, providing the Union army with greater access to Manchester and the Southside.[232] Anderson realized that any hope of regaining control over Tredegar (not to mention a presidential pardon) depended on reasserting his devotion to the United States, and he worked zealously to that affect; in addition to vehemently voicing his support for reunification, Anderson also participated in a number of Unionist activities held in Richmond, including a reception for Francis H. Pierpont, governor of the Restored Government of Virginia during the war and newly appointed provisional governor of Virginia proper.[233]

Anderson received support from a number of prominent Virginians who rallied to his defense, including the aforementioned Pierpont, as well as many among Richmond's business elites, who all emphasized the need for Tredegar's products in the rebuilding of southern infrastructure. On July 6, 1865, several of these men, including Charles Ellis (president of the Richmond, Fredericksburg and Potomac Railroad), Jonathan F. Fry (superintendent of the Richmond City Gas Works), James L. Davis (superintendent of the Richmond City Water Works) and Thomas H. Ellis (president of the James River and Kanawha Canal Company), penned a plea to President Andrew Johnson directly on Anderson's behalf, petitioning the president to both pardon Anderson and return the Tredegar to his capable hands:

> *The undersigned citizens of the state of Virginia respectfully state that the rail roads, factories, coal mines, buildings and other interests represented by them are greatly in want of The Tredegar Iron Works, in rebuilding,*

repairing and operating their several works, buildings and establishments and earnestly request if consistent with your public duties that you will grant pardon to the properties thereof Joseph R. Anderson, John F. Tanner, Robert Archer and Robert S. Archer and allow them to put their works in operation...We are informed that each of the persons named has taken the amnesty-oath, and from our personal acquaintance with them we are satisfied that you may rely on the oath being sacredly-kept and observed by each of them.[234]

When Secretary of War Stanton ordered that the Treasury Department be given control of the Tredegar property, Anderson renewed his entreaties for clemency in earnest and again rallied his voluminous support network, with the heads of several companies that relied on Tredegar products calling for his pardon and the return of the enterprise to his capable hands. Following a glowing letter from Pierpont to President Johnson, the president agreed to meet with Anderson personally. After four separate meetings, a period during which the likelihood of amnesty being granted teetered between certainty and total doubt, Anderson finally received his presidential pardon on September 21 and soon after was granted control of the works.

The Tredegar that was returned to Anderson's management was not in the best of shape; according to an April 28, 1865 inspection report by U.S. captain of ordnance D.W. Flagler, buildings and workshops that had been damaged by fire or accidents during the war, such as the carpenter shop and Crenshaw Woolen Mill, were never rebuilt. While much of the machinery was in fairly good working order, a considerable amount had been pushed to its limits, and this, combined with a wartime inability to obtain new machines from the North and repairs being less than adequate, meant that a large proportion of Tredegar's workings and infrastructure required extensive rehabilitation, leading Flagler to mirror other Union leaders' opinions that the ironworks be shut down permanently. While such an outcome was avoided following Johnson's pardon and Anderson's reacquisition of the works, the issue of Tredegar's condition remained. Tredegar was, in many ways, a shell of its former self and required a great deal of restoration—and capital—to return to its former levels of productivity.[235]

To this end, Anderson continued to voice his undying support for the Union, and President Johnson in particular, in the hope that he would be in a far more stable position from which to approach northern and western financiers, sorely needed in the face of the South's economic and infrastructural woes.[236] Anderson was able to raise some of the needed capital on his own. His brother-in-law, Captain Edward Archer, had run Union blockades to sell Virginia cotton abroad and returned shortly before war's close with caches of gold, and additional cotton sales in London in 1866 netted Anderson further funds—in all, sales of cotton resulted in about $190,000 toward Tredegar's revival.[237] Anderson also relinquished control of some of the company's landed assets, selling and leasing several blast furnaces in Botetourt County and selling off the 1,100-acre Dover coal mines property in Goochland County, which had been purchased by Anderson at the start of the war.[238]

Anderson understood that, in order to attract prospective northern investors, the company's business structure required a complete restructuring.[239] Initially, Anderson imagined a kind of iron/railroad trust, entitled the "Tredegar Scheme," which would create a partnership between the works and various railroad companies, with Tredegar producing, under railroad supervision, all the required tools and equipment for the industry—a system not all that dissimilar from the relationship Tredegar held with the Confederacy during the war.[240] Due to a lack of funds on the parts of both Tredegar and the region's railroad companies, this organization never materialized. In time, Anderson was able to attract the interest and support of several prominent northern financiers, particularly William Henry Aspinwall, a multimillionaire shipping magnate from New York. On Anderson's behalf, Aspinwall attempted to draft Gustavus Vasa Fox, assistant secretary of the navy, to be president of a reorganized Tredegar, at a salary of $10,000 per year, as part of Aspinwall's larger plan to broaden his influence along the Atlantic coast's shipping lanes. Fox, however, even after visiting the city on Anderson's personal invitation, stated that Aspinwall "would not tempt him to live among those secesh." Understandably, this arrangement did not appear either, leaving Anderson with no other choice but to reorganize the firm himself, relying largely on the same staff that had served under him before and during the war.[241]

The Tredegar Company

On February 27, 1867, Joseph R. Anderson and Co. was reorganized as the Tredegar Company, with Joseph R. Anderson and John F. Tanner as president and vice-president, respectively. Archer Anderson was named secretary and treasurer and served on the board of directors alongside Dr. Robert Archer

Notice regarding the reorganization of J.R. Anderson & Co. as the Tredegar Company, February 27, 1867. *Library of Virginia*

(Anderson's father-in-law) and his son Robert S. Archer. Aspinwall was also a board member for several months until his resignation, whereafter he was replaced by Francis T. Glasgow, who was also chief of the foundry at the time.[242]

All previous business-related holdings on the part of the Andersons and Archers (the Tredegar and Armory properties, respectively) were transferred by deed to the newly incorporated commercial entity. The semblance of stability that Anderson sought in reorganization began to produce returns, as several other prominent northern financiers joined Aspinwall in investing in the company, helping to ensure Tredegar's restoration. The

TREDEGAR IRON WORKS.

TREDEGAR COMPANY, Proprietors,

JOSEPH R. ANDERSON, President.

ARCHER ANDERSON, Secretary and Treasurer.

R. S. ARCHER, Superintendent Rolling Mills.

F. T. GLASGOW, Supt. Foundry and Machine Shops.

The Tredegar Company of Richmond, Va. (Successors to J. R. Anderson & Co.), continue to Manufacture at their Works in that city,

RAILS of any required section, including Street Rails.
PATENT ROLLED CONTINUOUS LIP CHAIRS.
BEST CHARCOAL BAR IRON, of high tensile strength.
TRUCKS of any desired pattern ready for the Car bodies.
FISH PLATES, with Bolts and Nuts for same.
RAIL-ROAD CARS.
CASTINGS, including the heaviest descriptions, of Iron & Brass.
IRONS complete for Fink's, Bollman's, or Howe Truss Bridges.
RAIL-ROAD AND BOAT SPIKES.
RAIL-ROAD AXLES.
MARINE AND STATIONARY ENGINES of all sizes.
NAILS AND CUT SPIKES.

The great capacity of the Tredegar Iron Works — Some 30,000 tons per annum,— their location on tide-water, in the midst of the rich Coal and Iron deposits of Virginia, their unequalled advantages for shipment by Rail, Steamer, or Sail Vessel, without interruption during any part of the year, and an active experience of thirty years enable the Proprietors to guarantee the promptest and most economical execution of orders, which are solicited from all parts of the United States.

Address
THE TREDEGAR COMPANY,
RICHMOND, VA.
Or
60 BROADWAY, NEW YORK.

Tredegar advertisement, 1870. *Library of Virginia.*

largest northern shareholder was John F. Winslow, the former president of Maryland's Lulworth Iron Company, who, ironically, had personally funded the construction of the USS *Monitor* and was also among the first American ironmakers to secure patents for and successfully implement the Bessemer steel-making process. He was also a Tredegar board member from May 1870 to April 1873.[243]

Even before the official reorganization of the company, Anderson had begun to search out the best talents—many foreign-born, as had been the case prior—to help rebuild the former "Krupp of the Confederacy." In addition to posting advertisements in northern newspapers, enticing newly arrived immigrants with high pay and steady work below the Mason-Dixon, Anderson also attempted to recruit such valued talent directly. In 1866, shortly before the reorganization, Tredegar actually sought, with the aid of an agent in Pennsylvania, to negotiate directly with European agencies in the hopes of acquiring six puddlers and their helpers. Tredegar would agree to pay for their travel across the Atlantic, and the workers were indebted to Tredegar regarding such until they paid this sum off.[244] Follow-up letters to the agent in Pennsylvania from Vice-President Tanner went unanswered, and no such arrangement ever materialized.[245] Anderson also wrote personally to several foreign ironworkers and engineers already established at northern sites, inviting them to see Tredegar firsthand, in hopes of luring new talent to Richmond.

David Eynon was one such engineer, a Welshman following in Rhys Davies's footsteps by coming to Richmond to work at the Tredegar Iron Works. Exactly when he immigrated to the United States is not known, although he was definitely in Harrisburg, Pennsylvania, by war's end, for it is here that Joseph Reid Anderson wrote to him in October 1866, requesting that he visit Richmond (all expenses paid by Tredegar) to inspect the Armory rolling mill.[246] Undoubtedly Anderson had learned of Eynon vis-à-vis the railroad-related patents he had applied for while employed in Pennsylvania, particularly one that improved on the method of manufacturing railroad chairs, one of Tredegar's top-selling products. After Eynon's short visit, Anderson offered Eynon the position of manager of the Armory rolling mill, with a salary of $2,500 a year, in addition to "a comfortable house at the works, and household fuel free of charge."[247] As a member of the upper management, Eynon was eligible to hold stock in the company and to receive yearly bonuses; in 1869, he received a bonus of $500.[248] It has been suggested by none other than Anderson himself that Eynon's success encouraged more Welsh immigrants to seek their livelihoods at Tredegar in the years following the war.[249] Eynon's tenure at Tredegar was short-lived; during his brief time there, however, he contributed immensely to Tredegar productivity. He was responsible and received a patent for an improvement on Tredegar's spike machines; Eynon's redesigned process allowed for the forging of railroad spikes but without the reheating of the blanks required by previous methods, thereby speeding up the entire process.[250] Before his departure in November 1870, Eynon was responsible for a number of improvements to Tredegar's infrastructure, most importantly overseeing the repair and installation of several turbines across the site.

SALES AND PROMINENCE: SOARING

The standard Tredegar railroad spike was five and a half inches long, and $^9/_{16}$ of an inch thick, one of the most commonly used type of spikes throughout the American railroad industry. Although Tredegar manufactured numerous other varieties and sizes of spikes, these were the models most in demand. In 1868, Tredegar bought outright for $12,000 two manual spike machines it had previously been leasing from a Pittsburgh-based company—a reasonable price to pay for the increased production of spikes, a product which had netted the company hundreds of thousands of dollars over the last several years.[251] By 1873, with close to two thousand employees, Tredegar was Richmond's largest employer.[252]

The occasional labor disputes that had plagued Anderson before and during the Civil War continued into the postwar arena, although the large-scale disruption to operations previous strikes had caused was, for the most part, not repeated. The last major labor disturbance Anderson had to contend with occurred in 1867, just as J.R. Anderson & Co. was reorganized as the Tredegar Co. The mostly foreign iron puddlers demanded a one-dollar raise in pay, from six dollars per ton of iron puddled to seven dollars per ton; the puddlers were among the most valued and skilled of Anderson's employees, and a strike on their part would have brought the entire site to a near standstill.[253] Instead of attempting to find comparable foreign workers on such short notice and at such a critical and questionable juncture in terms of Tredegar's future survival, Anderson relented and agreed to the one-dollar pay increase.[254] In March 1870, a second strike that would have crippled Tredegar on the part of the Moulder's Society, a "loosely-structured union" of those based in the pattern shops, was threatened. While a walk-out was called for, it never occurred, and Anderson was able to dodge another confrontation with organized labor.[255]

In March 1868, fueled by its role in the nationwide railroad boom, Tredegar established a sales office in the center of New York City at 60 Broadway. This office allowed the company access to both the economic heart of the country as well as the latest information regarding the state of iron production the world over.[256] From its inception to the beginning of 1870, John F. Tanner was placed in charge of the New York office and managed the various agents that served throughout the country. A deal was reached with various merchants that if they were selling Tredegar spikes, there was an understanding they would sell only Tredegar spikes, allowing Anderson to potentially corner a portion of a very lucrative market. Each agent had his specific "turf" and would receive 2.5 percent of any sales of Tredegar spikes.[257] Among the merchants that acted as Tredegar agents were Post and Company of Cincinnati, M.M. Buch and Company out of St. Louis and, most significantly, Chicago's Crerar, Adams, and Company, one of the largest railroad supply companies in the country and a firm that would continue to do business with Tredegar far into the future.[258] In 1868, the Old Dominion Steamship Company received exclusive rights to carry Tredegar products from Richmond to New York City.[259] Tredegar sold railway and other iron products not only in America but also to Canada and several countries in South America and the Caribbean.[260] Business and name recognition beyond the city limits of Richmond were so strong that there were even (brief) talks concerning the opening of a secondary Tredegar location in Rome, Georgia, in 1872.[261] As for the Tredegar site itself, Anderson was actively enlarging its scope and size, buying up surrounding land to further augment the works. In 1872 alone, Tredegar inked land-purchasing deals worth over $25,000 for several lots adjacent to the property.[262] In 1868, a company store was built to the south of the James River and Kanawha Canal wall, to the east of the Spike Mill, and provided workers with groceries and dry goods, as well as any supplies they may need for the job. Unlike stores located in "company towns" elsewhere across the country, the Tredegar Company Store did not issue any scrip but rather simply acted on credit, deducting what was owed from the workmen's next paycheck.

The years since the end of the Civil War and the reorganization of J.R. Anderson & Co. into the Tredegar Company were a time of growth, both physically at the site but also financially, with orders and profits mounting every year. A year after reorganization, in 1868, Tredegar sold 1,217 tons of bar iron; by 1872, that had increased to 4,531. The sales of finished railroad spikes totaled 2,411 tons in 1868, and in five years, that number had more than quadrupled to 9,676. All told, the total amount of finished iron products sold annually jumped in that five-year period from 11,130 tons to over 85,000.[263] Between 1867 and 1872, yearly profits rose threefold at Tredegar, to the tune of $417,669 in 1872 alone.[264] Orders were piling up in both Richmond and in the New York office, and it seemed as if the boom would only reach ever higher. As with all such booms, however, a bust was never far behind.

1873

At the onset of the 1870s, railroads were universally accepted as "the nation's economic bellwether." If one had to invest in anything, the railroad industry was the safest bet.[265] As is the case in any booming economy, speculation ran amok, and in 1873, a financial panic led to an economic depression that, in many ways, far eclipsed the one that occurred sixty years later in the 1930s. The railroad industry was thriving, certainly, but it relied on an expansion that moved far beyond actual demand. The railroading business was dependent (not surprisingly) on laying railroads; whether they went to areas that could potentially create the shipping/transportation revenue needed to cover the actual expenditure of laying the road in the first place was, at the time, inconsequential. With a comment that overflowed with common sense, the logic of which was realized by many only too late, shipping magnate Cornelius Vanderbilt remarked at the height of the impending crisis: "There are a great many worthless railroads started in this country, without any means to carry them through. Respectable banking houses in New York, so called, make themselves agents for the sale of the bonds of these railroads and give a kind of moral guarantee of their secureness…Building railroads from nowhere to nowhere at public expense is not a legitimate undertaking."[266]

The railroad boom was subsidized in part by the government but to a large degree on credit supplied by financing firms. Such was the dependence on bonds, stocks and other forms of industrial-grade IOUs that, in a very short expanse of time, a quite precarious situation developed, wherein the failure of a single, small enterprise could potentially cause ripples throughout an entire industry, affecting even the largest of firms. There are myriad factors that can lead to economic catastrophes such as the one that occurred in 1873, but the following is an attempt at summarization of a situation that, adequately addressed, could fill an entire tome in and of itself. Several railway lines began running into trouble meeting their pecuniary obligations (partly due to a loss in credit from Europe, which was starting to feel its own economic pinch and had been responsible for nearly $2 billion worth of investments in American railroads in recent years), which led to serious pains on the part of financing firms, the bulk of whose business was in the loaning of money to these railroads. With the demand for loans on the part of railroads decreasing, since their own financial futures were being called into question, the financing companies began to suffer.[267] In September 1873, one such firm, the New York Warehouse & Security Company, announced its insolvency to investors, a trend that rapidly spread throughout America's financial infrastructure, with the First National Bank of Washington, the New York & Oswego Railroad and, most significantly, Jay Cooke & Co., a bank that was heavily involved in the sales of both U.S. treasuries and railroad company bonds, all declaring insolvency.[268] Reassurances and calls for calm on the part of names such as "Commodore" Vanderbilt and Hetty Green intended to halt or at least slow the momentum of insolvencies did nothing, and President Grant's attempted bulwarks against collapse proved just as ineffective—before the year was out, over five thousand companies had gone bankrupt.[269] Through both snap decisions and well-planned strategies, some individuals—including Vanderbilt, Jason "Jay" Gould and John Pierpont Morgan—survived and even prospered following the panic and resulting depression. For the majority of Americans, however, the hard times were just beginning. The boom was over, and Tredegar was going to suffer for it.

There were worries at Tredegar for some time and warnings that the boom years could not last forever, but little was done on the part of Anderson or other senior management to prepare for such a development. As historian Dennis Maher Hallerman spoke of the situation, Anderson seemed to have followed a "carpe diem" approach to business: take today for what it's good for, and whatever happens tomorrow will happen.[270] This is a fundamental example of the Tredegar business structure under Anderson, something more akin to a modest family business than the large-scale corporations of the Gilded Age—very little of what could have been done to further strengthen the company itself was taken into account, with the family's prosperity and societal status paramount. This is not to say that Anderson cared nothing for his employees or for the health of the Tredegar as a commercial entity (Anderson spent prodigiously on fire insurance and other business precautions) or to paint him as some sort of Scrooge-like ogre but rather to emphasize a differences to be found between Tredegar and other companies and corporations rising in the latter years of the 1800s. Nothing could have prevented Tredegar's being affected by the Panic of 1873, but less expansion, some investment in newer technologies (mainly steel) and a lower dependence on credit are but a few of the actions that may have, at the very least, mitigated the damage.

Defaults on payments for products had begun appearing before 1873 at Tredegar's office, and as stated, nervous mumblings did begin, but the full impact was not realized until the fall of 1873. Much like the railroads, Tredegar was expanding its operations and landholdings in the years immediately prior to the panic, and this dependence on bonds and credit in place of actual cash revenue would prove to be a debilitating hindrance. In 1872, a new car factory was constructed. One of the most profitable railroad-related ventures aside from the famous Tredegar spikes were the railroad cars and gondolas the site began producing in the late 1860s, and with demand for these cars rising alongside the nationwide railroad expansion, an expanded facility for car fabrication was deemed a necessity.[271] From January 1872 to January 1873, Tredegar accepted orders for 1,123 railway cars, mostly boxcars and flat cars but also a number of coal cars and gondolas.[272] A large portion of these sales were on lines of credit, which quickly dried up once financing firms began collapsing in September 1873. One such company, the New York & Oswego Midland Railroad, was a recurring and significant customer that operated largely on credit, having ordered 250 railway cars from Tredegar between June and September 1872 alone.[273] The New York & Oswego Midland's collapse in 1873 constituted a major fiscal blow to Tredegar, and the failures of other companies from which Tredegar held notes of debt only exacerbated the situation.

The Richmond & Danville Railroad had co-invested with Tredegar in the construction of a bridge across the James River in 1870. In exchange for Tredegar's shouldering a portion of the cost (as well as constructing the bridge itself), the R&D agreed to both carry coal from the Chesterfield mines to Tredegar and ship iron and other materials to and from the depot at Rockett's Landing at discounted rates.[274] With the R&D's sudden default on the remaining portion of its obligations regarding the bridge following 1873, Tredegar was left holding the outstanding $55,186 bag. Anderson was able to negotiate credit with an insurance company, placing the bridge itself as a security deposit—certainly a reprieve of sorts, but not an enviable situation by any means.[275] Aside from defaults and note cancelations, the downward turn in the industry also affected the value of Tredegar's products; the price of spikes on the open market hovered around $5\frac{1}{4}$¢ a pound before the collapse and plummeted down to $2\frac{3}{4}$¢ a pound in 1875. Several sources of local pig iron shuttered, further damaging Tredegar's ability to acquire raw materials.[276] In late 1873, liens against Tredegar began appearing on numerous parcels of land the firm had bought the previous year.

Tredegar Iron Works

From January 17 to January 24, 1876, Tredegar ceased operations entirely, as negotiations commenced concerning the firm's future. Pledges and bonds promising the entire site as collateral helped to some degree in stabilizing the situation but did nothing for the five hundred to six hundred men who were immediately laid off.[277] Fortunately for Anderson, Tredegar did not go out of business entirely—rather, it was placed into receivership. In a July 8, 1876 letter to Tredegar's stockholders explaining the conditions of the receivership settlement, Anderson attempted to explain the dire circumstances the company, and the management personally, found themselves in, leaving no other alternative, aside from total failure, to receivership.

> *Gentlemen, In submitting to the creditors of the Tredegar Company a plan for a settlement of their claims, which involves the winding up of the Company and loss of the stock, we feel sure the stockholders will not need to be told that we did not give up all hope of saving any part of investment till every effort and every resource had been exhausted…Business and the prospects of trade have grown worse from day to day, and the time has come when we have felt obliged to make the recommendations contained in this accompanying circular to creditors. We sincerely deplore the losses of our associates; but it is due to ourselves to say that we have spared no effort to avert this disaster, and that we have sacrificed all of our available individual means to sustain the Company's credit.*[278]

The Tredegar Company, with Anderson acting as receiver, faced an uphill battle toward solvency at a time when not only was it deeply indebted to several entities across the country but also when many of its most dependable customers (those that had not collapsed entirely), such as the Chesapeake and Ohio Railroad, were also under receivership themselves. Despite these challenges, Tredegar did indeed survive and was able to emerge from receivership in 1879 to a level of productivity that must have seemed unrealistic just a few short years earlier.

It is interesting to note that 1873 also spelled the end of, as well as a manner of resuscitation for, the original Tredegar Ironworks in Wales, which by that point had swelled into a massive industrial complex capable of producing more than fifty-two thousand tons of iron per year and boasted several rolling complexes and eighty individual puddling furnaces.[279] The original partnership formed seventy-three years prior was dissolved, in large part due to labor unrest and financial uncertainties throughout southern Wales, and a group investors formed a new firm, the Tredegar Iron and Coal Company, to assume the assets and operations of its predecessor.[280] The Tredegar Iron and Coal Company soon adapted to producing rails of Bessemer steel and survived another two decades before finally shutting down shortly before the end of the century.[281]

Even during the uncertain years of the 1876–79 receivership period, Richmond's Tredegar was still recognized as a leading industrial giant of the South, as evidenced by a glowing article detailing the reemergence of the former Confederate states that appeared in the July 1877 edition of *Scribner's Monthly*:

> *The activity of the Tredegar Iron Works since the war has been remarkable. Since the reorganization of the company in 1867 with a capital of $1,000,000...A more complete establishment of its kind is not to be found anywhere in the United States...The Works cover somewhat over fifteen acres of ground, and have an unlimited supply of water-power at all seasons of the year. The present capacity is more than double what it was before the war, the rolling-mills turning out over thirty thousand tons of railroad bars, spikes, etc., per annum, and the foundries between twenty and thirty thousand tons of castings, while the machine-shops are capable of an indefinite amount of work, depending upon the extent of force employed and the amount of orders they may have in hand.*[282]

Under Joseph Reid Anderson's guidance, the receivership period saw Tredegar bounce back to high and, in some cases, record earnings. In 1876, Tredegar's foundry operations alone recorded over $88,000 in sales; in 1880, that same department saw sales rise more than 102 percent to over $853,000.[283] Tredegar, like the rest of Richmond, had bounced back at a rather surprising pace; from the original forty-three manufacturers in the city before the war, the sixteen left in 1866 survived and were soon joined

Tredegar Iron Works after the war. From *Scribner's Monthly*, December 1872. *Nathan Madison*.

by others, many of which successfully weathered the panic.[284] In spite of the ravages of 1873 across the entirety of the nation, Richmond was still the second-largest manufacturing municipality in the southern states, after New Orleans, in 1880.[285]

One significant change at the ironworks was the discontinuation of all puddling operations. As evidenced by labor disputes throughout Tredegar's history (namely, in 1847, 1863 and 1867), puddlers were both the most skilled and oftentimes the most troublesome workers, as far as Joseph R. Anderson was concerned. Their presence, however, was a necessity as long as Tredegar's product line called for the use of new wrought iron. Despite constructing several new puddling furnaces in 1868, which brought the total number of such furnaces on site to twenty-five, Tredegar increasingly made use of scrap iron beginning in the late 1860s.[286] As each puddling furnace was phased out of operation over the course of the mid-1880s, Tredegar began increasingly to depend on the purchasing of scrap, recyclable wrought iron in lieu of producing it via puddling on site. The furnaces and surrounding forests in Botetourt that had supplied Tredegar for decades were leased to the Alleghany Ore and Iron Company in 1890 for ten years before the furnaces were shut down and the lands converted for use as small timber farms at the turn of the century.[287] As it could be melted down and reused regardless of its original purpose, scrap iron from any number of industries was readily available at relatively low cost, thanks in part to an excess of iron rails removed from service and replaced with those made of steel. Over five hundred tons of scrap T-rails, at twenty-six dollars per ton, were bought by Tredegar from a New York–based scrap supplier in late 1881.[288] In April 1887, the *Alexandria Gazette* reported that six hundred tons of old rail had been shipped to Tredegar by way of London, England.[289] In the two-week period between May 7 and May 22, 1892, alone, over one million pounds of scrap iron arrived at Tredegar.[290] During the latter half of the nineteenth century, Tredegar invested in several crushing machines used to break apart discarded car wheels, rails and other scrap items for later melting and recycling. The company also purchased thousands of decades-old and obsolete cannons from arsenals across the country to be melted down and reused.

During the 1880s, Anderson helped found two organizations: one commercial, through which he possibly hoped to gain better influence over Tredegar's standing on the national stage, and the other a continuation of the civic service he began decades prior when he first served on the Richmond City Council. In October 1885, at a meeting in New York City, representatives of several spike-producing firms—including J.R. Anderson, acting on behalf of the Tredegar Company—called for and established the United States Association of Spike Manufacturers. While other related organizations, such as the American Iron Association founded in 1855, existed largely to lobby for protectionist tariffs that would benefit the entire iron (and later steel) industry, the Spike Manufacturers' goal was to manipulate prices for a particular item. The purpose for the organization was succinctly explained in its constitution and bylaws: "believing that our only relief from incurring losses through the manufacture of spikes, consists in the proper regulation of the product of each spike maker, the undersigned hereby agree to the stipulations hereto attached; that the manufacturers of spikes in the United States do form an association for the protection of the trade."[291] As of this formative meeting, at which Anderson was elected chairman, the association consisted of nine members, Tredegar included. Other "big names" involved were the firms of Dilworth, Porter & Co., Ltd. of Pittsburgh; the Tudor Iron Works of St. Louis; and the Montour Iron and Steel Co. of Chicago. Essentially, the purpose of the group, as already stated in its bylaws, was to regulate the spike industry. By both naming the price at which all members would agree to sell and by setting the exact amount of spikes, per pound, that would be allowed onto the market, it was hoped that some stability in the price of railroad spikes across the industry could be established. Dilworth and Tredegar were granted the largest allotments allowed into the multi-company pool, with their contributions from August to October 1886 totaling 50,964 and 39,775, or 37.54 percent and 29.33 percent, respectively, of the totality of the pool. During successive meetings,

Archer Anderson, circa 1870. *Library of Virginia*.

many held in New York's prestigious Astor House, this number fluctuated over the succeeding few years, with several members, Dilworth and Tredegar included, threatening to abandon the venture on more than one occasion. Most often, the group could not agree on the most basic of decisions, such as the price of the standard 5½- by $^9/_{16}$-inch spikes. In June 1887, Anderson threatened to leave the organization unless several demands were met, particularly his suggestion that member firms not be bound to the price agreed on by the committee, which, obviously, would seem to negate the purpose of the entire association in the first place.

The appointment of an association staff, including a secretary and general manager with fixed salaries of $1,000 per annum each, apparently did nothing to form any tighter bonds between the various members. The association did exist for several more years until at least 1899, when in May of that year Tredegar contributed 14,200 kegs of spikes to the association's total 60,040 keg holdings for the month, but any later mentions of it are spotty at best, and the association seems to have dissolved within a few more years.[292] Evidence, both contemporary to the time and from the advantage of hindsight, suggests that Anderson's and the association's attempts at mimicking, on some small scale, the well-developed price-fixing strategies found in the steel and oil industries did nothing to bring any standardization to the spike business, with prices continuing to fluctuate throughout the remainder of the century.

A second organization Anderson helped form was one intended to help the central Virginia area continue to heal from the wounds of the Civil War. On September 6, 1888, he, along with son J.R. Anderson Jr. and a number of other Richmond leaders, founded the James River Valley Immigration Society, the purpose of which was to "procure and promote emigration to the James River Valley."[293] Anderson, who donated $500 to the society's coffers at its inaugural meeting, likely saw the organization as a possible means to reinvigorate sections of the region still affected by the aftermath of the Civil War, be that agriculturally, economically or industrially. The society created offices throughout and beyond what today would be called the Greater Metro-Richmond area—in addition to Richmond city itself, agents of the James River Valley Immigration Society were assigned to the counties of Goochland, Campbell, Fluvanna, Powhatan, Buckingham, Amherst and Bedford and to the city of Lynchburg.[294] It is doubtful that Anderson supported the society in the hopes of luring northern or foreign-born ironworkers and engineers to Tredegar. The times had changed, and many of the skills (and immigrants) that Anderson may have coveted in previous decades had been disseminated and assimilated across the country over the years, to the point that metallurgic know-how was just as advanced (if not more so) in America as it was in Britain or anywhere else in Europe. Anderson's participation in the James River Valley Immigration Society was likely an attempt, in the waning years of his life, to help further reinvigorate his city and his state.

Anderson, even in his advanced age, had apparently not lost his taste for founding new commercial ventures. In June 1889, with J.R. Anderson as president and Joseph Jr. as treasurer, the Glenmore Iron Company was incorporated, not in Richmond but just outside Green Brier, in southeastern West Virginia. Across an expanse of over three thousand acres (now the site of the prestigious Greenbrier Hotel), a mine and works for purifying iron ore was built; the site even boasted a direct connection to the nearest rail line via the Chesapeake and Ohio Railroad.[295]

TREDEGAR ON THE VERGE OF A NEW CENTURY

By 1890, Tredegar was on firm financial footing, with sales in the foundry alone totaling $536,334.59 that year. With some of its highest sales numbers in years, the company had extricated itself from an economic abyss to which many, many others had succumbed.[296] Indeed, a series of companies that appear in Tredegar's ledgers, such as the South Carolina Railway Co., were still in receivership due to troubles stemming from the 1870s. While the New York office had closed as of 1875, the Tredegar Company retained sales agents in New York until the 1890s, ensuring its stake in the national and even international iron market. In the spring of 1890, Tredegar was awarded a contract to produce rails, spikes, chairs and other items for the *Banco del Comercio, Ferrocarriles Unidos de La Habana & Almacenes de Regla* (The Bank of Commerce, the United Railways of Havana and the Regla Warehouses—joint partners in the endeavor). The United Railways of Havana was actually a British-owned firm operating in Cuba that was highly active in consolidating and maintaining the many railroads that were integral to the island's chief export, the sugar crop.[297] The Havana deal had likely been in the works for quite some time, as Francis Glasgow had traveled to Cuba "in the interests of the Tredegar Company" and remained there for several weeks in January and February 1886.[298] Between August and November, Tredegar recorded sales of nearly $119,000 in its foundry sales books to the United Railways of

Tredegar Iron Works

A view of Tredegar Iron Works from Gambles Hill. From *Harper's Weekly*, January 15, 1887. *Nathan Madison.*

Havana project alone, a little over 22 percent of the entire year's earnings. From 1890 to 1900, annual foundry sales never dropped below $160,000, with the lowest years corresponding to several large- and small-scale financial panics that afflicted both Europe and the United States in the closing years of the nineteenth century.

Tredegar's consumer base underwent noticeable alterations as well. While railroads continued to place the largest orders monetarily speaking, many local enterprises began placing larger and more frequent orders with the company. Municipal agencies such as the City Water Works, Gas Works and the City Engineers Department requested pipes and manhole covers, and growing industrial concerns, such as Belle Isle's Old Dominion Iron and Nail

1865–1892

Works, the Richmond Paper Manufacturing Company and the Virginia & Carolina Chemical Company placed orders for plates, bearings, boilers and other tools vital to their trades. The expanding Richmond Locomotive and Machine Works purchased Tredegar car wheels by the hundreds each year and used Tredegar iron in the construction of its locomotives.

Tredegar was also in a position to aid in the growth of an entirely new industry: the electric streetcar. Horse-drawn carriages and later steam-driven omnibuses had acted as public conveyances throughout Richmond since before the Civil War. However, in February 1888, the Richmond Union Passenger Railway, under the guidance of master-engineer Frank Julian Sprague, began operations, allowing Richmond to lay claim to having the first practical and dependable electric city trolley system in the world.[299] Despite doubts and setbacks facing the new system, especially after an early trip wherein several mules were needed to pull Sprague's stalled trolley up a particularly steep hill, the electric railway established itself in Richmond, and several different lines, a microcosm of the myriad railroads crisscrossing the continent, soon appeared throughout the city.[300] The several companies operating electric railways in Richmond, such as the Richmond City Railway Co. and the Richmond and Manchester Railway Co., in addition to Sprague's Union Railway, composed barely 0.17 percent ($903) of foundry sales in 1890. These companies' presence in Tredegar's order books increased only slightly within the next decade. The importance here, however, lies not in the pecuniary influence these nascent industries held over Tredegar's ledgers but rather in the fact that these new ventures began their lives in such proximity to a facility that could manufacture, with very few exceptions, everything they could conceivably require.

The Osterbinds

The Osterbind family's presence at Tredegar grew as well. Anton, having been at the works since the 1840s, was joined in the late 1860s by his firstborn son, Henry Carter. Born on April 19, 1851, at the family home at 623 South Belvidere (overlooking Tredegar), Henry Carter Osterbind, at the age of fourteen, became an apprentice in the spike mill and by 1869 was listed in city directories as a professional machinist.[301] On November 25, 1875, Henry Carter married Ellen Jane Clark, a niece of his stepmother, and in the following years, several children were born, including the couple's first son, Carter Clarke Osterbind, on September 30, 1881.³⁰² In 1886, Henry was appointed to head of the horseshoe shop by Joseph Reid Anderson, following the recommendations of foundry superintendent F.T. Glasgow:

> *I suggest that* [Henry] *Carter Osterbind be put in charge of the Horse shoe making, that he have supervision of the roll turning and fitting in the machine shop, of the rolling of the blanks and making and finishing the shoes. We are suffering now for want of a mechanical head having supervision & responsibility for the whole process from rolling blanks to completion of the shoe. With such an organization, I believe a large trade could soon be built up, giving employment to a train & making an important branch of the business.*³⁰³

Henry's assumption of this position was quite the promotion. Begun in 1873, Tredegar's Horse Shoes and Mule Shoes Department was a growing source of income for the postwar ironworks, alongside its railroad products. In the ensuing decades, horse and mule shoes increasingly claimed larger portions of Tredegar's portfolio—a 1913 Tredegar Co. catalogue from the firm's shoe division mentions no fewer than twenty-six different varieties of shoes offered by the works.³⁰⁴ Glasgow's suggestion that Henry lead the horseshoe department perhaps was made in part thanks to the first of three patents Henry applied for during his time at the works. In September 1886, a patent was granted to the younger Osterbind for improvements he made on a machine that prepared blank bars for molding into horseshoes, a project he collaborated on with fellow Tredegar worker John H. Snyder.³⁰⁵ By 1891, Henry Carter held the title of manager of Tredegar's rolling mill, directly under the superintendent and, by 1892, had moved out of Oregon Hill to the more "prestigious" 200 block of East Cary Street, as befitting his new position at the company.³⁰⁶

The Passing of Joseph Reid Anderson

On September 7, 1892, while on a trip to Isle of Shoals, New Hampshire, General Joseph Reid Anderson died of natural causes at the age of seventy-nine. The death of one of Richmond's leading citizens affected the city immediately and profoundly. Richmond newspapers promptly began to run lengthy biographies and glowing obituaries for the Tredegar's former proprietor:

1865–1892

> *When the sad news was received at the Tredegar by Major Robert Archer, General Anderson's brother-in-law, orders were given to shut down the works until after the funeral. By the men the announcement of the loss they had sustained was received with the most profound sorrow. Many of the employees of the establishment had been associated with General Anderson for long years, and had for him the deepest affection. To these his death was the breaking of a personal tie. By all he was regarded with respect and esteem, and to all he was ever kind, courteous, and approachable. To-day [sic] there will be a meeting of the force to make arrangements for attending the funeral.*[307]

The *Richmond Times*'s reporting of the grief to be found at Tredegar in the wake of Anderson's passing was not unwarranted. By all appearances, Anderson was well respected and well liked by a majority of the men in his employ. During the Christmas season of 1879, testimonials and dedications were written in Anderson's honor, by both a committee of men (led by Anton Osterbind, Henry Carter Osterbind and George Perrini) employed by Anderson for the past quarter of a century and another group composed of the sons of said longtime employees, wherein they requested that he "accept this slight testimonial, which weighted in the scales of ordinary trade and traffic its value may be insignificant, but when weighed in the affections of those who enjoy such friendly relations as exist between employer and employee, it carries with it the best and heartfelt prayers for future happiness and prosperity."[308]

In response to his workmen and the gold-headed cane they presented to him alongside their testimonials, Anderson warmly responded:

> *I have no hesitation in saying that is the proudest event of my life to receive the assurances contained in your letters, couched in such touching words, that in this long period you, my worthy, intelligent and honest friends and employees, have found so much to approve in my course towards you…I can only say in return that I most heartily reciprocate your kind wishes for myself and my family; and as in the past, so in the future, I will endeavor to remember what you have illustrated by your lives, that we do not live alone for ourselves, but are (each in the position in which God has placed him) accountable to Him for doing our duty to our fellow-man.*[309]

Two days after his death, a train arrived in Richmond bearing Anderson's remains, and from the Anderson residence, a procession carried the casket to

St. Paul's Episcopal Church, in the shadow of Capitol Square, where the funeral was held. Tredegar workmen, past and present, were welcome to attend, and over five hundred (with newspapers reporting almost half of them to be African American) met first at Monroe Park and marched to Anderson's home to pay their respects before accompanying the dirge on its way to St. Paul's.[310] Eight of Anderson's grandsons, including Archer Anderson Jr., Joseph Reid Johnston Anderson and St. George Anderson, served as pallbearers; honorary pallbearers behind the casket included current and former employees, such as Anton Osterbind, George Perrini, Edward Wade and William E. Tanner, as well as other Richmond industrial luminaries, including Joseph Bryan, Philip Haxall and James H. Dooley.[311] The Richmond Chamber of Commerce, which Anderson had led some years prior, convened a special ceremony in his honor and in a remembrance, recalled: "For nearly half a century General Anderson was actively engaged in business in this city, and during all that time he was at the head of one of the most important manufacturing establishments in the South. The Tredegar Company has contributed as much to make Richmond known as a manufacturing and commercial centre as any enterprise ever established here, and its capacity and usefulness in this direction was principally due to the ability, energy and character of its president."[312]

From St. Paul's, the procession made its way westward toward Belvidere Street and on to Hollywood Cemetery, not far from the Tredegar Works itself, where Anderson was laid to rest. In a brief testimonial drafted and sent to area newspapers by the employees themselves, the Tredegar's collective workforce resolved:

> *That in the death of our friend we and the entire community have sustained a great loss. To us he was kind, considerate and courteous all through his long connection with us, both in and out of the works…That we tender his bereaved wife, sons and daughters and their families our deepest sympathy, and while we lament ours and their loss, we rejoice in the fact that if we follow the example and imitate the noble Christian character of our beloved friend and employer we shall be united again with him in that home where toil is over and where all is rest and peace.*[313]

In a remembrance recalling the strike forty-five years prior regarding the employment of slave workers at the Tredegar and armory plants, Richmond's most prominent African American newspaper, the *Richmond Planet*, praised

Anderson for his business acumen, as well as for the magnanimity he showed his black workmen:

> *Thrown as he was daily among hundreds of workmen, there was not one who did not honour and revere him. He was particularly the friend of the coloured people. When great pressure was brought to bear for the purposes of dismissing the coloured men in his mills, his reply was, "Some of these men have been with me ever since I entered business and I shall never turn my back on them." His reply was his whole character. He was too great to know any prejudice, either on account of race or colour. The lowliest workman in his mills had the same access to him which the wealthiest merchant accorded.*[314]

CHAPTER 4

1892–1918

In 1892, Archer Anderson succeeded his father as president of the Tredegar Company, but the remainder of the company's upper management was left more or less unchanged in the sense that it remained a family affair—Robert S. Archer (Archer's uncle) served as superintendent of the rolling mills, while Francis T. Glasgow continued on as superintendent of the foundry and John Francis Thomas Anderson (Archer's younger brother) served as sales agent. But what was it exactly that Archer, now aged fifty-six, had inherited from his father? In this era of growing commercial ventures and ever-expanding monopolies, what Mark Twain had dubbed the "Gilded Age," where precisely did Tredegar fit? Even in its earliest incarnations under Deane, Mills and General Anderson, Tredegar was never focused on local sales alone but rather sought customers across the region and across the nation, unlike a majority of antebellum establishments. However, the ties that J.R. Anderson and his son Archer forged and cemented in Richmond made them more akin to antebellum merchants who, to quote business historian Oliver Zunz, "acquired their wealth and exercised their influence in the same place."[315]

The Old South was gone, but the Andersons still operated Tredegar in something of an antiquated manner, dealing with workers and situations either themselves or through superintendents or other lower-level managers but never through the professional, educated managerial class whose members were attending universities and becoming an ever-increasing presence at many American corporations, such as U.S. Steel or the

1892–1918

Tredegar workmen, circa 1890. *Library of Virginia.*

DuPont chemical company. The arguably moribund attitude Tredegar's management held regarding "fresh blood" in the company was mirrored by its seeming aversion to modernization. DuPont devoted a significant proportion of its profits to investment in product diversification and to the creation of departments devoted solely to research and development—two actions Tredegar, for the most part, never undertook.[316] Tredegar, in regard to its consumer reach and high sales, was a modern corporation, but in managerial practices, alongside an apprehension toward innovation, the company was still largely anchored in the nineteenth century.

The most glaring lack of innovation on Tredegar's part was, of course, the firm's continued reliance on iron during a period wherein American physical and economic infrastructure was being transformed thanks to the introduction of mass-produced steel. The strength and durability differences between cast and wrought iron depended on the distribution of carbon throughout the metal; both forms of iron contained trace amounts of carbon (as well as other impurities), and the ratio of carbon to iron determined its practical applications. Steel production required a specific ratio of carbon (1 to 2 percent) to iron, heated to a specific temperature that allows for diffusion evenly throughout the charge, to create an alloy stronger than either cast or wrought iron. Steel had been produced for centuries but was difficult and time-consuming to manufacture and could only be fabricated in small quantities.

So-called blister steel was the most common form of steel produced in colonial-era America. Named for the blisters that appeared on the metal during its formation, this process involved placing a bar of wrought iron into a chest made of stone, filled with charcoal dust (or some other carbonaceous matter) and sealed with clay and sand, which was then transferred to a specially constructed cementation furnace. The wrought iron was heated, allowing carbon from the charcoal dust to diffuse into the iron, creating an alloy on the outer surface, while the interior of the bar usually remained largely iron alone.[317] As would be expected, this process was arduous; the artisan had to constantly monitor the furnace to ensure that the iron's melting point was not reached, while also scrutinizing any changes so as to better ascertain the point at which the metal had "matured." Accuracy in the shearing off of the outer layer of alloy away from the still-iron core was labor intensive and took years to master. This blister steel could then be reheated and worked into the desired shape or melted in clay pots (or crucibles) in an attempt to remove any remaining impurities by way of slag, creating what was known as crucible steel. As long as such a laborious and time-consuming process was the only method through which steel could be attained, cast and wrought iron remained the preferred structural and commercial metals throughout American industry.

The metallurgic industries were revolutionized, however, in 1856, when Englishman Henry Bessemer applied for a patent on a new process of steel-making that would allow for mass production. In Bessemer's process, an oval-shaped cylinder lined with refractory brick (known as a convertor) was filled with molten pig iron and tilted into an upright position; cold oxygen was blown into the torrid charge through tuyeres located at the bottom of the convertor, which oxidized out silica, carbon, manganese and other impurities, creating the convertor's signature erupting "blast." This oxidization process produced heat, maintaining the iron's liquid form as it purified into steel, until it was ready to be poured out into ingots.[318] American ironmakers would not truly experiment with Bessemer's method until the conclusion of the Civil War. But once the Bessemer process was perfected and employed en masse by such firms as the Cleveland Rolling Mill Company (1868), the Cambria Steel Company (1871) and Andrew Carnegie's Edgar Thomson Steel Works (1875), steel readily filled needs and applications for which iron once reigned supreme. Eight years after war's end, no fewer than eight steel works had been constructed in the United States, a number that only grew in subsequent years.[319] Just as Bessemer was being embraced, an even more efficient method was undergoing experimentation. The year 1868 witnessed

1892–1918

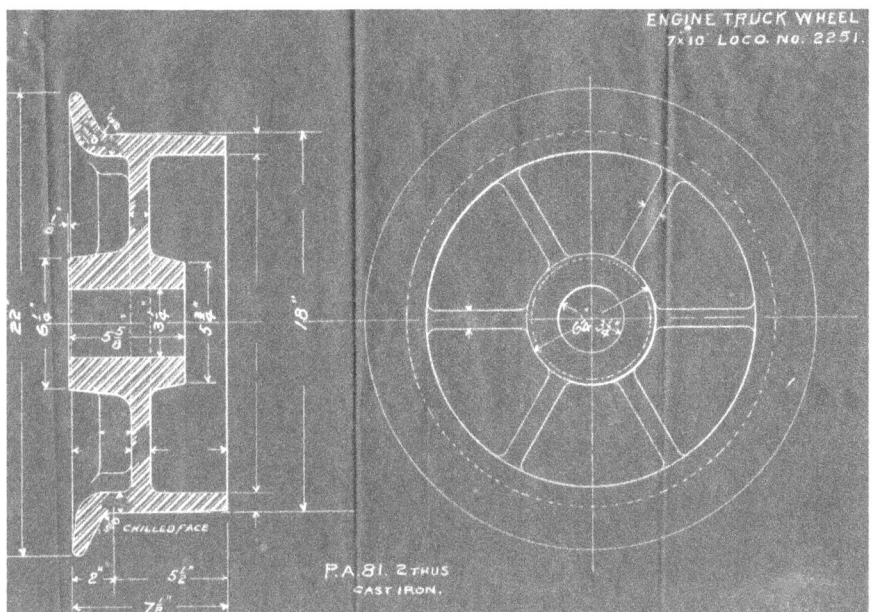

Railroad truck wheels, ordered by the Richmond Locomotive and Machine Works, 1891. *Library of Virginia.*

the first successful commercial application of Englishman William Siemens's open-hearth process, which acted much like an iron puddling furnace. It utilized a large, open "pool" of molten iron in which oxidization would take place and slag would form on the surface, conveying impurities away from the charge.[320] As with Bessemer's system, the open-hearth iron remained molten thanks to the oxidization process, allowing it the time and consistency required to mature into steel.

Despite the introduction and spread of steel manufacturing across the country, the iron industry was still going strong, due to the fact that the construction of steel did, after all, require pig iron. Furthermore, many industries did not adopt steel as readily as one may think, with railroads, machine tool makers and some construction firms still depending largely on wrought iron for years to come. There was no clear-cut, definite demarcation between the "end" of iron and the "beginning" of steel. The sum of pig iron produced in the United States rose from approximately 700,000 gross tons in 1855, just as Anderson was preparing to consolidate the myriad Tredegar operations under the banner of Joseph R. Anderson & Co., to nearly 14 million gross tons in 1900, several years after the general's passing.[321] Between 1860 and 1880, employment in the American iron industry rose from 40,000 to 140,000 workers; between 1870 and 1880, the amount of pig iron castings and rolling mill products collectively nearly doubled from 3,494,650 tons to 6,134,269 tons at the close of the decade.[322]

The railroad industry remained one of the ironworks' best customers in terms of spikes, car wheels, chairs and other related goods, but the age of iron rails traversing the country were long passed. One of the first actions undertaken by "Commodore" Cornelius Vanderbilt following the consolidation of his several railroad properties into the New York Central and Hudson River Railroad in 1870 was the complete overhaul of his iron rails and bridges and their substitution with those made of steel, a trend soon emulated by his many competitors.[323] In 1880, there were 466,917 tons of iron rails produced in the United States, compared to 741,475 tons of steel rails; this gap widened significantly in favor of steel, with its 2,076,325 tons in 1890 in contrast to iron's comparatively paltry 15,361 tons.[324]

The gradual encroachment on and then near overtaking of iron on the part of steel in many industries raises a question that is consistently and understandably posed regarding the history of the Tredegar Iron Works: why did Tredegar not convert to steel? Most of America's great steelworks of the latter nineteenth century were originally ironworks not dissimilar from Tredegar. The Cambria Iron Company adopted Bessemer convertors in 1871, reorganizing as the Cambria Steel Company in 1898; the Bethlehem Iron Company, founded in 1857 and reorganized under the title of Bethlehem Steel in 1899, had first begun producing Bessemer steel in 1873.[325] A $28-per-ton tariff against imported British steel implemented in 1870 only acted as further impetus for any aspiring American steelmakers.[326] The decade between 1865 and 1875 witnessed a rapid spread of conversion to Bessemer and open-hearth steel across America and across the globe. Prussia's famed *Krupp Gusstahlfabrik* (Krupp Cast-Steel Works), which was destined to become the largest iron and steel manufacturer in Europe and the centerpiece of a unified Germany, was in the process of adopting the Siemens open-hearth method in 1870, just as Wilhelm I's *Deutsches Kaiserreich* was proclaimed.[327] The success enjoyed by steelworks in Birmingham works beginning at the close of the century disproves the notion that a flourishing steel establishment was an impossibility in the South.

The answer, at best, is ambiguous. As of yet, there is no correspondence known to exist discussing any thoughts on Joseph Reid Anderson's part concerning the possibility of upgrading Tredegar so as to permit the fabrication of Bessemer or open-hearth steel. The time in which the plant would have been most likely (and most capable, from a financial standpoint) to make the transition to Bessemer steel would have been between 1866 and 1873, when profits were high, investors were available and the Bessemer process was gaining ground in America—it was also prior to the longtime financial stagnation that marked the 1870s, after which Tredegar lacked the capital itself for any such conversion.

So, why did Anderson not envision the same future as Henry Clay Frick or Andrew Carnegie? There are several possible reasons why there was never a Tredegar Steel Works along the banks of the James. As William T. Hogan notes in his *Economic History of the Iron and Steel Industry in the United States*, a conversion to the Bessemer process could not be accomplished piecemeal or in small stages, as the increased costs of the process itself required large-scale production in order to cover overhead while also retaining some profit.[328] Furthermore, Tredegar, for the entirety of its existence, relied on water power for the majority of its machinery, at rates that were extremely favorable to the company. The machinery needed to create steel, from the hot blast of the Bessemer convertors to the hammers required for further forming, could not be powered by water alone—if Tredegar were to upgrade via Bessemer convertors, it would have necessitated a near-complete overhaul of the company's power systems at a cost that would probably have come close to, if not equaled, the cost of acquiring the convertors, related patents and knowledgeable workmen themselves. If this were not an attractive proposition before 1873, it certainly would not have been after the panic and the austerity of receivership.

On a lesser and more personal level, it is entirely possible that Anderson desired to retain ownership of the company within the family. Andersons, Glasgows, Archers and other relations make up the majority of Tredegar stockholders throughout the company's existence, with J.R. Anderson, Robert S. Archer and Dr. Robert Archer holding 4,722, 771 and 661 shares of Tredegar stock, respectively, in 1868.[329] Following receivership and reorganization from 1876 to 1879, these three, their children and other relations and their estates following their passing continued to hold a preponderance of available Tredegar stock. The selling of shares to and recruiting of investors to acquire the needed capital for any updates or expansions of operations may not have been as attractive to Anderson in his later years as it had been during the 1840s and 1850s. In short, keeping a profitable, local enterprise in the hands of his children and grandchildren may have, as his years progressed, held more purpose for Anderson than in achieving the nationwide clout of a Carnegie or a Morgan, particularly after nearly losing Tredegar once in 1865 and yet again in 1876. This explanation is lent some credence by the fact that, even after emerging from receivership and returning to relatively high profits in the 1880s and 1890s, there seemed to be absolutely no interest on Anderson's part to invest in or seek investors for either Bessemer or open-hearth steel processes, a period during which many other ironworks were successfully undertaking such transitions.

Archer Anderson, however, apparently took note of the direction the iron and steel industry was inevitably headed. Soon after his investiture to the presidency, he began inquiries into the possibility of bringing Tredegar into the steel age. Early in his tenure, Archer even proposed further outside investment in the company for the purposes of steel conversion. In 1898, a mortgage placed on the Tredegar property following its emergence from receivership in 1879 had nearly matured, with over three-fourths of the total $1 million paid back on the part of the company; in May of that year, Archer Anderson proposed to bondholders that the mortgage be extended, that the remainder ($294,000) be augmented by further investment upward to $400,000, raising the bondholder's annual dividends from 4 to 6 percent. According to Archer, the reason for this further injection of funds was clearly evident:

> *Within a short period it may be advisable to erect an open hearth steel plant, this manufacture having already been successfully established at Birmingham, Ala., and our Virginia pig irons being better for the purpose than those of Alabama. This will cost a considerable sum, and in connection with this improvement and other extensions of business already made, additional working capital will be required.*[330]

If Tredegar was to convert to steel-making this late in the game, the open-hearth system would have proved ideal, partly because it had overtaken Bessemer steel, in terms of prevalence and production numbers, by the time of Archer's proposal but also because its simplified process had lessened costs associated with steel conversion significantly. Twenty years prior, a conversion to steel-making along the Bessemer method could have run as high as $300,000, while an open-hearth system, albeit of somewhat smaller capacity, could cost as low as $150,000; between the 1880s and Archer Anderson's appeal to bondholders in 1898, that cost had lessened even further.[331] The mortgage's renegotiation did not result in the installation of open-hearth furnaces, although several improvements to Tredegar's traditional, iron-based production infrastructure, in the form of new buildings and machinery, did appear in the immediate years. A small recession and downturn in industrial production from 1902 to 1904 following a 1901 stock market panic may have acted as a deterrent on Anderson's part for such a significant overhaul of the enterprise; just as reasonably a reason, Tredegar's management may have determined that sales and profits were decent enough as they were and saw no need, at the time, to make such a leap. Further flirtings with a possible change to steel continued in succeeding decades, but, as with those of his father, Archer's reasons for never attempting a conversion to steel cannot be gleaned conclusively from company or personal records.

Still one of the South's largest iron establishments, Tredegar continued as it had under the guidance of General Anderson, servicing local and nationwide customers, and was affected by distant events as well as those closer to home. Edward "Cap'n Ned" Archer, longtime Tredegar engineer and son of Dr. Robert Archer, noted in his diary the effects of the 1902 strike by the United Mine Workers of America throughout the anthracite mines of Pennsylvania on Tredegar's operations: "We have enough soft [or bituminous] coal enough to keep running daily," Edward wrote, but he expressed anxiety in the event the strike was not resolved quickly, taking note of all happenings related to the strike and its ongoing negotiations.[332]

More local concerns involved periodical ebbs and flows of the James River, which affected Tredegar's power supply; a February 1903 fire that completely destroyed the Spike Mill and shut down spike manufacturing entirely for nearly a month; and a particularly harsh winter of 1904, during which several turbines on site were completely frozen, forcing the closure of the Central Foundry for several days.[333]

Tredegar spikes, chairs, fishplates and particularly horseshoes continued to be successful sellers throughout the country. Archer Anderson inherited a sprawling complex, amplified far beyond the limits of the works his father assumed ownership of in the 1840s. The former site of the Confederate Arsenal, to the east of the Tredegar mills and destroyed during the evacuation fires of April 1865, had been incorporated into Tredegar proper decades earlier and now held, in addition to the Merchant and Bar Mill (formerly Dr. Robert Archer's Armory rolling mill), a forge shop, a pay office, a carpenter shop and several storage buildings. The early years of Archer Anderson's presidency saw further expansion. Nine new buildings were erected at the site between 1900 and 1905.

Of the nearly forty structures in operation across the Tredegar complex in 1905, four were dedicated solely to spike production and five to horseshoe manufacture; the remaining buildings included everything from forges to several blacksmith, carpenter and machine shops.[334] Tredegar also purchased in 1907 for the sum of $10,000 an additional four hundred feet of property

TREDEGAR IRON WORKS

between the Bar (Armory) Mill and the river's edge in anticipation of further expansion.[335] In the spring of 1903, all management offices, from those of the president down, were temporarily relocated to the nearby pattern storage building while the Tredegar offices were renovated and refurbished. The office building actually predated the ironworks, having been built in 1816 initially as part of a small tanyard business operating on the grounds and repurposed later as Tredegar's offices (and occasional dwellings) as early as 1844; during the five-month renovation period begun in May 1903, workmen discovered hidden in the walls several long-forgotten notebooks and ledgers, including reports of the initial meetings of the Tredegar stockholders in 1837.[336]

SALES REPORTED BY THREE TREDEGAR COMPANY DEPARTMENTS, 1890–1900 (BEFORE TAXES, WAGES, ETC.)[337]

YEAR	FOUNDRY SALES	ROLLING MILL SALES	HORSESHOE MILL SALES	TOTAL FOR ALL DEPARTMENTS
1890	$536,334.59	$962,094.09	$40,001.44	$1,538,430.12
1891	$238,135.59	$736,720.56	$62,679.70	$1,037,535.85
1892	$433,933.83	$899,885.38	$75,471.14	$1,409,290.35
1893	$215,454.24	$700,663.73	$75,854.89	$991,972.86
1894	$165,999.87	$524,703.51	$74,538.66	$765,242.04
1895	$180,017.05	$548,804.69	$48,814.99	$777,636.73
1896	$179,606.15	$481,143.61	$68,208.72	$728,958.48
1897	$180,657.39	$413,435.96	$117,625.83	$711,719.18
1898	$258,902.38	$475,643.18	$162,434.39	$896,979.95
1899	$268,830.20	$829,614.32	$315,677.40	$1,414,121.92
1900	$368,641.50	$809,493.36	$162,707.40	$1,340,842.26
Total for Department	$3,026,512.79	$7,382,202.39	$1,204,014.56	$11,612,729.74

UNIONS

Labor unions began to appear at Tredegar during the waning years of General Anderson's leadership and fully asserted themselves during his son's tenure. As far back as 1866, small beginnings of a labor movement appeared at Tredegar in the form of the Young Men of Liberty, a secret society founded by workmen John Stokes and Henry Johnson and composed entirely of newly emancipated African American Tredegar employees.[338]

In 1881, at the height of the "Readjusters" era in Virginia politics, branches of the Amalgamated Association of Iron and Steel Workers (AA, today known as the United Steelworkers, or USW) were formed at Tredegar. Founded in 1876 with the merger of several smaller unions including the influential Sons of Vulcans, the AA was a union limited not to a particular trade or craft but rather open to any worker nationwide who happened to be affiliated with the iron- and steel-making professions. AA Richmond Lodge No. 2 at Tredegar was composed entirely of white workers, while Lodge No. 3 represented black workers only. These groups did make an impact on Tredegar's policies in a number of ways. In 1885, the *Labor Herald*, an organ for the nationwide, universal union the Knights of Labor, reported that significant strides in workers' rights had been made at Tredegar with regard to hours and wages. Despite being segregated on the basis of race, the two lodges of the AA did come together at times when workers' rights were concerned. Near the end of 1882, both groups jointly protested the firing of a white iron roller and argued for the reinstatement of his position. In October of the same year, an assemblage of four hundred Tredegar workers, white and black alike, went on strike for higher wages. Although only about two hundred of these strikers were actually in the AA, and the strike ultimately failed, the event did display a racial solidarity not found in many other aspects of Richmond life at the time.[339]

By the early 1890s, labor organizations representing ironworkers and affiliated tradesmen were among the most numerous of unions in Virginia, with lodges belonging to such groups as the Brotherhood of Locomotive Engineers, the National Association of Machinists and the International Brotherhood of Boiler Makers, Iron Ship Builders and Helpers of America appearing in the city.[340] In Richmond alone, the number of labor unions had risen from one in 1865 to thirty-nine in 1905, with those of ironworkers and/or railroad workmen comprising a majority.[341] Ironworkers counted among their ranks many of Richmond's most vocal labor organizers; during the 1887 House of Delegates election, boilermaker and labor leader Joseph Devine (who may have worked at Tredegar, in addition to the nearby Tanner & Delaney Engine Company) evoked such hatred following comments he made at a labor rally seemingly in praise of the 1886 Haymarket bombers that at least one public official called for his public lynching.[342] In 1896, the National Association of Machinists began representing Tredegar workers, within its Richmond Local 10, eight years after the union's

TREDEGAR IRON WORKS

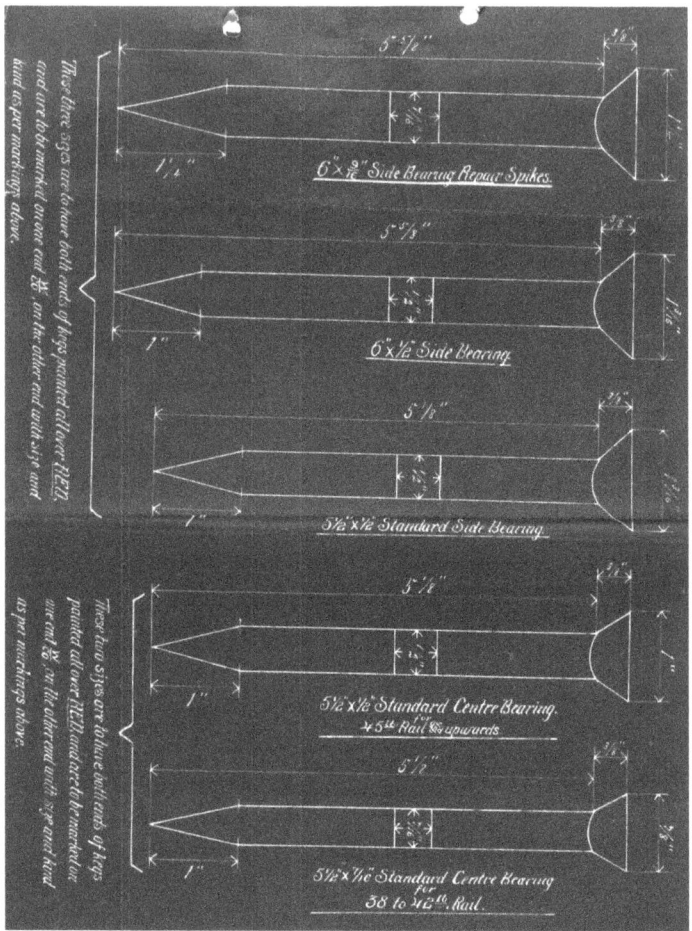

A few examples of the wide variety of railroad spikes offered by the Tredegar Company, 1889. *Library of Virginia.*

formation and one year after it merged with the American Federation of Labor (AFL) and relocated its headquarters from Richmond to Chicago.[343] This union, throughout various name changes, represented many Tredegar workers for the remainder of the company's existence.

Unions were, of course, bulwarks against the exploitation of workers in relation to wages and working hours but also offered collective aid in the event of a work-related injury, something quite common at many American industrial sites at the turn of the century, and Tredegar was no exception. Between 1866 and 1910, Richmond's newspapers reported no fewer than forty-five serious injuries (with many more likely never reported) being sustained at the works and no fewer than sixteen fatalities. Hot iron falling onto eyes and faces; fingers, hands and even entire limbs caught in the path of rollers or hammers; and skull fractures as a result of falling tools, iron bars or rafters were among the most common of injuries to Tredegar workmen, with the most severe cases requiring amputation. As gruesome as these injuries were capable of being, they paled in comparison to the many ways one could be killed on the job. On September 19, 1887, thirteen-year-old employee Charlie Mann was crushed to death when a four-ton shoe-bending machine in the horseshoe shop detached from its operating belt and collapsed onto the youth. On August 25, 1905, a twenty-eight-foot-diameter flywheel attached to the turbine powering the Bar Mill suddenly broke loose of its moorings while in full operation, destroying its enclosure and quickly fragmenting into several large, jagged projectiles, which flew outward far enough to clear the canal and land in nearby Gamble's Hill Park. Workman Samuel Owen's body was cleaved in two, killing him instantly, and five other workers were badly injured.[344] To the firm's credit, Tredegar's board of directors and management often approved dispensing monetary compensation to injured workmen, sometimes offering full or reduced salary for temporary absenteeism due to injury or illness. In the case of deceased workers, the company at times either helped subsidize funeral expenses or provided widows with some amount of monetary recompense, as was the case with several members of the Osterbind family.[345]

Those Who Called Tredegar Home

As Tredegar approached seven decades of (near) uninterrupted operation, the works became a place of continual employment for individual workmen not only from successive decades but also across generational lines, fathers followed by (or at times working side by side with) sons. This was certainly the case for both the upper management—Andersons, Glasgows, Archers—and also for the foremen, superintendents and other employees. Charles Wade, who had helped roll the iron plating for the CSS *Virginia*, worked at Tredegar for twenty-five years, alongside his brother and his father, Edward Wade, whose tenure at the works spanned half a century.[346] Elwood and Hugh, the

Tredegar Iron Works

Tredegar Management, 1908. Identification courtesy of Anne Hobson Freeman. *From left to right, front row*: Frank Glasgow Sr., Edward "Uncle Ned" Archer, Graham B. Hobson, Joseph J. Anderson (hands in pockets), Frank A. Hobson, William Porter; *second row*: Jake Anderson, William Trainham, Henry Carter Osterbind, Matthew DeGraffenried Hobson, St. George Mason Anderson (bowed head), Archer Anderson, Frank Glasgow Jr., Archer Anderson Jr. *Library of Virginia*.

two sons of Tredegar's stablemaster and yardmaster at the turn of the century, Hugh H. Harris, joined their father at his workplace when old enough. General Anderson's children had, in many ways, grown up around the works and the workmen it employed; his children matured alongside these workers' children, forming bonds that followed them into adulthood as this second generation also found their livelihoods at Tredegar. The Osterbind and Anderson families were particularly close and were often invited to one another's parties, weddings or other events. Aside from the extensive number of male family members already at the workplace, Anton Osterbind's daughters and granddaughters married into the families of other Tredegar workmen, increasing the familial ties throughout the enterprise.

When Augustus "Gus" Krengel, a worker who had first arrived at Tredegar around 1866, finally retired in April 1925, Tredegar's management decided to provide monthly payments of half his original salary for several months "in

1892–1918

A view of the Tredegar complex from the east, circa 1890. *Cook Collection, The Valentine.*

view...of your long service with us and the esteemed affection we all have for you." Gus's son, John Ernest Krengel, worked alongside his father beginning in the 1890s and remained at Tredegar for half a century, eventually becoming the company's chief patternmaker.[347] When Augustus's mother died in May 1904, the foundry was shut down on the day of her funeral to permit workers to pay their respects.[348] During the 1980s, Elwood O. Harris recalled a turn-of-the-century childhood growing up around his father's workplace, riding with worker Willie Nash, who would make deliveries of groceries and other goods to the Tredegar company store; bringing food to the families of sick or injured workmen; and picking wild strawberries with other children and Tredegar employees along the wall of the James River and Kanawha Canal.[349] As Elwood later recalled, "Our family felt that the Tredegar was the 'Papa' of all who worked there. It was home, the place you went when you had problems. Everyone knew each other."[350]

Tragedy struck one of the Tredegar's most prominent families on April 7, 1909, when former lawyer and then-department manager Frank T. Glasgow, son of Francis T. Glasgow and brother of novelist Ellen Glasgow, committed suicide at the age of thirty-eight, shooting himself in his Tredegar office.[351] Several years after his son's untimely death, the eighty-three-year-old elder Glasgow retired in 1912, concluding sixty-three years at Tredegar. Francis Glasgow, a nephew of Joseph Reid Anderson, had been an early partner and investor in both the Tredegar and Armory Iron Co. ventures and had remained with the company throughout the trials of the Civil War and

Tredegar Iron Works

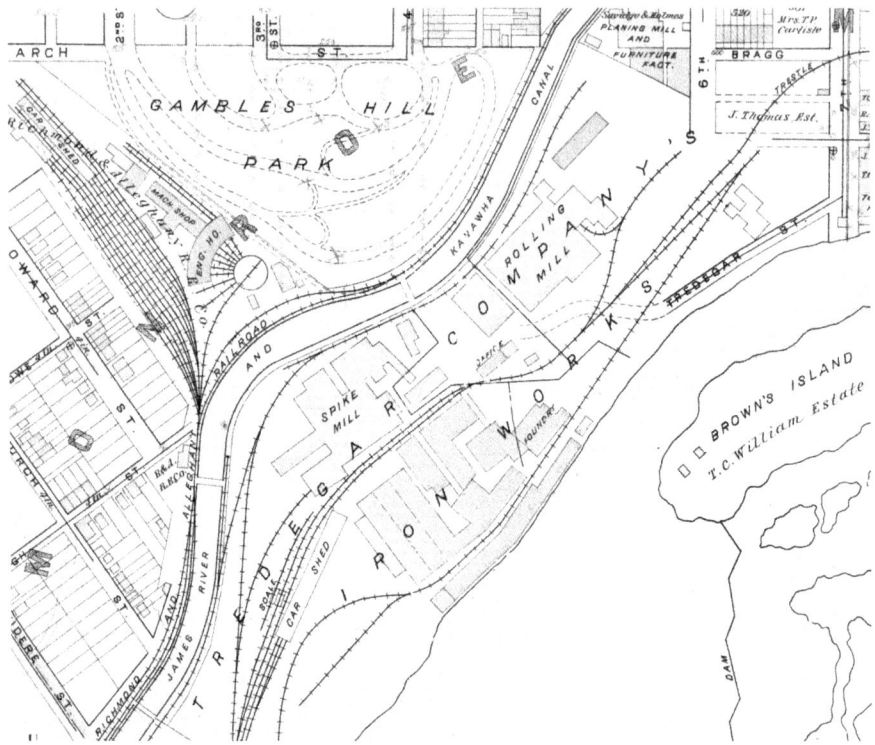

The Tredegar Iron Works, Sanborn Insurance Map, 1905. *Virginia Commonwealth University Libraries.*

receivership, holding several positions throughout his tenure, including that of foundry superintendent, secretary, treasurer and vice-president.

Anton, the patriarch of the Osterbind family, died while still employed at Tredegar, as foreman of the Chain and Bar Mills. After suffering from an illness, Anton passed away at his home in Oregon Hill on March 25, 1902.[352] Obituaries praised both his long tenure at Tredegar and his dedication to his church and community, and adornments covered his grave site at Hollywood Cemetery in a family plot not far from one belonging to the Anderson clan. Henry Carter Osterbind, Anton's eldest son, worked as an apprentice from 1867 through 1872 in Tredegar's machine shops and quickly moved up through the company ranks to the position of manager of Tredegar's horseshoe division.[353] In June 1893, Henry applied for a second patent; this time, he applied through the auspices of Tredegar. The patent costs for his invention, which improved the method by which railroad coupling pins were formed, were paid by Tredegar, and its rights were held in the firm's name.

1892–1918

In return, Henry was paid "twenty five cents per ton of 2240 lb. on all pins headed & pointed" using his new device.[354] The last patent that can be attributed to Henry was in March 1912 for a device that streamlined the production of wedge keys for railroad brake shoes.[355]

The younger Osterbind remained a valued employee of the Tredegar firm throughout the years and became close friends with the upper management. Andersons, Archers and others were invited to family functions and ceremonies, and Henry's wife, Ellen, frequently presented baked goods as gifts to management. According to a thank-you letter from Mary Mason Anderson, wife of Archer Anderson, "There is no fruit cake like Mrs. Osterbind's…Mr. Anderson ate the very last crumb of the one you sent us before."[356] Henry also received several bonuses and periodic raises throughout his career, including a $150 bonus in January 1900, and was granted a $25-a-month raise in 1902, followed by a $200 bonus and a further $10-a-month raise in 1910.[357] By 1908, Henry had been promoted yet again to superintendent of the rolling mill. Henry's position at Tredegar required a fair amount of company travel, and he made several trips to Washington, D.C.; Alexandria; Harrisburg; and other cities representing Tredegar's interests.[358]

In late June 1914, a beam in one of the buildings at Tredegar fell and severely injured Henry; despite the efforts of doctors treating him for well over a month, gangrene seized the injured leg, and Henry succumbed to the infection and died on August 1, 1914, at the age of sixty-two.[359] Many Richmond industrial and civic leaders attended the funeral and offered condolences to Ellen, in particular Archer Anderson, who, in a remembrance addressed to her personally, recalled Henry's "remarkable technical skill as a mechanical engineer and mill manager [and] his inflexible integrity and resolute will in the performance of duty." Anderson also included a check for $300, roughly the equivalent of almost $7,000 in 2015, to cover funeral expenses.[360]

In addition to Henry, three other members of the Osterbinds' second generation in America and two members of its third worked at Tredegar during and after Reconstruction in the Bar Mill, one of Tredegar's most important divisions.[361] William James Osterbind, born on March 15, 1849, was the first child of Anton's elder brother, Berend (Barney) Osterbind, and the first Osterbind child to be born in the United States. Shortly after the end of the Civil War, William began an apprenticeship at Tredegar, possibly under the auspices of his uncle, Anton. As opposed to a number of his relatives, William did not seem to specialize in any particular aspect of metallurgy at Tredegar but rather was something of a "jack of all trades."

By 1870, he was a nail cutter and also held positions as spike cutter, puddler, canvasser, machinist and ironworker.³⁶² Berend Osterbind Jr., following his father in "Americanizing" his name to Barney, was born in 1857. In his late teens, as early as the mid-1870s, he began an apprenticeship at Tredegar. Like his brother William, Barney Jr. held several differing posts at Tredegar, varying from watchman to machinist to roller. He began work as a machinist in Tredegar's Spike Mill by at least 1887.³⁶³ The youngest son of Anton and Mary, "Bee" (named after his uncle Barney) was born on July 21, 1868. Bee began work at Tredegar in the 1880s and spent several years working alongside his family in the Bar Mill before his death in 1911.³⁶⁴ The fourth member of the Osterbind's second generation at Tredegar, James Reinhold Osterbind (son of Barney Sr.), affectionately known as "Uncle Jim" by his co-workers in later years, began work at the site in 1888, after leaving a two-week stint at a nearby cigarette factory.³⁶⁵ In 1895, James was made supervisor of the workers and machinery that created the angle bars that connected railroad tracks to one another, a position he maintained for the remainder of his time at Tredegar. Lawrence Osterbind, born on September 3, 1900, and son of Barney Jr., worked alongside his father and uncles in the Bar Mill for several years, beginning in 1918.³⁶⁶

Carter Clarke Osterbind, a third-generation Osterbind at Tredegar and son of Henry, was born on September 30, 1881.³⁶⁷ He received a greater degree of formal education than his grandfather or father, attending McGuire's School, a college preparatory school near Monroe Park. Following graduation in 1898, he began classes at Virginia Polytechnic Institute in Blacksburg (today's Virginia Tech).³⁶⁸ Carter seemed to have enjoyed collegiate life, as he was elected to many extracurricular positions, such as treasurer and later president of the Lee Literary Society and vice-president of his class.³⁶⁹ In 1903, he graduated with a degree in mechanical engineering.³⁷⁰

For a little over a year following graduation, Carter worked at the American

Henry Carter Osterbind and son Carter Clarke Osterbind outside Tredegar machine shops, circa 1913. *Library of Virginia.*

1892–1918

Locomotive Company's Richmond branch. In the summer of 1905, however, he followed in the family tradition and, at the personal request of his father to the American Locomotive Company's Richmond superintendent H.A. Gillis, was let go in order to work under his father at the Tredegar Iron Works.[371] Like his grandfather and father, Carter rose through the ranks, first as foreman and then as engineer, and within a few years of his arrival at Tredegar, Carter was made manager of the Bar Mill.

On November 11, 1915, barely a year after the death of his father, Carter died of a sudden heart attack at the age of thirty-seven while on a trip to Battle Creek, Michigan, to visit his sister Minnie Osterbind Kimball. On November 20, 1915, an obituary and remembrance appeared in the pages of the *St. Luke's Herald*, a newspaper founded by Jackson Ward businesswoman and bank president Maggie L. Walker:

> *Though feeling the great weight of sorrow, which the death of our Manager and Friend, Carter C. Osterbind has placed upon us, we feel constrained to offer some slight testimonial to his disposition and character as seen by us.*
>
> *His life was such as to cause the employees of the Steam Forge, Bar and Guide Mills to say that a Christian gentleman has passed away.*
>
> *He was punctual to duty and always pleasant to meet.*
>
> *We shall miss him, and feel that his place cannot be easily filled.*
>
> *May we emulate his noble virtues, hoping to meet him, "Some sweet day by and by."*
>
> *Resolved, That a copy of this resolution be sent to his bereaved Family, and published in the* St. Luke Herald.
>
> *Done by order of the colored employees of Steam Forge and Bar and Guide Mills of the Tredegar Iron Works.*
>
>   *Morton Deane, Joseph N. Myers and Jack Robinson—Committee*[372]

While the Osterbinds remained at Tredegar for decades to come, other workers struck out on their own to try to make a name for themselves in rebuilding the South's shattered infrastructure after the Civil War. Shortly after his naturalization as a U.S. citizen in Henrico County in 1851, Alexander Delaney, nephew of locomotive engineer Matthew Delaney, joined his uncle at Tredegar, where he moved up the managerial ladder, heading his own department by 1861.[373] That same year, Alexander resigned from his position in order to join the newly formed Confederate army but was immediately removed from active service and returned to his post at Tredegar by order of Confederate secretary of war Judah Benjamin, citing the need for skilled engineers at the works. He was still able to serve in the Confederate army in some capacity, however, as a first sergeant in the Tredegar Battalion. During and long after the war, he was praised for his ability to aid in the Tredegar's continuance of ordinance production, despite constant shortages of both manpower and raw materials.[374] At war's end, Delaney joined the Metropolitan Iron Works, a small venture co-founded by former Tredegar workers William E. Tanner and Jacob Otto Ehbets. By 1869, Delaney had become a senior partner in the firm, now called Tanner, Ehbets & Delaney & Co. After several name changes following Ehbets's departure in 1870, the firm was renamed the Tanner & Delaney Engine Co. in 1882.

Chester Alexander (C.A.) Delaney, son of Matthew Delaney and first cousin of Alexander Delaney, was born in Richmond, Virginia, on June 22, 1852. Chester's father died while he was a small child, and he was placed in the guardianship of his cousin Alexander, who by that time was working at the Tredegar Iron Works, where Chester more than likely learned the trade of locomotive and engine machinist, before joining his cousin at the Tanner & Delaney Engine Co. While his cousin Alexander left Tanner & Delaney shortly before a major restructuring in 1886, C.A. stayed on, eventually becoming first assistant superintendent and later chief superintendent of the firm by then known as the Richmond Locomotive and Machine Works. The Locomotive and Machine Works used Tredegar iron in everything from wheels and axles to boilers and other locomotive components.[375] In 1898, Delaney moved to Pennsylvania, following his appointment to the position of superintendent of the Dickson Locomotive Works, in Scranton.

At the turn of the twentieth century, the American locomotive industry was dominated by a single company: the Baldwin Locomotive Works, based in Philadelphia, Pennsylvania. In an attempt to compete with Baldwin, several smaller locomotive manufacturers combined to form a larger, amalgamated entity, the American Locomotive Company, in 1901. That same year, the Dickson plant became a part of the American Locomotive Company (ALCO), as did the Richmond Locomotive and Machine Works. Delaney initially remained in Scranton following Dickson's absorption into ALCO as sales representative but later relocated to Chicago following his promotion to ALCO's western representative, a post he held until his retirement in 1925.[376]

1892–1918

African Americans continued to compose a significant portion of Tredegar's workforce, skilled and unskilled. Former slaves, already highly trained in a variety of occupations, stayed on at Tredegar following emancipation and aided in forming the earliest of formal trade unions at the works, paving the way for the succeeding generation of black workers at Tredegar. This second generation included Morton Deane, one of the signers of Carter Osterbind's remembrance in the *St. Luke's Herald*. Educated in business at some of the first schools in Richmond to cater specifically to African American students, Deane was born free in 1852 in Buckingham County and moved to the city while still a youth, possibly shortly after the fall of Richmond in 1865.[377] By 1871, Deane had begun working at Tredegar as a laborer, before rising to the position of mechanic in the rolling mill.[378] Having worked at Tredegar for over half a century, Morton Deane died on April 28, 1924. Aside from his extensive tenure at Tredegar, Deane was a well-respected and active participant in Richmond's African American community, serving as first a clerk and then a deacon and trustee of Richmond's Second Baptist Church, and in 1894, he was one of five African Americans elected to Richmond's city council that year.[379]

A Return to War

In late 1897, Tredegar received its first government ordnance contract since the end of the Civil War, supplying shot and shell during the build up to what would become the Spanish-American War. As the United States continued to grow as a military power throughout both the Eastern and Western Hemispheres following the turn of the twentieth century, Tredegar's share of military contracts grew concurrently, for itself but also in some cases as a subcontractor to other firms such as Bethlehem and Crucible Steel.

The 1861 Gun Foundry, circa 1913. Note the piles of scrap car wheels and the nearby car wheel crushing tripod. By this point, the Gun Foundry had ceased operations as a functional foundry. *Library of Virginia*.

Between 1908 and 1913, Tredegar was awarded approximately $1,428,534 worth of government contracts, on behalf of both the army and the navy, predominately for cast-iron shot and shell for naval guns, ground howitzers and mortars ranging in size from three to sixteen inches.[380] So many orders were received that in 1915 Tredegar constructed two buildings solely for shell storage.[381]

As in years past, a portion of Tredegar's success in winning government contracts was owed to its ability to retain a profit while simultaneously underbidding all other contenders. As demonstrated by one military contract in particular, Tredegar challenged, and often won out against, many of the principal armament manufacturers of the day, including the behemoth Bethlehem Steel.

April 1914 Ordnance Department Contract for Six Hundred Twelve-Inch Mortar Shells (1046 lbs.), Model 1907[382]

Firm	Lowest Bid (per shell)	Total
American & British Manufacturing Company	$45.25	$27,150
Bethlehem Steel Company*	$35.98	$21,588
Mobile Stove & Pulley Manufacturing Company	$33.00	$19,800
Tredegar Iron Company	$29.00	$17,400

* Bethlehem Steel Company actually offered shells of steel, as opposed to cast-iron, but was still rejected in favor of Tredegar's lower offer.

The Tredegar management, however, refused to fill any foreign orders for ordnance after the Great War's outbreak in July 1914. In the words of a company spokesman: "We were forced to decline on that [European] account…There was a possible chance of getting entangled with the neutrality laws, and we do not intend to violate them, even in spirit. We have all we can handle, and are content to keep clear from entangling alliances."[383]

Tredegar's potential for future ordnance production in the event of American involvement in the war might have caught the eye of several larger industrial concerns, particularly that of Charles M. Schwab's Bethlehem Steel, which was looking to expand after accepting sizable orders from the British government. In October 1915, Richmond newspapers carried rumors that Schwab was interested in purchasing the entire Tredegar operation, and that Archer Anderson had offered an option valued at $2.5 million.[384] Several

1892–1918

investors at the time had spoken of building a steel works in Richmond, and the Old Dominion Iron and Nail Works on Belle Isle, then under the direction of Frank Jay Gould, son of nineteenth-century railroad speculator Jay Gould, was in the process of installing electric steel convertors at its site, so such an expansion into steel, and particularly one facilitated by financial luminaries on the level of Gould and Schwab, was not outside the realm of possibility. Rumors involving possible purchases of Tredegar on the part of the Bethlehem Steel Company and even the United States Steel Corporation continued to circulate throughout the month of October, but by November, such talk had petered out, and no such acquisition ever took place.[385]

In the years immediately preceding 1917, a significant percentage of Tredegar's shot and shell (an estimated $532,000 worth) was ordered on behalf of the Frankford Arsenal. A sprawling military-industrial compound established in 1816 just outside Philadelphia, spanning 91.5 acres by 1922 and employing approximately six thousand workers during World War I, the Frankford Arsenal had, by the early 1900s, became the government's premier ordnance testing, research and ammunition-manufacturing facility. Tredegar shells arrived empty at Frankford, where they were then filled and readied for use.[386] Tredegar's association with Frankford continued following America's entry into the conflict on April 6, 1917, as the value of military contracts coming Tredegar's way rose substantially, from $1,594,013 to $3,281,196 between 1917 and 1918, respectively.[387]

While manpower and material shortages are always concerns in wartime, two occurrences in particular threatened to derail Tredegar's ordnance production and its ability to fulfill its contractual obligations to the

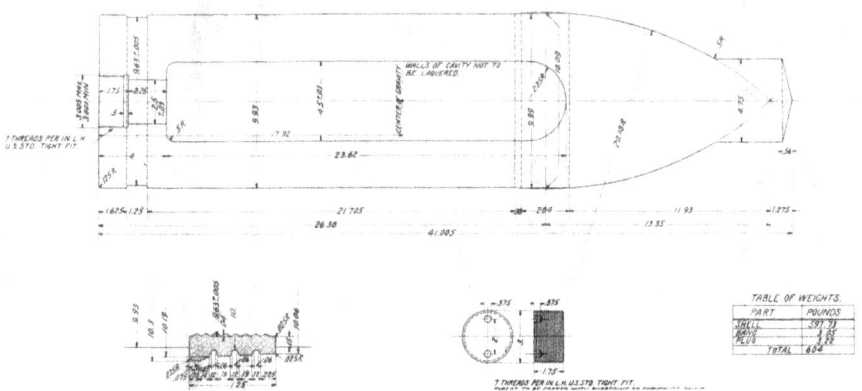

Design plans for one of Tredegar's most-produced items during the early twentieth century, the Model 1907, ten-inch naval projectile. *Library of Virginia.*

government. Due to the chronic inability of railroads to meet America's sudden wartime needs, President Woodrow Wilson placed the entire nation's railroad system under direct government control in December 1917 with the formation of the United States Railroad Administration, naming former secretary of the treasury William Gibbs McAdoo as director general of railroads.[388] Many railroad-dependent industries such as Tredegar stood to benefit from the creation of McAdoo's office, as evidenced by Archer Anderson's citing of "uncertainty of the railway transportation, the difficulty of assembling materials in proper time and the great scarcity of labor due to the present war" as the chief causes of production delays.[389] A second catalyst behind the establishment of the Railroad Administration was constant and destabilizing fluctuations in wages throughout the industry, as workers' pay was being rapidly outpaced by costs of living. Railroad workmen's wages had oscillated over the previous few years, and any modifications in wages dictated by McAdoo's office were often taken into account by related industries (iron making included) when managing their own pay scales.[390] In the spring of 1918, during the Tredegar's busiest period of that year, the workmen of the machine shops, as represented by the International Association of Machinists (IAM, formerly the National Association of Machinists), pressed for higher wages in line with what was expected to be announced for the railroads in McAdoo's next ruling on the subject. In response to their demands, Tredegar's management issued a statement that was a bit softer in tone (and certainly more forgiving) than the reply Joseph Reid Anderson sent his striking workmen some seventy years before:

> *While the Company is always willing to talk over affairs of the shop with the Shop Committee it is fair to tell you that this Company is unwilling to consider the question of a claim for increased wages until Mr. McAdoo has announced formally his decision as to the Railroad wages and this Company has considered such decision to see what, if any, bearing it has on wages in our Shop…I am frank to tell you, however, that even if our wages are not the same as Mr. McAdoo makes the railroad wages, we shall not consider the railroad wages as governing our Shop…Our desire is to pay not only fair wages, but the most liberal we can pay and still obtain work on competitive bidding. We hope our decision, when made, will be satisfactory to our employees, as of course, we do not expect any one to work for us, if he can do better elsewhere.*[391]

1892–1918

IAM representatives held meetings with Tredegar's management as well as government officials, reaching as high as Acting Assistant Secretary of the Navy Louis N.H. Howe. Negotiations proved productive, and a settlement, without strike, was reached that August. IAM general executive board member Thomas Savage wrote to the local IAM chairman, congratulating the union on its victory but also emphasizing the workmen's responsibilities: "I feel that the machinists and toolmasters are indeed fortunate and I cannot impress upon you too strongly that it is your duty as well as the duty of each and every machinist employed at the Tredegar plant to put forth his energy and best efforts in order that maximum productivity is maintained."[392] The machinists did indeed obtain the wage hike they desired; upper-level blacksmiths received a raise, from $0.68 to $0.78 per hour; tool room and fixture men both received $0.78 an hour, up from $0.72 and $0.68 respectively; and first- and second-class machinists wages were raised by $0.05, to $0.73 and $0.67 per hour, respectively. Bonuses based on production levels were also granted to some workers. Per the agreement, all wage changes were

Tredegar workmen machining World War I naval shells, circa 1918. *Cook Collection, The Valentine.*

retroactively effective back to June 1, 1918, so the government, in August 1919, compensated Tredegar $13,000 to offset any differences in pay for ordnance workers.[393]

In addition to short-lived labor woes, Tredegar was also impacted by the worldwide influenza epidemic that had already killed hundreds of thousands across the country and had made its way to Richmond by October 1918; St. George Anderson, superintendent of the foundry, wrote to the Ordnance Department that between 30 and 40 percent of his workmen had been stricken with the flu and had called out of work for several days, leading to an estimated 50 percent decrease in productivity at the works. Fortunately for Tredegar and Richmond, the epidemic made its way to the city rather late in its cycle, and production returned to its established levels within a matter of weeks.[394]

Signifying the growing importance of munitions to Tredegar's portfolio, a new foundry was constructed exclusively for the production of shells and other projectiles in 1917. Located to the southeast of the Bar Mill (originally the site of the old Armory Mill) and just slightly north of the former millrace that separated Brown's Island from the "mainland," which by this point had been expanded into a power-generating canal for the Virginia Railway & Power Company (the predecessor to the modern-day Dominion Power), this foundry contained two large cupola furnaces, both fifty-six inches in diameter. It additionally boasted four ovens specifically for producing cores, sand inserts that would be placed into molds to form cavities and other features during casting. The 1917 Shell Foundry was capable of being converted rather easily into a second car wheel foundry if orders for shells ever reached low enough levels.[395] This new foundry fulfilled orders for American forces, and as a sub-contractor to other firms such as Bethlehem, Crucible Steel and DuPont, Tredegar manufactured shells that were used by the British, Russian and Brazilian navies. An official inspector was sent to Tredegar on behalf of the federal government and would inspect shells on a weekly basis, confirming they were of the correct diameter by means of several measurement gauges he carried with him, one set for each type of shell manufactured.[396]

Military contracts continued to pour into Tredegar over the remainder of the war. As soon as hostilities ceased, however, the government recognized the need to cancel outstanding contracts with armament manufacturers not only to conserve materials and labor but also to hasten the return to a peacetime economy. As a result, Boards of Contract Adjustments were established within each of the military branches to ensure that all remaining contracts were concluded to the satisfaction and fair treatment of both government and industrial interests.[397] Through the use of such boards, the government compensated Tredegar for contracts cancelled at war's end. The government purchased whatever munitions were already finished under the contract, and any additional materials purchased by Tredegar to fulfill the order could be kept by the company and sold as scrap, with the government covering the difference between the current market price and the inflated costs Tredegar had paid during wartime. While Tredegar was compensated for whatever items it had already completed, it was nonetheless something of a loss to win a contract for $33,671.90, only to receive $865.25 for it several months later, as was the case regarding a cancelled June 1918 Ordnance Department order for 2,465 six-inch cast-iron shells.

Naval contracts, however, were less likely to be cancelled than army contracts. Shortly after the sinking of the RMS *Lusitania* in May 1915 by German U-boats, President Wilson pushed for the creation of more robust U.S. Navy. The Battle of Jutland, between British and German dreadnaughts in the North Sea and arguably the largest sea battle in history, had just concluded the day before Congress voted on (and likely helped to ensure the passage of) the Naval Act of 1916, which called for an unprecedented expansion of the U.S. Navy. The act authorized the construction of 10 dreadnaught-class vessels, 6 battle cruisers and 50 destroyers, all fully equipped with the most powerful armament available at the time. In all, over 150 navy vessels were expected to be constructed between 1919 and 1923.[398] The completion of this most modern of fleets was not dependent on the outcome of the war; in fact, the loss of the Allies to the Central powers would have made such an armada all the more necessary. Thanks to the passage of this bill years earlier, and in response to the naval arms race that soon began between the United States, Great Britain and Japan in the early 1920s, many naval contracts were not cancelled following the end of World War I. This favored Tredegar greatly—the single largest contract awarded to the Richmond works during this era was a July 1918 naval order: 50,500 individual pieces, including 20,000 six-inch projectiles and 10,000 eight-inch projectiles, in an agreement that totaled $1,653,815.[399] Tredegar continued to receive a sizable number of government orders even after war's end—over $2 million worth between the signing of the armistice in November 1918 and the multinational Washington Naval Conference of 1921–22, which was intended to curb remilitarization on the part of all signatories, the United States included.

Like many U.S. industries, Tredegar's bottom line was augmented thanks to America's entry into the war. In the four years between 1910 and

Tredegar Iron Works

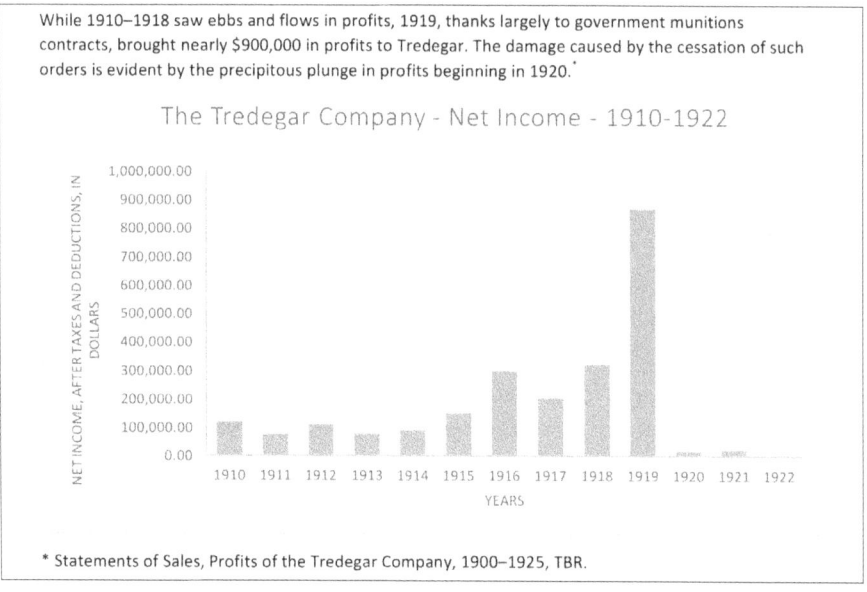

1914 combined, Tredegar reported a taxable income (gross income, less expenses, wages and any deductions) of $495,696. If counting the year of the sinking of the *Lusitania* (1915) and the period of military preparation and rearmament that followed, the company's total taxable income from that time to 1919, the year of the Versailles Treaty, was $1,858,000—more than a three-fold increase.[400] The amount that Tredegar collectively paid its approximately 1,300 workmen also jumped, from $506,404 in 1916, to $1,212,341 in 1918.[401]

Conversely, the end of a war economy had an adverse effect on Tredegar's finances; the company had not diversified its product line as had other manufacturers, and deprived of military orders, Tredegar relied mostly on the sale of horseshoes, railroad spikes and other small implements, which, while still in demand, was a significant decrease from the level of productivity the company once maintained. Profits dropped to $18,516 in 1920 and $1,269 in 1922 and then actually reached into the negative for two years before returning to the black in 1925 and onward for the remainder of the decade.[402]

Chapter 5

1918–1957

Changing of the Guard

The fourth president of the Tredegar Company, Archer Anderson, died at his home on January 4, 1918, at the age of seventy-nine following a sudden illness. As was the case with his father, Tredegar ceased operations so that workmen could attend the funeral, which was held at St. Paul's Episcopal Church and followed by a burial ceremony in the Anderson family plot at Hollywood Cemetery. The Richmond papers praised Archer's role in leading Tredegar and his unwavering dedication to that position, and that position alone:

> *Colonel Anderson was one of the most prominent business men* [sic] *of Richmond, and was an important factor in the reconstruction of this city and section in the years that followed the close of the War Between the States…It is known that Colonel Anderson, who for more than a quarter of a century has been recognized as one of the most distinguished citizens of Richmond, because of his extraordinary ability, his scholarly attainments and his brilliant military record, could have occupied several public offices within the gift of the city or State, but he consistently refused all such overtures. He was considered one of the foremost citizens of Virginia, and always took great interest in the affairs of the State.*[403]

Anderson was continuously praised for the eloquent dedication he provided at the 1892 unveiling of the Robert E. Lee statue that now resides

Archer Anderson, circa 1913. *Courtesy of Anne Hobson Freeman.*

along present-day Monument Avenue. His service to various historical organizations, such as the Stonewall Jackson Monument Corporation, the Southern Literary Society and the Virginia Historical Society, was also recognized.

Within a few days of Archer Anderson's death, Archer Anderson Jr., at the age of fifty-two, was promoted from vice-president to president of Tredegar by the board of directors. Archer Jr. was born on December 28, 1866, the third child of Archer Sr. and Mary Mason Anderson, at the family home in Richmond. After following his father to the University of Virginia and graduating with a master of arts degree in 1888, Archer Jr. studied law before being admitted to the Virginia state bar in 1890. In March 1899, Archer Jr. joined the Tredegar Company, first as assistant to the president, followed by stints as superintendent of the horse shoe department and then vice-president (following the resignation of Francis T. Glasgow in 1912), before his appointment to president on January 11, 1918.[404] After becoming president, Archer Jr. apparently felt it was unethical to take on any more of the company stock than what he already held, something he was entitled to do as president (and which his predecessors readily did), out of a fear of profiting from "an inside knowledge of the company's affairs."[405]

To fill the void left by Archer Anderson Jr.'s vacating his previous post, the new president decided to maintain the familial domination of Tredegar's management, not with an Anderson, an Archer or even a Glasgow but rather a Hobson and appointed Joseph Reid Anderson Hobson as vice-president. Born on June 27, 1867, J.R.A. Hobson was the grandson of General Anderson and the son of Colonel Edwin Lafayette Hobson and the general's daughter, Fannie Anderson. Colonel Hobson was a native of Greensboro, Alabama, who had enlisted in the Confederate army shortly after Fort Sumter and remained in service through the entirety of the Civil

1918–1957

Archer Anderson Jr., circa 1890. *Library of Virginia*.

War, participating in such battles as Cedar Creek, Chancellorsville and Spotsylvania Court House. He married Fannie Anderson at the close of 1865 and soon after came to work at Tredegar. He also managed a portion of J.R. Anderson's agricultural holdings in Goochland for several years.[406] The younger Hobson attended the University of Virginia Law School and graduated in 1890, after which he worked for the Bell Telephone and Telegraph Company before returning to Richmond and taking his place directly under his cousin Archer Jr.

The same year Archer Anderson died, Tredegar also witnessed the passing of Edward Richard Archer. Born on March 9, 1834, and the son of Dr. Robert Archer, Edward died on March 13 from a severe illness from which he had suffered for little under a month. Apprenticing at the Tredegar in the late 1850s, Edward left the company to serve first in the United States and then in the Confederate navies. After the war, he returned to his brother-in-law's firm as chief engineer, assisting David Eynon in the installation of several turbines that powered Tredegar's postwar recovery. Edward remained one of Tredegar's chief engineers until the day he died, at the age of eighty-four.[407] Despite the fact that he was actually a brother-in-law, Edward was the "young nephew of Gen. Joseph Reid Anderson, Cap'n Ned Archer"

TREDEGAR IRON WORKS

Edward "Cap'n Ned" Archer, 1913. *Courtesy of Anne Hobson Freeman.*

mentioned in a 1943 *Saturday Evening Post* article highlighting Tredegar's history and wartime production. "Cap'n Ned," a captain in the Confederate navy, ran the Union blockades, carrying to London Southern cotton that was intended to be sold to fund the war effort but was instead exchanged for gold, some of which was once again run back through the blockades by Cap'n Ned to Richmond and provided Anderson with much of the funds that he used to restart Tredegar following his pardon in 1865.[408]

By the early 1920s, the changes in management were complete, and the executive officers were Archer Jr. and J.R.A. Hobson as president and vice-president. Archer Jr.'s younger brothers rounded out the top management; Joseph Reid Johnston Anderson was named secretary and treasurer, and St. George Mason Anderson became superintendent of the foundry. St. George, holding a degree in mechanical engineering from Stevens Institute in Hoboken, first came to work at Tredegar in 1901 as superintendent of the rolling mills before being promoted to overseer of the foundry and machine shops in 1911; he also assumed the vacant position on Tredegar's board of directors following the retirement of Francis Glasgow.[409] The only non-Anderson (or related kin) in the senior management, W.R. Trainham, served in the newly created position of auditor. J.R.A. Hobson's younger brother, Matthew DeGraffenried Hobson, served as an assistant superintendent.[410] John F.T. Anderson, uncle to Archer Jr., served as general sales agent of Tredegar until September 3, 1920, when he committed suicide at the age of sixty-two; he was soon succeeded by Edward Hanewinckle Trigg, who would hold that post for many years to come.[411]

With the passing of Archer Anderson and Edward Richard Archer, the Tredegar's top positions, for the first time in its history, were devoid of leaders with significant military backgrounds and experience, and lacked any veterans of the Civil War for the first time in over half a century—its two top executives were of the generation born immediately after the war. This was a turning point in the company's history; the presence of university-educated men, with years of prior business experience and training in modern business practices, placed Tredegar alongside the majority of companies operating in America at the time. Its transition from post-bellum ironworks to modern, professionally managed industrial plant was, however, a decade or two behind other firms in regard to similar evolutions—a fact that, when combined with a lack of innovation in the recent past (particularly in regard to adopting steel), as well as the presence of nothing resembling the professional, managerial class already present at a number of other contemporary firms for more than forty years, signaled a possible, albeit slow, decline in the coming decades.

In 1922, Tredegar's operational area encompassed roughly twenty-three acres, with seven outlaying acres surrounding the works also under the company's ownership. Many of the buildings were connected with cobblestone roads, while much of the property was also covered with standard-gauge rail tracks, about three and a half miles worth, upon which several yard engines and switching locomotives ran, ferrying materials into Tredegar and between shops and finished products out of the plant. The cars attached to these engines, between forty and fifty in number, were loaded by use of two magnetic cranes, capable of lifting ten and twenty tons. Up to thirty thousand tons of scrap and pig iron and six thousand tons of fueling coal and coke could be stored on the numerous storage yards scattered across the property.[412] Sixteen water turbines operated on site, the most powerful a forty-two-inch, 247-horsepower McCormick-model vertical turbine used in the Merchant Mill. Collectively, over 1,960 horsepower could be generated by Tredegar's turbines, powering everything from spike cutters and horseshoe rolls to cupola bellows.[413]

Tredegar Iron Works

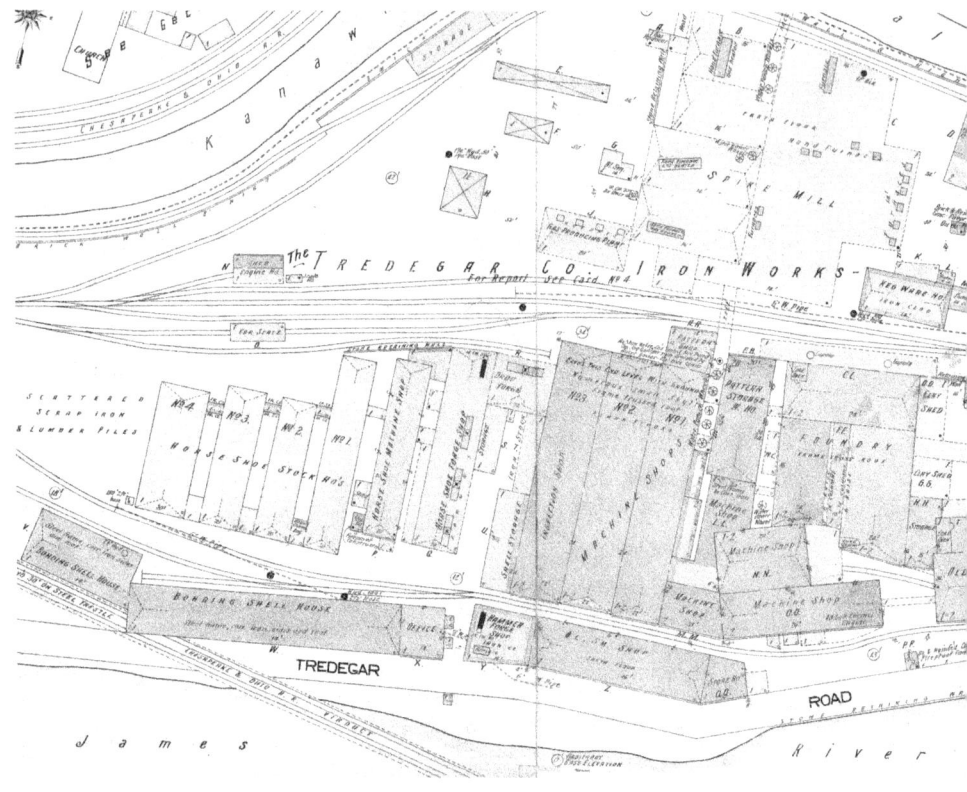

The Tredegar Iron Works, Sanborn Insurance Map, circa 1922. *Library of Virginia.*

In addition to the New Shell Foundry constructed on the far eastern end of the property in 1917, several new small shops and sheds appeared, and many existing departments received much-needed upgrades. The shop previously used for the construction of car axles had been repurposed as a steam forge, in which scrap iron was heated and pounded, using two 3,000-pound and one 2,500-pound steam hammers, into blooms; blacksmithing and millwright shops were also located in the new steam forge. The spike factory now boasted seventeen spike machines (twelve hand-operated, five automatic) and a machine shop dedicated solely to repairs needed in the spike department; the horseshoe department had seven machines, and an on-site cooper shop could produce up to 1,500 kegs a day for both shops to use. The central Tredegar foundry (now often called Foundry No. 1, or the Old Foundry), with many of the original 30,000-pound capacity cannon cranes still in use, had been largely refitted for the production of car wheels as

1918–1957

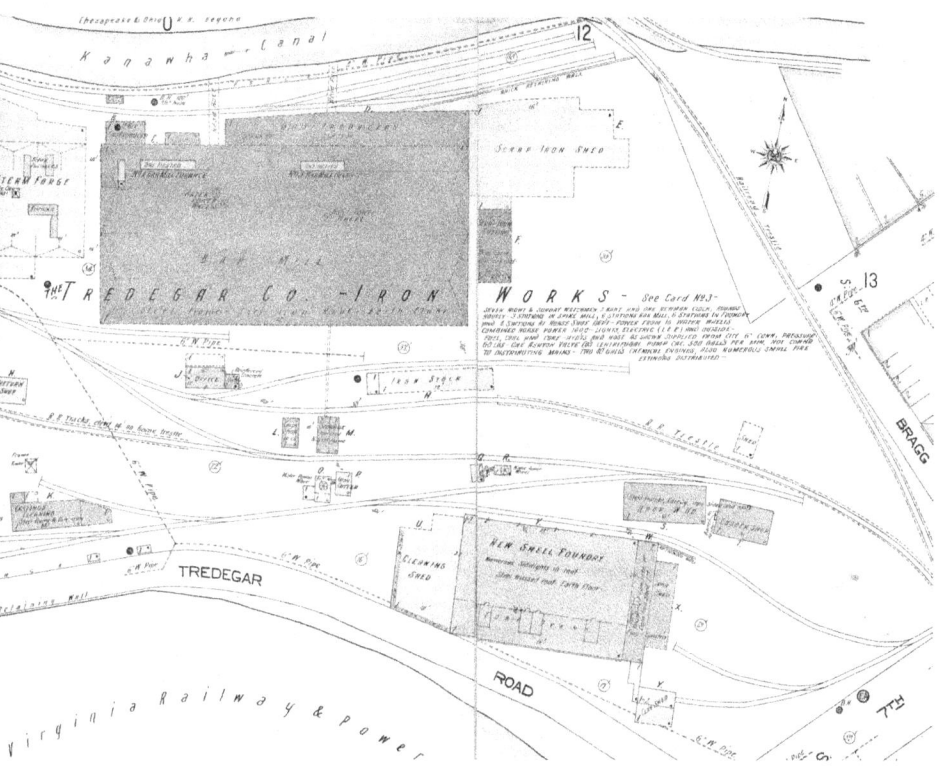

well as other castings, with the use of two cupola furnaces, sixty-four inches and fifty-four inches in diameter. The pattern storage building, now three stories high following several successive fires over the previous few decades, still acted as a repository for all needed moulds and patterns. The Pattern Building was not alone in suffering the ravages of fire, an endemic scourge that plagued the works, in varying levels of severity, throughout the entirety of its existence. Between 1920 and 1931, no fewer than seven major fires struck Tredegar, the worst occurring in April 1924 and destroying numerous freight cars, a locomotive and several horseshoe storage sheds, amounting to a complete loss of all horseshoes stored on the grounds.[414]

Archer Anderson Jr. was acutely aware of Tredegar's historical significance. While president, he began work on a "History of Tredegar" notebook, compiling over one hundred years' worth of deeds, contracts, advertisements and correspondences, all for the purpose of chronicling the firm's history. He tracked down men who had served under his grandfather during the Civil War, both at Tredegar and on the battlefield, and requested whatever

Tredegar Iron Works

Throughout the late nineteenth and early twentieth centuries, one of the Tredegar's most frequent customers was the nearby Richmond Locomotive and Machine Works, which produced, among other engines, the Richmond Compound Locomotive shown here. *Nathan Madison.*

information or documents possible from companies that had worked with or ordered from Tredegar in years past. Alongside this appreciation of his inheritance, Archer Jr. also recognized the need for modernization at the aging plant. Shortly after assuming the leadership of Tredegar, he sought two avenues toward modernization (one successful, one not) intended to bring Tredegar, competitively speaking, into the twentieth century.

Beginning in the summer of 1919, as the remaining army and navy contracts kept Tredegar at full operational capacity, Archer Jr. began to seek consultation regarding the possible conversion of Tredegar's machinery "from the use of iron to the use of steel billets only."[415] As has been noted, Tredegar never transitioned from an ironworks to a steel works; that is not to say, however, that Tredegar did not produce steel products or products that contained a fair amount of steel in their composition. Some variations of horse and mule shoes, as well as particular models of fishplates and other railroad components, required the use of steel, and Tredegar met these demands, placing orders with Monongahela River steel producers such as Carnegie's steel works in Duquesne and the Jones & Laughlin Steel Company outside Pittsburgh for new and scrap steel to supplement these needs. What Archer Anderson Jr. proposed was a slight upgrade from a simple (and by that point nearly archaic) ironworks, not quite a full-scale steel works but rather a middle ground—simply put, a steel-processing and finishing firm, able to meet the changing demands of the industry. Anderson and senior officers wrote to companies such as Crucible Steel, Bethlehem Steel and others

1918–1957

inquiring as to the possible mechanical and personnel changes under such a modernization, citing the limited nature of their business as long as it relied solely on recycled scrap iron. By September, Tredegar was already making offers to potential new mill managers and making supply arrangements with steel producers. "Having made a favorable arrangement with one of the largest steel producers in the country for such steel as we may require," St. George Mason Anderson wrote to a colleague in Flint, Michigan, "we are shortly giving up the working of iron in our mills entirely to work nothing but steel billets on all mills."[416] Within a few months, however, the officers showed some doubts as to its success, and it does not reappear in company correspondences until May 1921, when Archer Jr. blames the scheme's failure on "overwhelming difficulties brought about by the bad spirit of our employees…trying to kill the job and…doing all they could apparently to limit production."[417] Fears of lessened or terminated employment on the part of lifelong ironworkers in the event of a transition to steel would be expected, although Tredegar's sudden drop in revenue, in part due to a lessening of government contracts combined with the nationwide recession that struck the country in 1920–21, is likely the overriding explanation for the company's continued reliance on iron alone. Archer Jr. continued to show interest in upgrading Tredegar's output for several more years, inquiring about the American Rolling Mill Company of Middleton, Ohio (ARMCO) and its "ARMCO iron," a product only slightly softer than basic Bessemer steel, in 1924 and even looking into the possibility of installing at least one open-hearth steel furnace in late 1925.[418]

Archer Jr.'s other attempt at modernization was far more successful. In the spring of 1924, he pushed for a complete overhaul of Tredegar's accounting and record-keeping system, seeking to replace the simple account ledgers and sales books used since the company's inception with practices that reflected more contemporary standards and procedures, particularly those demanded by the relatively new federal income tax laws. After several months of consultations with both the accounting firm Price, Waterhouse & Co. and the Bethlehem Steel Company, Tredegar hired, at a cost of $4,000 a year, an accountant to aid in the complete reorganization of the company's bookkeeping practices along the lines followed by many of the era's most successful firms, Bethlehem in particular.[419]

Owing to the depression of 1920–21 and an iron market Anderson referred to as "deadly dull," Tredegar, beginning in December 1920, laid off a fair amount of its workmen, levied a 10 percent reduction in wages and temporarily shut down several departments intermittently, including the Bar

Tredegar Iron Works

Small automatic spike machine, produced by the Youngstown Foundry and Machine Company of Youngstown, Ohio. This machine was first tested at Tredegar in April 1922 and several similar machines came to be used at Tredegar alongside traditional, manual spike machines. *Library of Virginia.*

and Spike Mills; the foundry and machine shops remained open only thanks to the need to fulfill outstanding government contracts.[420] Thankfully, by the winter of 1922, all shuttered departments had reopened, a 10 percent raise was given to all workers and Tredegar was slowly returning to its normal operating capacity. In 1922 alone, even in light of temporary department shutdowns, Tredegar's workmen were, during eight-hour shifts, three hundred days a year, capable of producing 73,000 gross tons of finished iron products, including 225,000 kegs (22,500 tons) of railroad spikes and 150,000 kegs (7,500 tons) of horse and mule shoes. Nearly everything the plant needed for repairs or modifications could be made on site, with many Civil War–era lathes being fitted with newly fabricated parts and tips rather than being replaced. For the most part, the lower-skilled jobs at Tredegar, particularly those at the rolls and furnaces, were held by African Americans, while the higher-skilled positions, including those of blacksmiths, shell-production and foremen, were reserved for Caucasians.[421]

The Great Depression

The iron and steel industries were among the hardest hit following the October 24, 1929 stock market crash and were, on some level, victims of their own success. The prosperity of the 1920s, small recessions throughout the decade aside, benefited companies like Bethlehem Steel and U.S. Steel, as orders for large-scale products such as locomotives and other industrial equipment piled one on top of the other; likewise, dependence on the sale of such items spelled disaster for these companies' bottom lines when orders dropped off suddenly and significantly. The year of the crash, the iron and steel industries, collectively the largest source of employment in America at the time, produced 63 million tons of steel—in 1932, this had dropped precipitously to barely over 15 million tons.[422] The market for finished iron products had lessened dramatically ever since mass-produced steel had become a reality, but interestingly enough, Tredegar's avoidance of transition to steel may have actually helped the firm weather the Great Depression on some level. While behemoths such as Bethlehem saw orders for massive products like steel locomotives drying up, Tredegar's manufacturing portfolio was, comparatively speaking, composed of a variety of cheaper, smaller items that could potentially still find buyers in hard times.

Tredegar Iron Works

This is not to suggest, however, that Tredegar was unharmed by the Depression. In 1929, Tredegar's reported profit was approximately $123,000, dropping to $78,000 in 1930. In 1932, profits dropped to barely $650, and in 1933, Tredegar once again reached negative profits, with a reported loss of nearly $64,000.[423] The number of railroad spikes, by the ton, decreased from 5,106 in 1928 to barely 1,000 by 1932; likewise, angle bar sales, by ton, went from 3,000 down to 960 during the same time period.[424] The sale of iron rebar used on concrete structures peaked for the time period at 108 tons in 1929 but fell drastically to only 1 ton in 1932. The fact that the horseshoe department's output was as high as it was during the Depression is something of a miracle. Horseshoe production was hindered for several years by a disastrous fire that had occurred on April 24, 1926, which destroyed part of the horseshoe shop, several storage buildings and much of the department's tools and machinery, including a Baldwin switching locomotive; losses in terms of horseshoes alone, roughly 2 million pounds' worth, was estimated to be around $77,000 after whatever could be sold (or used) as scrap was salvaged.[425] The buildings and required equipment were rebuilt or replaced over the next several years. Despite both a department only just recently returned to full operational capacity and a nationwide economic depression, horseshoe sales were not nearly as low as those of other items during the Depression. Horseshoe sales dropped to 571 tons sold in 1932, from 844 tons five years prior. In all, the tonnage of finished iron products produced by Tredegar dropped by 6,523 tons, from 9,094 in 1928 to 2,571 in 1932.

Not surprisingly, the Depression years reveal a lessening of government contracts coming Tredegar's way. In years prior, a multitude of contracts were awarded each year; for most of the 1930s, this slowed to one contract a year, if any at all. A $74,520.00 naval order for six thousand six-inch projectiles was awarded in July 1930, followed in 1931 by a $400,000.00 contract for the production of live shells for the navy. In December 1933, a contract worth over $150,000.00 was granted for naval ordnance, followed by another worth $2,798.00 in July 1934; in January 1935, Tredegar underbid other companies for a contract to once again produce practice shells for the navy. Large munitions contracts did not return until tensions escalated in Europe once again, with a $44,393.50 Ordnance Department order in June 1939.[426]

In a move that undoubtedly was meant to aid the company and its shareholders (which was largely still the Andersons, Archers and related branches) during the Great Depression, Tredegar's board of directors approved a stock repurchase plan in October 1932. The company offered a fixed price tender repurchase directly to its stockholders (Tredegar stock was rarely listed on any exchange), wherein Tredegar would buy back 50 percent of all outstanding stocks from all shareholders at fifty dollars per share, with all returned stocks retained as treasury stock by the company.[427]

One way in which companies increase the value of a seemingly undervalued stock by creating a scarcity of shares available on the open market (particularly during lean economic times, when it was possible to buy low), this stock buyback provided a double boon to Tredegar's investors in that not only did they receive payment for the stocks they sold back, but also the limited number of outstanding stocks could yield a higher dividend in the future. With every stockholder's shares halved, across the board (Archer Anderson Jr.'s shares were reduced from 392 to 149 and St. George M. Anderson's from 321 to 161), Tredegar, in terms of stocks outstanding, and the shareholders, in terms of compensation and possible dividend returns in the future, stood to gain from this move, which helped in weathering the Great Depression, which was to reach its lowest depths the following year.[428] In 1933, as was the case with previous depressions, many Tredegar workers were let go as several shops and departments shut down temporarily, coinciding with across-the-board pay cuts: a 5 percent reduction for all salaried employees making $125 a month or less, a 10 percent cut for those making more and a 15 percent diminution in pay for the president himself.[429]

C&O Lawsuit

The dual threats of an ongoing economic depression and a complete drought of government contracts were only compounded by a lawsuit brought against the Tredegar Company that accused the firm of no less than outright fraud stretching back decades.

Before and definitely after the conclusion of the Civil War, it was apparent to the majority of American businessmen, entrepreneurs and investors that the steam engine and its miles of rails were destined to completely supplant canals as the chief carrier of America's freight and future prosperity. Many canals across the country were being drained, and the towpaths once used by horses to pull boats upstream were now being laid over with steel and iron rails; in this, the James River and Kanawha Canal was no different. A series of catastrophic floods throughout the 1870s, repairs from which drained the company's already-limited coffers, resulted in the dissolution of the James

River and Kanawha Company in 1878 and the creation in its stead of the Richmond and Alleghany Railroad, intended to both absorb the assets of its predecessor and to construct a railway along the canal's path.[430] Construction was begun on opposite ends of the line (at Clifton Forge and in Richmond) to meet in the middle, while the canal remained open to traffic and shipping until the completion of the rail line. A promise was made on the part of the Richmond and Alleghany to honor all hydropower contracts with which the late James River and Kanawha Canal Company (JRKC) had entered into agreement to supply water power for another century. In the fall of 1881, all 193 miles of the railroad were completed, and the canal finally ceased all operations, with the exception of the continuance of supplying water power. A decade later, in 1891, the Chesapeake and Ohio Railroad (C&O) purchased the Richmond and Alleghany line, along with the canal and its obligations to its hydropower beneficiaries, Tredegar included.

As early as October 1924, the C&O had expressed concerns regarding Tredegar's water usage, suggesting that the ironworks was using more water than contracts allowed, a complaint that appeared frequently in succeeding years. In 1933, when Tredegar's management complained to the C&O that it was not maintaining the structural integrity of the canal, thus causing fluctuations in the amount of waterpower it received to power its machinery, the C&O once again raised the water rights issue and threatened legal action if no adjustments were adopted on Tredegar's part. This was the beginning of a litigation that would last for the next three years, the defense from which would cost Tredegar dearly, but a defense was needed if it hoped to remain in operation. The low rates Tredegar had been paying the JRKC and its successors in the form of the C&O (reported in 1919 to be only $8,000 a year) had allowed it to maintain a competitive stance in relation to northern iron establishments (increasing expenses in shipping and materials, which were offset by lower power costs) for decades, and the loss of that power source would have necessitated the near-complete overhaul of the Tredegar site to accommodate electric generators, a prospect that the company simply could not afford.[431]

Each side hired its own historical consultants, tasked with poring over city and company records to try to determine just what Tredegar was allowed per its myriad agreements, which reached back all the way to Colonel Harvie's original arrangement with the JRC in the late eighteenth century. What may have otherwise been a fairly straightforward exercise in historical and industrial research quickly presented its own hindrances. Several grants used various descriptions of "inches" of water allowed, and the nature of the "inches"—whether the size of the aperture in the canal, the width of the waterwheel that would use the water or even the width of the raceway—was never defined. The more modern method of measuring hydroelectric power, cubic feet per second (cfs), was not in use at the time of the original grants. As a result, the question of how much water Tredegar was actually allowed per its agreement became a search to define exactly what "inches" meant. The C&O argued that "inches" referred to the size of the aperture, which, if that was indeed the case, would have resulted in Tredegar being forced to increase the amount of water it purchased from the railroad if it hoped to maintain current levels; Tredegar, on the other hand, claimed that the inches in question referred to the width of the waterwheel and gates that the water flowed through and across—the size it had (for the most part) always used and which was still in use by the early 1930s, signifying (in Tredegar's opinion) continued compliance with the initial grants. Tredegar spared no expense in its defense and hired the services of two highly respected engineers to argue its case: Roswell D. Trimble, of the Richmond-based engineering and consulting firm of R.D. Trimble & Co., and Robert Horton, formerly of the U.S. Geological Survey and New York Department of Public Works and a leading expert of the day in hydraulic engineering.[432] After months and then years of wrangling between the two sides about the definition of "inches," interestingly enough it was none other than Tredegar's original president, Francis B. Deane, who, in a manner of speaking, provided the most significant evidence in Tredegar's favor.

In 1854, Deane had requested and received a grant from the original James River and Kanawha Company for an aperture grant equaling 606 square inches, as he was in the process of replacing his overshot wheels with turbines. The 606 square inches was a conversion from an original 100-inch grant Deane had used for the original waterwheel, which was itself 100-inches in diameter. The language in this renewed grant seemed to suggest that, in similar cases, the canal company used waterwheel-width as a basis for grant measurements, casting some doubt on the railroad's interpretation of the water grants.[433]

In 1936, a settlement agreeable to both parties was reached that included a renegotiation of Tredegar's water rights, which retained the amount of water power the company had held previously, albeit with a slightly higher price tag. The company still enjoyed a relative bargain when compared to the potential upgrade and operating costs if the water was replaced entirely with electricity. Tredegar continued to run on water power for the remainder of its existence, using both turbines and electric generators powered by the canal's ebbs and flows. In the late 1930s, Archer Anderson Jr. anticipated the eventual necessity of transitioning to electricity alone, a process that was never implemented. By 1938, Tredegar was tied into the Virginia Electric and Power Company's (VEPCO) grid, which supplied power in the event of some obstruction of the canal's supply, and the ironworks even began selling excess water-generated power, at two cents per kilowatt, back to VEPCO.[434]

THE SECOND WORLD WAR

Along with the greater majority of American industries, iron and steel bounced back from the Great Depression following the massive industrial build-up preceding the Second World War; from 15.2 million tons in 1932, American steel production rose to just under 90 million tons by 1944.[435] As pig iron is needed for the making of steel, the need for iron grew alongside the demand for iron, and despite the growth of "big steel" over the previous

Tredegar workmen, 1939. *Richmond Times-Dispatch*.

seventy years, Tredegar proved it could still compete with larger, more modern firms in the cutthroat arena of government contracts.

Following the dearth of government contracts for munitions that permeated most of the Depression years, ordnance contracts began to trickle into Tredegar by the end of the 1930s and increased as the new decade dawned. Between June 1940 and July 1941, contracts totaling at least $1.4 million were awarded to the Richmond firm, largely for army and navy target projectiles, and as America came closer to and finally joined the Second World War, these orders expanded to include live shells to be manufactured at Tredegar (one of only four firms nationwide producing shells of cast iron) and filled elsewhere before shipment to the front lines.[436] Shortly after Tredegar returned to its role as a wartime supplier of ordnance, an era that had begun nearly one hundred years before came to an end.

On January 30, 1942, Archer Anderson Jr. died of a heart attack at the age of seventy-five. As with previous presidents, Tredegar's management released an impassioned memorial to his personality, temperament and leadership abilities.

> *He was deeply consecrated to his calling which he felt to be invested with dignity and responsibility. He set extremely strict standards of conduct for the customers and suppliers of the Company no less than for the Company and himself as its chief officer…His feelings to his associates were affectionate, and his relations with them informal and most friendly, so that they enjoyed their contacts with him and will miss him and mourn his loss…During his incumbency problems of labor, materials, and outlets for products became more complicated than they had previously been, and increasing competition rendered constant improvement of methods of operation a condition of survival. The success of the Company during his tenure of office reflects his adequate meeting and dealing with these various problems.*[437]

For the first time since 1849, the president of Tredegar had no son to pass the position on to; Archer Anderson Jr. lived the entirety of his adult life in the Anderson family home in which he had grown up, a lifelong bachelor with no heirs. The number of experienced family members still at the top had dwindled in recent years, particularly with the passing of St. George M. Anderson and Vice-President J.R.A. Hobson in 1936 and 1938, respectively.

The presidency passed to sixty-year-old Paul E. Miller, who had served as vice-president since the death of J.R.A. Hobson and whom many saw as being groomed for the presidency by Anderson himself.[438] Miller was not

Western Union message sent in the name of General Dwight D. Eisenhower to the men and women of the Tredegar Company on May 15, 1943. Several women worked in the Tredegar offices as clerks during the war years. *Library of Virginia.*

a member of the Anderson family, nor was he even from Virginia. Miller, a native of Ohio, had worked as the manager and superintendent of the Bryden Horse Shoe Works, of Catasauqua, Pennsylvania, for thirteen years before leaving to accept a manager's position at Tredegar in 1922.[439] Begun in 1882 and affiliated with the massive Catasauqua Manufacturing Company, Bryden was a major producer and licensor of horse and mule shoes at the turn of the century, a manufacturer with which Tredegar had numerous dealings, both being members of the national Horse Shoe Manufacturers Association; Miller also was not the first transplant from Bryden to Tredegar, as Peter F. Greenwood, a manager of Tredegar's Horse and Mule Shoe Department until his death in 1902, had worked at Bryden for several years before relocating to Richmond.

Upon assuming the presidency, Miller followed in Anderson's lead, ensuring that all of Tredegar's 650 workers dedicated themselves fully to the war effort. "I know that I speak for every real man and woman in this plant when I say that we can and will do even more to supply our small share," Miller wrote to the U.S. Navy's Admiral C.C. Bloch, "of the materials needed to bring this war to a finish, which will be embarrassing to Herr

1918–1957

Shickelgruber [*sic*]."⁴⁴⁰ Regarding his workforce, Miller seemed to take pride in the predominance of aged workers within the ranks; some years prior, Archer Anderson Jr. had begun a practice, followed by Miller, in showing preference to those aged fifty or older in new hires, believing them to be better skilled and more reliable in their production methods, albeit noting occasional spikes in absenteeism due to many workers being unable to keep up with a six- and seven-day workweek.⁴⁴¹ This overabundance of workers in their fifties through their seventies, however, did not deter Tredegar from meeting and exceeding its wartimes expectations in regard to quantity and quality. "Quantity is not enough," wrote Colonel Hauseman. "Never in the history of war has there been a more exacting life-and-death demand for top quality in ordnance production…Tredegar's magnificent tradition of craftsmanship over the years is graphically reflected today in its splendid job for Army ordnance. Tredegar has been an inspiration to us all."⁴⁴²

Tredegar had the honor of earning one of the navy's first "E" awards. The "E," or Army-Navy Production Award, was a special recognition given to industrial sites that excelled far beyond expectations regarding the production of military equipment. While the navy offered to host a ceremony unfurling a navy "E" banner at the works, the management seemingly did not desire a great public "hullaballoo" and instead awarded every Tredegar employee with a special lapel acknowledging the achievement, as well as a copy of a congratulatory letter sent to the firm by Secretary of the Navy William Knox.⁴⁴³ Tredegar, in addition to supplying munitions to the war effort, also served in other ways. Throughout the war, the company was praised for the aid it generously provided to both the Red Cross and the Naval Relief Society. In June 1945, Miller donated several kegs of horseshoes to Camp Lee, just south of Richmond, so

Tredegar workmen repairing a flywheel, March 1945. *Richmond Times-Dispatch*.

that the soldiers stationed there could participate in horse-riding, one of their "favorite recreational diversions."[444]

For Tredegar, the 1940s saw renewed conflicts with organized labor, which had made considerable inroads at the site over the last several decades. In April 1944, the understanding between Tredegar and the American Federation of Labor (which had absorbed the IAM years prior) Local #23004, composed entirely of African American workmen, was renewed after much negotiations, guaranteeing a five-cent-per-hour raise for all unionized employees, per the recommendation of the National War Labor Board.[445] One year later, a strike over further wage adjustments was threatened on the part of a number of Tredegar's #23004 members but was averted thanks to renewed dialogues, as well as a warning issued by AFL president William Green that such actions "would be in violation of the no strike pledge which we made to President Roosevelt at the beginning of the war."[446]

In 1944, while large government contracts awarded to Tredegar were making headlines in local newspapers, the plant itself attracted reporters for a wholly different and unforeseen reason. Tredegar had become a crime scene, linked to a case that was later labeled by Richmond police as "one of the dirtiest murder cases in the history of the city."[447] On September 6, 1944, the body of John "Johnny" Krengel was discovered in the pattern storage building, severely beaten and shot in the head.[448] John Krengel, aged sixty-nine, began working at Tredegar in the 1890s and was the firm's chief patternmaker; he was also the son of August Krengel, who had come to Tredegar just after the end of the Civil War and had retired in 1925. During the subsequent police and FBI investigations at the site, which saw turbine water pits drained in search of a murder weapon and the questioning of every single Tredegar employee, rumors ran high regarding the

Government inspectors visited Tredegar on a weekly basis during wartime in order to ensure the proper size and conformity of all shells produced. March 1945. *Richmond Times-Dispatch.*

1918–1957

possible motive behind Krengel's murder. Some believed he was killed for the large amount of money he carried on his person (and from which he made loans to other employees in need), while others suggested that he came across a foreign agent "snooping" about the patterns used in shell manufacture and was thus silenced.[449] Leads were followed for more than a decade after the crime, and a $500 reward was offered for any information leading to a break in the case. No leads panned out, no one claimed the reward and the wartime murder of John Krengel remains unsolved to this day.

In the face of an aging workforce, labor concerns and even the murder of a longtime and cherished employee, Tredegar under Miller's guidance powered through the remainder of the war, producing tens of thousands of shells for the American military, even eliminating time off for holidays to meet production demands.[450] By 1943, Paul Miller estimated that 75 percent of all Tredegar sales were to the navy and army in the form of ordnance contracts, outstanding contracts of which, the following year, were valued at over $1.5 million.[451]

NEARING THE END

While Tredegar stockholders were receiving dividends of anywhere between 5 and 7 percent from 1943 through 1946 and a dividend of 12 percent in 1947, Tredegar had, in Paul Miller's words, "lost money each year since the war."[452] From 1946 through 1950, income losses were reported on the company's tax returns—nearly $164,000 in 1949—and while ordnance contracts were indeed still being sought and won by the company, it was not nearly to an extent that emulated the successes of previous years.[453] Additionally, the cost of production was outpacing the value of goods sold; a gross income of $683,321.34 in 1947 was offset by production costs totaling $725,354.55, resulting in a net loss for the year of over $130,000.[454] Continuing labor difficulties, and the high costs they extracted from the company, did little to help. In the summer of 1946, 160 spike, horseshoe and clinch bar workers did not report to work, resulting in the entire cessation of all operations at the plant for several days, alleviated only after negations resulted in a raise of twelve cents per hour for striking workers; further disruptions to production were threatened in 1949 when the Local #23004 again petitioned for a raise in pay. Tredegar, which argued that a wage cut was needed to remain competitive, was actually forced to increase all hourly

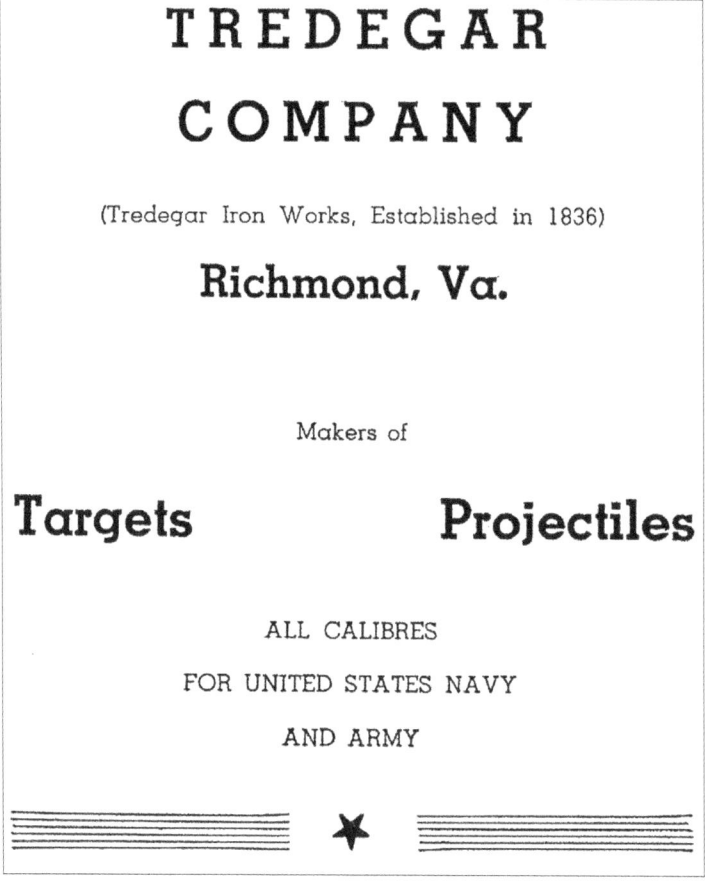

An advertisement for Tredegar Products, circa 1945. *Library of Virginia.*

wages by four and a half cents, "with adjustments of inequities amounting to as high as 24½¢ per hour," and provide double time for weekend work.[455] Beginning in 1951–52, Tredegar had once again returned to the black financially, albeit at levels that did not inspire great confidence regarding the firm's future.

Paul E. Miller informed the board of directors in August 1947 that he intended to resign no later than the following October. Miller's resignation was a result of constant clashes with Tredegar's board of directors over his inability (despite his best attempts) to procure new markets for Tredegar products outside of its rapidly evaporating ordnance business. A 1946 attempt at producing graphite-heavy (but easily machinable) gray iron and a later attempt at reworking scrap steel into concrete rebar met with both failure and considerable monetary losses.[456] Miller was succeeded as president of Tredegar by Raymond Worth Krise, a sixty-one-year-old former executive at the Milton Manufacturing Company. Milton, located in the Pennsylvania town of the same name, was an ironworks that, in addition to nuts, washers and bar iron, also produced munitions during World War II and belonged to the same wartime Philadelphia Ordnance District as Tredegar; it is likely through this link that Krise came to Tredegar's attention.[457] Miller, however, did not sever his ties with Tredegar completely. He remained one of the company's largest stockholders, with four hundred shares to his name by the mid-1950s, and received compensation as a "consulting engineer" to the new president for several months.[458] Isaiah Kinsey, who had served as vice-president under Miller, retired in the fall of 1949 and was succeeded by Francis "Frank" D. Williams Jr., who had started at Tredegar the previous year and was the first J.R. Anderson descendant to serve in the upper management for quite some time.[459]

Krise seemed somewhat of an aloof manager, staying primarily in the office and largely removed from the day-to-day operations on the floors of the machine shops, far more distant than the presidents who preceded him.[460] There is a possibility that the board believed a leader more experienced in modern business management, as opposed to production-level iron "know-how," could serve as a better steward of the company's fortunes as it entered the second half of the twentieth century. While business and stockholders meetings continued as usual, the writing on the wall had to be obvious to many at the site, which had witnessed a lessening of products offered and reduction in those employed, many of whom were not permanent workmen but rather temporary employees brought on when a government contract was secured and let go as soon as the contract had been fulfilled.

The site itself had seen better days; as Paul Miller reported to stockholders as early as 1947, "the physical plant had been allowed to depreciate beyond the point which the Directors felt wise."[461] Several fires had destroyed many machine shop buildings and storage sheds in the preceding years, and the flooding of the James River and Kanawha Canal in 1951 briefly placed the floors of several shops under nearly two feet of water. A particularly harsh storm at the beginning of the decade caused damage to several of buildings, particularly the Tredegar offices, where one of its chimneys collapsed through the roof, barely missing the desk of ordnance production manager Charles Miller.[462] Many of the structures on the ground were not in use or had ceased to function under their original intention; for decades, the 1861 gun foundry, unused as a foundry since the nineteenth century, had been used alternatively as a shed for cleaning car wheels and as a storage and shipping depot. As of July 1950, the original central foundry had ceased all operations, and the only foundry still in use was the 1917 shell foundry.[463] Beginning in the early 1940s, concerns regarding the relative brittleness of chilled cast-iron car wheels (a Tredegar mainstay) when compared to those made of steel led to at first a lessening of their demand on the part of railroad companies and finally legislation banning their use on the railroad.[464] Tredegar halted construction of car wheels in 1946.[465] Some small ordnance work continued for the United States Armed Forces following the end of the Korean War (twenty-five-pound bomb casings and sixteen-inch projectiles, as well as 175-millimeter proof shot), formed in the shell foundry and finished in the machine shops located to the immediate right of the pattern storage building. Spike, angle bar and horseshoe production continued, albeit on a much-depreciated scale.[466] The former brass foundries and machine shops that bordered Tredegar Street had all been repurposed by 1951 for the finishing of shells, with the military inspector's office at the far southeastern corner of the property. In fact, many of the complex's structures were on borrowed time; according to Tredegar's 1915 federal tax filings, the entire compound, as it was then, had a "probable life" of ten to twenty years at most, but it outlived that expectation by a further two decades.[467]

Even the Osterbind family, who, over several generations, had proved unwavering loyalty to Tredegar, was absent by the mid-1950s. Carter Osterbind Haase was born on September 10, 1909, to Mary Copeland Osterbind Haase (sister of Carter Clarke Osterbind) and William Frederick Haase, a second-generation German immigrant who, with his father, ran a furrier business in Richmond.[468] As a young man, Carter Haase displayed impressive engineering abilities, successfully constructing an airplane himself in the family's garage. Using spare parts and a second-hand Ford Model A engine and appropriately naming the plane *Patches*, Carter successfully flew the aircraft several times before crashing it a few months after its first flight.[469] Carter Haase's time at Tredegar was extremely brief when compared to those of his relatives. After leaving his family's furrier shop, Carter went to work for competitor Miller and Rhoades in 1940 only to leave the following year to begin work at Tredegar manufacturing shells for the war effort. For four years, he continued that vocation, leaving Tredegar in the fall of 1945 when he took a job as a machinist at the American Tobacco Company's Lucky Strike factory in Richmond.[470]

James Reinhold Osterbind, at Tredegar since 1888, had helped produced munitions for four wars and had seen five different men occupy the company's presidency. James was the last of his family to leave Tredegar and was one of the longest-serving Tredegar employees, retiring in June 1953, sixty-five years after his first day on the job.[471] James was one of a number of Tredegar employees honored at a 1944 ceremony recognizing the work of eight ironworkers at the site who boasted a combined history of 428 years on the job.[472]

Tredegar's approximately 270 employees in 1955, working a combined total of 601,000 hours over the course of the year, continued producing many of the same goods that the site had supplied for the last century. Contracts with the armed forces for target projectiles comprised 63 percent of the plant's output, with rail joints (21 percent), spikes (10 percent), merchant bars (4 percent) and horseshoes (2 percent) rounding out the rest of the company's remaining product line.[473] But as was noted in a 1956 stockholder's report, even ordnance contracts—the lifeblood of the company in recent years and quite possibly the only reason it had not shuttered years earlier—were no longer viable production avenues. The stockholder report concluded, "There is no prospect at present for additional target projectiles; in fact the outlook is poor for gun ammunition since defense procurement now covers largely the electronic types such as rockets and guided missiles. This situation may necessitate closing the shell foundry."[474] Lower sales, a depleted market share and a series of devastating fires were obstacles to any further revitalization of Tredegar's fortunes. Krise's attempts at modernization and diversification met with as much success as those of Miller before him. In 1952, Tredegar accepted an order from the Pontiac and Oldsmobile Divisions of General

James Reinhold Osterbind, upon his retirement from Tredegar in 1953, after more than sixty-five years on the job. *Richmond Times Dispatch*.

Tredegar Iron Works

Tredegar Yard Engine, one of the small locomotives that carried products across the works from one shop or shipping depot to another, circa 1950. *Nathan Madison.*

Motors to furnish steel for automobile crankshafts. The recycled carbon steel, however, was rejected by GM due to its substandard quality. Tredegar was forced to reroll the 115,000 pounds of steel into bars, in an effort to salvage some profit from what was otherwise a complete disaster.[475] Additionally, outdated and obsolete machinery, something that had plagued the company for the last several decades, posed a serious impediment to any future profitability, as Raymond Krise told stockholders in February 1956: "A large investment in machinery and in forging equipment is needed to enable Tredegar to produce modern ordnance; and several million additional dollars are required for electric steel-making furnaces, among other things, to put Tredegar in a position to compete effectively and profitably under present day conditions."[476]

Tredegar's 1955 tax returns showed a reported profit of $146,977, certainly an improvement from the negative numbers of years earlier but still a far cry from the successes of the firm's heyday. Not surprisingly, talks of mergers and acquisitions were in the air, and one company, a literal next-door neighbor to the Tredegar Company, displayed the greatest interest.[477]

Albemarle Paper

In February 1887, with an initial capital of only $22,000, the Albemarle Paper and Manufacturing Company was formed and incorporated in Richmond and soon built its first paper mill on the banks of the James River just below

1918–1957

Hollywood Cemetery. As had been the case for Tredegar, the choosing of this location was heavily dependent on access to the James River and Kanawha Canal for hydroelectric power.[478] Also similarly to Francis Deane, Captain James F. Chalmers and Edward B. Thaw, president and secretary, respectively, sought guidance from abroad regarding the construction of their mill in the form of James Lishman, the latest in a lineage of expert British papermakers. Like Rhys Davies at Tredegar seventy-odd years prior, Lishman not only came to Richmond to design and construct a mill but also stayed on as the site's first superintendent. At first, the Hollywood Mill specialized in newsprint before expanding into blotting and other absorptive paper products.[479]

Shortly after the turn of the century, Albemarle's leadership began programs of both horizontal and vertical integration, an ambitious series of expansions that differed heavily from that followed by Tredegar, which, arguably from the late nineteenth century onward, did not seek expansion to any large degree. In 1907 and 1912, the mill equipment underwent several refits and improvements, and in 1919, Albemarle purchased a plant then owned by the Dixie Paper Mills located on nearby Brown's Island, the former site of the Confederate laboratories. Six years later, a third Albemarle Mill, the Riverside Mill, was built near the original Hollywood site. In 1937, Albemarle extended its reach into neighboring

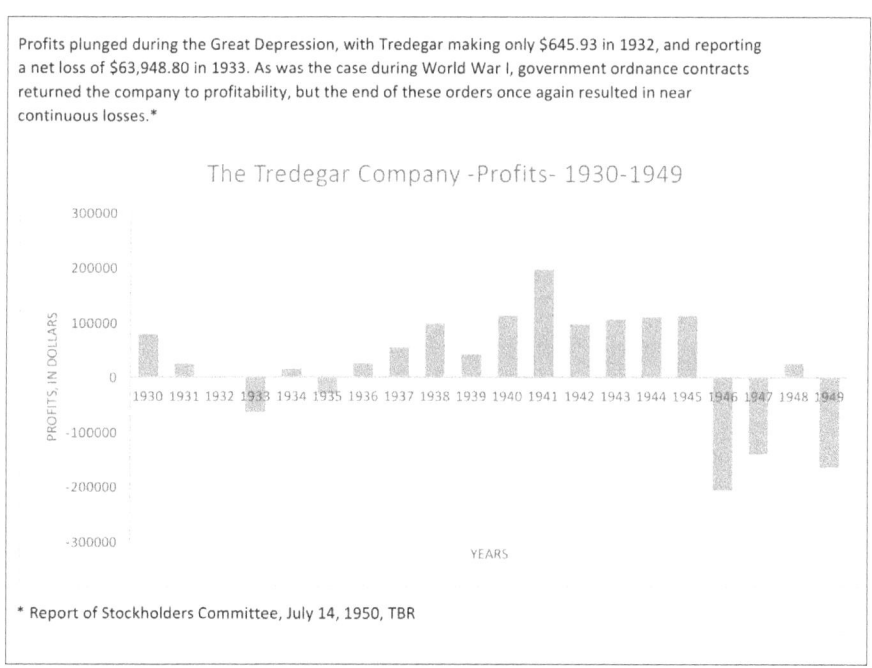

Profits plunged during the Great Depression, with Tredegar making only $645.93 in 1932, and reporting a net loss of $63,948.80 in 1933. As was the case during World War I, government ordnance contracts returned the company to profitability, but the end of these orders once again resulted in near continuous losses.*

* Report of Stockholders Committee, July 14, 1950, TBR

states, acquiring the Halifax Paper Company of North Carolina and the Raymond Bag Company in Middletown, Ohio, in 1955. It was at this point, after nearly half a century of continuous expansion, that Albemarle approached the Tredegar Company.

Albemarle sales between its various operations, including the plants in Richmond, the Halifax Paper Company and the Raymond Bag Company, totaled $30 million in 1955. The company was looking to expand its operations, particularly in Richmond, where its three plants were separated from one another by only one obstacle: the Tredegar Iron Works.[480] Albemarle was certainly in a position to buy, with its total assets in 1956 over $26 million, compared to Tredegar's of barely $2 million.[481] Rumors concerning the possible talks between the two firms had existed for some years, but actual overtures, followed by concrete negotiations, from Albemarle to Tredegar did not occur until mid-decade. Negotiations almost broke down in late 1956 over a draft agreement concerning proposed compensation of Tredegar's executives. Tredegar's board of directors argued that since it had been approved on the part of stockholders and that the executives had not received a "substantial" raise since the end of the Second World War, the generous severance package they suggested to Albemarle was not only fair but also due them. The severance pay was agreed on, as well as a pension for Tredegar's directors and office workers (1 percent of their pay over the course of their entire tenure at Tredegar, to commence at age seventy), due to the understood fact that, owing to their advanced age, most of the Tredegar executives would not be carried over for employment at Albemarle. When the merger was put to the stockholders of both companies for a vote, 93 percent of Albemarle shareholders and 96 percent of Tredegar shareholders voted in favor of the acquisition.[482]

The actual sale of Tredegar to Albemarle was solely in terms of stocks, in that each share the Tredegar stockholders held in the company was replaced with both preferred (10,118 total) and common (51,096 total) stock in Albemarle, giving Tredegar stockholders a 9.37 and 28.64 percent ownership, respectively, of Albemarle's aggregate stock.[483]

Acquisition and Closure

With the financial aspects decided, the fate of the physical Tredegar plant itself was left to be determined. While some of the buildings were in questionable shape, there was a large amount of machinery that still held years, if not decades of profitable use in them, and neither firm wanted to scrap them entirely (although some were repurposed for Albemarle's purposes). The fact that Albemarle was solely interested in acquiring Tredegar for its land, which would connect all three of Albemarle's milling properties in the city, was not in dispute; Albemarle held no interest in expanding into the iron and steel trades. Per the merger agreement, Tredegar's machinery, as well as the company's extensive land holdings in Craig, Alleghany and Botetourt (including the Grace, Jane and Rebecca former furnace tracts, which totaled 14,513 acres alone), were to be assumed by an entirely new subsidiary called the Tredegar Timber Company.[484] The land was conveyed to the new company, and all of Tredegar's machinery and inventory (that was not needed by Albemarle to fulfill orders already placed) was bought by Tredegar Timber for a lump sum of $5,000; those holding stock in the former Tredegar Iron Works were also given stock in the new Tredegar Timber Company, which amounted to 10,118 shares, half non-cumulative preferred and half common stock.[485] In accepting the $5,000 option, the Tredegar Timber Company was allowed to operate "any one or more of the following kinds of businesses: a railroad supply business, spike manufacturing, ordnance, a general iron or steel business, scrap, a fabricating business, [or] a machine shop business," keeping, at least, the idea of a Tredegar ironworks alive beyond the Albemarle acquisition.[486]

On February 19, 1957, following the acknowledgement of the incorporation of the Tredegar Timber Company, and after it was observed that all agreed-upon severance payments had been made, the last meeting of the board of directors of the Tredegar Iron Company was called to a close. The minutes of that meeting do not record any sort of ceremony acknowledging the end of a company, with a history over 120 years in the making, that witnessed America's industrial growth, the nation torn asunder by civil war and then reunited and the rise of the United States to the status of global superpower. Rather, a fairly commonplace finale closed out those final minutes:

> *Mr. Krise, on behalf of himself and the other officers and employees of the corporation, expressed their gratification at having served this company, and the Board of Directors expressed their appreciation for the services rendered by the officers and employees. There being no further business to come before the meeting, on motion duly made, seconded and adopted unanimously, the same was adjourned.*[487]

EPILOGUE

The Tredegar Division of Albemarle Paper Manufacturing Company continued production, fulfilling a handful of orders that had been accepted before the merger, while others were transferred to the newly created Tredegar Timber Company. The merchant mill, spike mill and horseshoe departments operated until mid-February 1957; by the end of June, all departments had been shut down, and the hammers, furnaces and other machinery of the old Tredegar finally fell silent.[488] Tredegar master mechanic Ernest "Buddy" Bradshaw was kept on by Albemarle at the site, as were Tredegar's former locomotive engineer and four other workers, who not only maintained the site but also worked in Albemarle's new maintenance shop, located in the former 1917 shell foundry. The former pattern storage building was also used for maintenance work required by Albemarle's nearby paper mills, and the old Tredegar offices were repurposed briefly to serve as a research and development laboratory.[489] Rolls of paper needed for Albemarle's mills were stored in the vacant Central Foundry, and pulp was kept in former Bar Mill sheds, an area once occupied by the Virginia Manufactory of Arms.[490]

Several weeks after the merger between Tredegar and Albemarle Paper was sent to and approved by the State Corporation Commission of Virginia, Frank D. Williams Jr., former vice-president of Tredegar and now president of Tredegar Timber, met with Albemarle's upper management and accepted the option allowing the new company to claim former Tredegar machinery. In total, $130,000 worth of machinery and $30,000 worth of inventory was

Epilogue

transferred to the "new Tredegar": the original $5,000 paid as part of the option was credited to this purchase, with the remaining balance to be paid in installments.[491] Forty-one outstanding orders, totaling $53,000, were also transferred to Williams's Tredegar as it began operations across the James River in nearby Chesterfield County.[492] The succeeding years bode well for the new firm, which officially rechristened itself as the Tredegar Company in 1958. In 1959, it began pulping operations, under the supervision of the Virginia Forestry Service, in the former furnace properties in Botetourt. Back in Chesterfield, Williams signed a contract with the Reynolds Metal Company for the production of aluminum, a first for any company called "Tredegar."[493] In December 1959, the Tredegar Company acquired Houck & Greene Steel Company in nearby Oilville, Virginia, which subsequently operated under the title of the Houck & Greene Division of the Tredegar Company and produced prefabricated steel structures, structural steel, reinforcing bars and other products.[494] For nearly another three decades and under the uninterrupted guidance of Frank D. Williams Jr., the Tredegar

The Tredegar Central Foundry in 1971, shortly before Hurricane Agnes and the loss of its roof. *Courtesy of Ray Potter.*

Epilogue

By 1971, the 1861 Gun Foundry suffered from a missing roof, leaning walls and constant floods. *Courtesy of Ray Potter*.

Company continued to produce iron and steel railroad spikes, fishplates, steel bars, steel rail clamps and more until finally ceasing operations in 1987. Much of the machinery, used first in Richmond and then in Chesterfield, was sent to Ohio, purchased by Cleveland Track Materials, Inc., and put to use once again producing implements for the railroad industry.

In Richmond, the original Tredegar site was falling further into decrepitude, compounding the dilapidated state the works exhibited during the last years of its operation. Following the 1962 purchase of Pennsylvania's Ethyl Corporation by Albemarle Paper, the surviving firm (taking the former's name) began to diversify out of simple paper products, embracing such avenues as aluminum production, chemical, polyethylene and plastics manufacture and research into petroleum additives. With operations

Epilogue

at the Richmond paper mills winding down, Ethyl's use of the Tredegar site lessened significantly. Between 1957 and 1970, fires damaged several surviving buildings, particularly the pattern storage building and the 1861 gun foundry; these same fires also gutted the former horseshoe and machine shops, which were finally torn down following a complete flooding of the property in 1969.[495]

Hurricane Agnes, tearing its way across the south in 1972, wrought even more damage to the few remaining structures. That same year, prompted by the suggestion of the Richmond City Council and well aware of the historical value Tredegar represented, Ethyl began an ambitious and extensive restoration and rehabilitation of the surviving buildings, overseen personally by Ethyl president Floyd D. Gottwald Jr. and Ethyl executive Roy E. Johnson.[496] While many structures—including the pattern storage building (and adjacent carpenter shop), the 1861 gun foundry, the company store, the 1917 shell foundry and the Tredegar offices—could be saved, many buildings, including the original central Tredegar foundry, had to be razed simply due to their instability. The foundry, its origins dating back to the 1830s, did survive in some sense, however—bricks taken from its walls were used to reconstruct the 1861 foundry's smokestack.[497]

The 1861 gun foundry, with its collapsed roof, bowing south wall and perennially flooded floor, was singled out in particular for reconstruction owing to its historical connections to the Civil War and also as a unique juxtaposition with the many high-rises and corporate towers that now claimed the Richmond skyline.[498] By the mid-1980s, the remaining Tredegar buildings had been restored, still surrounded by remnants of turbines, raceways and other industrial artifacts, and the 1861 gun foundry was available for the hosting of public and private events, such as a 1985 art exhibit; in 1986, the 1917 shell foundry was torn down to accommodate a new water main for the city of Richmond.[499]

Recognizing the importance of Tredegar to Richmond, Virginia, and American history, the Valentine Museum, founded in 1898 and dedicated to the history of the city, launched a satellite museum at the restored Tredegar in May 1994. In addition to a merry-go-round and an ice skating rink, the new attraction, called Valentine Riverside, boasted exhibits and films exploring Tredegar and Richmond's history, including a sixty- by eighty-foot film projected against the eastern side of the pattern building. Valentine Riverside, however, failed to attract enough visitors to remain viable and closed in September of the following year.[500] In 2000, the National Park Service relocated its main visitors' center for Richmond National Battlefield

Epilogue

The 1971 remnants of a Tredegar machine shop, with the pattern storage building visible behind. *Courtesy of Ray Potter.*

Park from its Chimborazo Medical Museum in nearby Church Hill to Tredegar's pattern building, which had lain largely unoccupied since the closure of Valentine Riverside. The National Park Service was joined in 2006 by the American Civil War Center, a private, nonprofit museum operating out of the 1861 foundry and dedicated to exploring the Civil War and its legacies from the three perspectives that defined the conflict—Union, Confederate and African American.

The history of the Tredegar Iron Works has no definitive conclusion. It is still evolving and will continue to do so in the years and decades to follow. A company named Tredegar still claims Richmond as its corporate headquarters; in 1994, Ethyl (as of 2004, known as New Market) spun off its plastics and films division into a new company—the Tredegar Corporation. At what is now appropriately called Historic Tredegar, a new museum is slated to be constructed on the site, following the 2013 merger of the American Civil War Center and the Museum of the Confederacy, which has operated at the former White House of the Confederacy, the wartime home of Jefferson Davis, since 1896.

Tredegar's fires have long since been extinguished. Around its remnants, however, loom edifices of the modern American economy: central offices

Epilogue

The Tredegar Iron Works site in the early 1990s following massive restoration. *Virginia Commonwealth University Libraries.*

Tredegar Iron Works site in 1996, following the closure of Valentine Riverside. Visible is an ice-skating rink just downhill from the preserved company store. *Virginia Commonwealth University Libraries.*

Epilogue

of several Fortune 500 companies and the Richmond branch of the Federal Reserve. Over half a century after Tredegar's demise, its land and the surrounding area is still home to many of Richmond's most important economic entities, and within its surviving buildings its story, its unique role in American industrial and military history, is told and retold to curious visitors. In various ways, determined historical conservation, along with simple luck, defeated the ravages of war, conflagrations, neglect and time to ensure that Tredegar survived into the present, and beyond into posterity.

NOTES

ABBREVIATIONS FOR MANUSCRIPT COLLECTIONS

LVA: Library of Virginia, Richmond, Virginia.
MLG: Mary L. Geschwind Papers, 1845–2006. Accession 50461. Personal papers collection, the Library of Virginia, Richmond, Virginia.
TBR: Tredegar Iron Works Records, 1801–1957. Accession 23881, 24808, 26601. Business records collection, the Library of Virginia, Richmond, Virginia.
WHS: Wisconsin Historical Society, Madison, Wisconsin.
VHS: Virginia Historical Society, Richmond, Virginia.
VM: The Valentine Museum, Richmond, Virginia.

INTRODUCTION

1. Diane Telgen, "Major Entrepreneurs and Companies," in *Industrial Revolution in America—Iron and Steel*, edited by Kevin Hillstrom and Laurie Collier Hillstrom (Santa Barbara, CA: ABC-CLIO, 2005), 62.
2. Fritz Redlich, *History of American Business Leaders, Vol. I: Theory, Iron and Steel, Iron Ore Mining* (Ann Arbor, MI: Edward Brothers, Inc., 1940), 83, 106.
3. Clay Bailey, "Joseph R. Anderson of Tredegar," *Commonwealth*, November 1959: 2.

CHAPTER 1

4. William Coxe, *A Historical Tour through Monmouthshire* (Brecon: Davies and Co., 1904), 79; Evan Powell, *The History of Tredegar* (Tredegar: Blaenau Gwent Heritage Forum, 2008), 2.

5. Coxe, *Historical Tour*, 79; J.A. Giles and A. Thompson, trans. and ed., *The British History of Geoffrey of Monmouth* (London: James Bohn, 1842), 3.
6. Powell, *History*, 3.
7. Ibid., 2–4.
8. Ibid., 16.
9. Prys Morgan and David Thomas, *Wales: The Shaping of a Nation* (Newton Abbot: David & Charles, 1984), 110.
10. Ibid., 111, 115.
11. Ibid., 114.
12. A.H. John, *The Industrial Development of South Wales: 1750–1850* (Cardiff: University of Wales Press, 1950), 192.
13. Robert B. Gordon, *American Iron, 1607–1900* (Baltimore, MD: Johns Hopkins University Press, 1996), 90.
14. Ibid., 15.
15. Bradley Stoughton, *The Metallurgy of Iron and Steel*, 4th ed. (New York: McGraw-Hill Book Company, Inc., 1934), 26.
16. Ibid., 12, 29–35.
17. Gordon, *American Iron*, 134.
18. Powell, *History*, 20; Charles Wilkins, *The History of the Iron, Steel, Tinplate and Other Trades of Wales* (Merthyr Tydfil: Joseph Williams, 1903), 136; John, *Industrial Development*, 34.
19. Francis Trevithick, *Life of Richard Trevithick—With an Account of His Inventions* (London: E.&F.N. Spon, 1872), 222.
20. Powell, *History*, 24–25.
21. Ibid., 30–31.
22. Chester G. Hearn, *Circuits in the Sea: The Men, the Ships, and the Atlantic Cable* (Westport, CT: Praeger Publishers, 2004); Blaenau Gwent Heritage Forum, *The Henry Hughes Story* (Tredegar: Blaenau Gwent Heritage Forum, 2009), 12.
23. Powell, *History*, 22.
24. Howard Templin, correspondence with author, August 14, 2013.
25. Anne Kelly Knowles, *Mastering Iron: The Struggle to Modernize an American Industry, 1800–1868* (Chicago: University of Chicago Press, 2013), 112.
26. *Hereford Times*, November 24, 1838.
27. Kathleen Bruce, *Virginia Iron Manufacture in the Slave Era* (1930; repr., New York: Augustus M. Kelley, 1968), 3.
28. Charles E. Hatch Jr. and Thurlow Gates Gregory, "The First American Blast Furnace, 1619–1622: The Birth of a Mighty Industry on Falling Creek in Virginia," *Virginia Magazine of History and Biography* 70, no. 3 (July 1962): 259–96.
29. Jeffery C. Turner, "Cloverdale Furnace: A Century of Iron Manufacture in Botetourt County Virginia, 1789–1889" (master's thesis, Virginia Polytechnic Institute and State University, 1984), 1–2; Virginius Dabney, *Richmond: The Story of a City* (Garden City, NY: Doubleday & Company, Inc., 1976), 5; John Bezis-Selfa, *Forging America: Ironworkers, Adventurers, and the Industrious Revolution* (Ithaca, NY: Cornell University Press, 2004), 49.

30. Klaus Wust, *The Virginia Germans*, 2nd ed. (Charlottesville: University of Virginia Press, 1975), 3; Thomas Sowell, *Ethnic America: A History* (New York: Basic Books, 1981), 21; Bruce, *Virginia Iron Manufacture*, 9.
31. Telgen, "Major Entrepreneurs and Companies," 49.
32. Gordon, *American Iron*, 58; Laura Croghan Kamoie, *Neabsco and Occoquan: The Tayloe Family Iron Plantations, 1730–1830* (Prince William, VA: Prince William County Historical Commission, 2003), 14.
33. Bruce, *Virginia Iron Manufacture*, 114–17.
34. Douglas C. Macleod, "Lynchburg's Man of Iron: The Forgotten Career of Frances B. Deane Jr., (1796–1868)," *Lynches Ferry*, Fall/Winter 1991/1992: 14–17.
35. Ibid., 14.
36. Ibid., 14.
37. Gordon, *American Iron*, 45.
38. F.R. Wadleigh, "Story of the Richmond Coal Fields" Richmond Coal Basin Project File, 1811–1953, The Library of Virginia (LVA); Sean Patrick Adams, *Old Dominion, Industrial Commonwealth: Coal, Politics, and Economy in Antebellum America* (Baltimore, MD: Johns Hopkins University Press, 2004), 26–27.
39. Wadleigh, "Richmond Coal Fields," 34.
40. Gerald P. Wilkes, *Mining History of the Richmond Coalfield of Virginia* (Charlottesville: Commonwealth of Virginia, 1988), 22.
41. T. Gibson Hobbs Jr., *The Canal on the James: An Illustrated Guide to the James River and Kanawha Canal* (Lynchburg, VA: Blackwell Press, 2009), 2–5; Steven J. Hoffman, *Race, Class and Power in Richmond, 1870–1920* (Jefferson, NC: McFarland & Company, 2004), 19.
42. Captain Thomas F. Hahn, T. Gibson Hobbs Jr. and Robert S. Mayo, *Towpaths to Tugboats: A History of American Canal Engineering* (York, PA: American Canal and Transportation Center, 2004), 29.
43 Bruce, *Virginia Iron Manufacture*, 97.
44. Douglas C. Macleaod, "Iron Initiative for the Commonwealth: The Life and Times of Francis Browne Deane Jr.," (unpublished manuscript, 1991), Virginia Historical Society (VHS); Stephen Taber, *Geology of the Gold Belt in the James River Basin, Virginia* (Charlottesville: University of Virginia Press, 1913), 246.
45. Taber, *Geology of the Gold Belt*, 247.
46. Dabney, *Richmond*, 1.
47. Ibid., 6.
48. Mary Newton Stanard, *Richmond: Its People and Its Story* (Philadelphia: J.B. Lippincott Company, 1923), 23; Thomas S. Berry, "The Rise of Flour Milling in Richmond," *Virginia Magazine of History and Biography* 78, no. 4 (October 1970): 387–408.
49. Berry, "Rise of Flour Milling," 392; *Journal of the House of Delegates* (Richmond: Thomas Ritchie, 1821), 234.
50. Emily J. Salmon and Edward D.C. Campbell Jr., ed., *The Hornbook of Virginia History* (Richmond: Library of Virginia, 1994), 130; Reverend Robert Douglas Roller, "Genealogy of Mrs. Virginia Harvie Patrick," in *West Virginia Historical Magazine Quarterly* 2, no. 4 (October, 1902): 43–57.

51. Thomas Rutherfoord, *Autobiography of Thomas Rutherfoord, Esq. of Richmond, Virginia: 1766–1852*, edited by James Moore III (Richmond, VA: Maylocks Publications, 1986), 40.
52. Berry, "Rise of Flour Milling," 398.
53. Ibid., 404; Michael S. Raber, Patrick M. Malone and Robert B. Gordon, *Historical and Archaeological Assessment—Tredegar Iron Works Site: Richmond, Virginia* (South Glastonbury, CT: Raber Associates, 1992), 17.
54. Berry, "Rise of Flour Milling," 404.
55. Articles of Agreement between the James River Company and Thomas Green, June 16, 1828, Tredegar Business Records, LVA (TBR), Notes of the James River Company, TBR.
56. *Acts Passed at the General Assembly of the Commonwealth of Virginia* (Richmond, VA: Thomas Ritchie, 1837), 217.
57. Archer Anderson Jr., *Memorandum for Penelope Anderson McBride*, December 2, 1935, TBR.
58. Proposals for Uniting the Virginia Foundry Company with the Property owned by Messrs. Deane & Cunninghams, TBR.
59. Bruce, *Virginia Iron Manufacture*, 153; Acts of the General Assembly of the Commonwealth of Virginia, Passed at the Session of 1838 (Richmond, VA: Thomas Ritchie, 1837), 190.
60. Proposals for Uniting, TBR.
61. Oliver Jones, *The Early Days of Sirhowy and Tredegar* (Risca: Starling Press Ltd., 1975), 58.
62. *Richmond Enquirer*, February 6, 1838.
63. *Baltimore Gazette and Daily Advertiser*, August 23, 1837.
64. *Richmond Whig*, March 21, 1840.
65. *Richmond Enquirer*, February 22, 1838.
66. Ibid.
67. *Richmond Compiler*, September 18, 1838.
68. *Hereford Times*, November 24, 1838.
69. Bruce, *Virginia Iron Manufacture*, 159–61.
70. Robert Sobel, *Panic on Wall Street: A History of America's Financial Disasters* (New York: Macmillan Company, 1968), 41.
71. George Brown Tindall, *America: A Narrative History*, Vol. 1 (New York: W.W. Norton & Company, 1988), 437.
72. Charles B. Dew, *Ironmaker to the Confederacy: Joseph R. Anderson and the Tredegar Iron Works*, 2nd ed. (Richmond, VA: Library of Virginia, 1999), 4.
73. Langhorne Gibson Jr., *Cabell's Canal: The Story of the James River and Kanawha* (Richmond: Commodore Press, 2000), 170.
74. John N. Ingham, *Biographical Dictionary of American Business Leaders: A–G*, Vol. 1 (Westport, CT: Greenwood Press, 1983), 17.
75. Henry Hall, ed., *America's Successful Men of Affairs: An Encyclopedia of Contemporaneous Biography*, Vol. 2 (New York: New York Tribune, 1896), 29.
76. Dew, *Ironmaker to the Confederacy*, 4.
77. Ibid., 6–7.

78. Ingham, *Biographical Dictionary*, 17.
79. Agreement between J.R. Anderson and Tredegar, February 27, 1843, TBR.
80. Dew, *Ironmaker to the Confederacy*, 10, 11; Botetourt County Heritage Book Committee, *Botetourt County Virginia Heritage Book, 1770–2000* (Summerville, WV: Wadsworth Publishing Company, 2001), 6–7.
81. *Richmond Enquirer*, June 28, 1839.
82. Edwin Olmstead, Wayne E. Stark and Spencer C. Tucker, *The Big Guns: Civil War Siege, Seacoast and Naval Cannon* (Bloomfield, ON: Museum Restoration Service, 1997), 16; Dew, *Ironmaker to the Confederacy*, 10.
83. *Daily National Intelligencer*, November 28 1842.
84. *Richmond Whig*, December 7, 1847.
85. Steven G. Collins, "System in the South: John W. Mallet, Josiah Gorgas, and Uniform Production at the Confederate Ordnance Department," *Technology and Culture* 40, no. 3 (July 1999): 517–44.
86. *Richmond Whig*, July 16, 1841.
87. Wilkes, *Mining History*, 22.
88. Agreement, Cunningham to William H. Macfarland & Holden Rhoades, Trustees, October 1, 1840, Richard E. Cunningham Papers, 1790–1978, VHS; Bruce, *Virginia Iron Manufacture*, 170, 171.
89. Dew, *Ironmaker to the Confederacy*, 12.
90. *Daily National Intelligencer*, December 25, 1844.
91. Andrew C.A. Jampoler, *Sailors in the Holy Land: The 1848 American Expedition to the Dead Sea and the Search for Sodom and Gomorrah* (Annapolis, MD: Naval Institute Press, 2005), 3–4; United States Coast Guard, Department of Transportation, *Records of Movements—Vessels of the United States Coast Guard, 1790-December 31, 1933* (Washington, D.C.: Coast Guard Historian's Office, 1989), 128.
92. J.R. Anderson to Charles Knop Jr., November 16, 1843, Letterbook 1881, TBR.
93. Macleod, *Lynches Ferry*, 15; *The Commonwealth of Virginia, Acts Passed at a General Assembly of the Commonwealth of Virginia* (Richmond, VA: Samuel Shepherd, 1847), 196.
94. Macleod, *Lynches Ferry*, 16.
95. Ibid., 17.
96. Douglas C. Macleod, "The Iron Trade on the James River and Kanawha Canal, 1840–1865," *The Tiller*, Spring 1994: 8–15; Dew, *Ironmaker to the Confederacy*, 222.
97. Dew, *Ironmaker to the Confederacy*, 12.
98. Production and Labor Records—Units Produced, 1843–1849; 1870–1872; 1871–1872, TBR.
99. Bruce, *Virginia Iron Manufacture*, 214–22.
100. J.R. Anderson to Governor William Smith, February 1, 1848, Virginia Commandant of the Public Guard, Armory Iron Company Records, 1846–1848, LVA.
101. Dr. Robert Archer, *Archer and Silvester Families—A History Written in 1870* (Richmond, VA: William Byrd Press, 1937), 20; Bruce, *Virginia Iron Manufacture*, 222.
102. H. Jackson Knight, *Confederate Inventions—The Story of the Confederate State Patent Office and Its Inventors* (Baton Rouge: Louisiana State University Press, 2011), 237.

Notes to Pages 45–51

103. Raber, Malone and Gordon, *Historical and Archaeological Assessment*, 52.
104. Ibid., 50.
105. Ibid., 57.
106. Dew, *Ironmaker to the Confederacy*, 12; J.R. Anderson to the Committee for Disposing of the Tredegar Iron Works, March 1, 1848, Letter book 1881, TBR.
107. Anderson Family Papers, stock certificates, TBR.
108. Agreement between Tredegar Iron Company and Joseph Reid Anderson, April 4, 1848, TBR.
109. Units Produced, Castings, 1843 May–1849 September, TBR.
110. Keith L. Bryant Jr. and Henry C. Dethloff, *A History of American Business* (Englewood Cliffs, NJ: Prentice-Hall, Inc, 1983), 56.
111. John Chamberlain, *The Enterprising Americans: A Business History of the United States* (New York: Harper & Row, 1963), 48.

Chapter 2

112. Dabney, *Richmond*, 140–45.
113. T. Tyler Potterfield, *Nonesuch Place: A History of the Richmond Landscape* (Charleston, SC: The History Press, 2009), 61, 73.
114. Andrea Mehrländer, *The Germans of Charleston, Richmond and New Orleans during the Civil War Period, 1850–1870: A Study and Research Compendium* (Berlin: De Gruyter, 2011), 58.
115. Steven J. Hoffman, "The Decline of the Port of Richmond: The Congress, the Corps, and the Chamber of Commerce," in *Virginia Magazine of History and Biography* 108, no. 3 (200): 255-278.
116. Dabney, *Richmond*, 133; Mehrländer, *Germans of Charleston*, 46, 58.
117. Interview with Anne Hobson Freeman, July 20, 2015.
118. Dew, *Ironmaker to the Confederacy*, 41; Charles F. Ritter and Jon L. Wakelyn, eds., *Leaders of the American Civil War: A Biographical and Historiographical Dictionary* (Westport, CT: Greenwood Press, 1998), 3.
119. Reverend William Duval to Governor William Smith, September 11, 1846, October 30, 1846, Executive Papers of Governor William Smith, 1846–1848, LVA; George D. Fisher, *History and Reminiscences of the Monumental Church, Richmond, Virginia, from 1814–1878* (Richmond, VA: Whittet & Shepperson, 1880), 221–22; *Daily Dispatch*, June 3, 1852; Margaret Meagher, *History of Education in Richmond* (Richmond, VA: Works Progress Administration, 1939), 108.
120. Dew, *Ironmaker to the Confederacy*, 26; Bruce, *Virginia Iron Manufacture*, 281.
121. Robert D. Trimble, "Report on the Water Rights of the Tredegar Co.," 44–45, *C&O v. Tredegar* Suit Papers, TBR.
122. Raber, Malone and Gordon, *Historical and Archaeological Assessment*, 103.
123. J.R. Anderson to F.&I.W. Slaughter, September 22, 1851, Letter book, 1881, TBR.
124. Paul F. Paskoff, *Encyclopedia of American Business History and Biography: Iron and Steel in the Nineteenth Century* (New York: Facts on File, 1989), 19.
125. Sobel, *Panic on Wall Street*, 80.
126. Ibid., 79.

127. Production and Labor Records, Payroll Ledger 1852 July–Oct, TBR.
128. Ibid.
129. Ibid.
130. Werner H. Steger, "United to Support, but Not Combined to Injure: Free Workers and Immigrants in Richmond, Virginia, During the Era of Sectionalism, 1847–1865," (dissertation, George Washington University, 1999), 132.
131. Kamoie, *Neabsco and Occoquan*, 9.
132. Ibid., 11.
133. James Peter Lesley, *The Iron Manufacturer's Guide to the Furnaces, Forges and Rolling Mills of the United States* (New York: John Wiley, 1859), 64.
134. Charles B. Dew, "David Ross and the Oxford Iron Works: A Study of Industrial Slavery in the Early Nineteenth-Century South," *William and Mary Quarterly* 31, no. 2 (April 1974): 189–224.
135. Ibid., 194.
136. John Bezís-Selfa, "A Tale of Two Ironworks: Slavery, Free Labor, Work, and Resistance in the Early Republic," in *William and Mary Quarterly* 56, no. 4 (October 1999): 677–700.
137. David R. Roediger and Elizabeth D. Esch, *The Production of Difference: Race and the Management of Labor in U.S. History* (Oxford, UK: Oxford University Press, 2012), 32, 36.
138. Brady Banta, "Joseph Reid Anderson," in Paul F. Paskoff, ed., *Encyclopedia of American Business History and Biography: Iron and Steel in the Nineteenth Century* (New York: Facts on File, 1989), 24.
139. Bruce, *Virginia Iron Manufacture*, 239.
140. Ibid., 240–41; interview with Viola Baecher, May 1, 2015; Rudolph M. Lapp, *Blacks in Gold Rush California* (Binghamton, NY: Vail-Ballou Press, Inc., 1977), 202.
141. Dew, *Ironmaker to the Confederacy*, 27.
142. Joseph Reid Anderson to Workmen, May 26, 1847, TBR.
143. Dew, *Ironmaker to the Confederacy*, 26; Steger, "United to Support," 90.
144. *Richmond Whig*, May 28, 1847.
145. Howard Templin, correspondence with author, August 14, 2013.
146. J.R. Anderson speech to the American Society of Mechanical Engineers, 1890, Administrative Records, TBR.
147. Vertical Files, Matthew Delaney, The Valentine (VM).
148. J.R. Anderson speech, 1890, TBR.
149. Chas. E. Fisher, "Locomotive Shops in the United States in 1855," *Railroad History*, no. 8 (1924), 29.
150. Agreement July 1, 1854, Estate of Joseph Reid Anderson, TBR.
151. Ibid.
152. Contracts between Anderson, Delaney & Co. and U.S. Navy, 1854–1855, Estate of Joseph Reid Anderson, TBR.
153. Dew, *Ironmaker to the Confederacy*, 15, 16.
154. Vertical File, Delaney, VM.

155. Mary L. Geschwind, *The Osterbind Family of Oldenburg and Richmond* (Greensboro, NC: self-published, 1997), 39.
156. Archer Anderson to Minnie Osterbind Kimball, April 2, 1914, Osterbind Connection to Tredegar Iron Works, Mary L. Geschwind Papers, 1845–2006, LVA (MLG).
157. Mehrländer, *Germans of Charleston*, 47.
158. Wust, *Virginia Germans*, 205, 207.
159. Geschwind, *Osterbind Family*, 41.
160. Anton Guenther Osterbind Notes, MLG.
161. C. Bancroft Gillespie, *Illustrated History of South Boston* (South Boston, MA: Inquirer Publishing Company, 1900), 110, 112.
162. John H. White Jr., *A History of the American Locomotive—Its Development: 1830–1880* (New York: Dover Publications, Inc., 1979), 451.
163. D.M. Ellett, "Report on the Financial Condition and Products of the Tredegar Company, Richmond, Va." (thesis, University of Virginia, 1942), 15.
164. John Leander Bishop, *A History of American Manufactures from 1608 to 1860* (Philadelphia: Edward Young & Co., 1864), 666.
165. Dew, *Ironmaker to the Confederacy*, 15.
166. *Index to the Miscellaneous Documents of the Senate of the United States for the Session of the Thirty-Sixth Congress* (Washington, D.C.: George W. Bowman, 1860), 15.
167. "Plan of That Portion of the Armory Lot Leased to Archer and Company," 1850, Virginia State Government Records Collection, LVA; Dew, *Ironmaker to the Confederacy*, 16.
168. Contract between Morris and Anderson, effective January 1, 1859, Sales and Shipping Contract Book, TBR.
169. Contract Book, 1859 July–1865 April, Sales and Shipping Records, TBR.
170. Ibid.
171. Contract with Thatcher Perkins, April 13, 1859, TBR.
172. Joseph Snowden Bell, *The Early Motive Power of the Baltimore and Ohio Railroad* (New York: Angus Sinclair Co., 1912), 149.; Joseph Snowden Bell, "Individual Paper of Feed-Water Heaters and Their Development," in *Report of Proceedings of the Annual Meeting of the American Railway Master Mechanics Association* (Chicago: Henry O. Shepard Company, 1918), 115.
173. Bell, *Early Motive Power*, 116; "Early Locomotive Works," *Railroad Age Gazette* 45, no. 15 (September 11, 1908), 915.
174. Contract with James Todd, July 4, 1859, Contract Book, 1859 July–1865 April, TBR.
175. Contract with William T. Francis, October 1, 1859, ibid.
176. Contract between Uri Haskins and J.R. Anderson & Co., August 7, 1860, ibid.
177. Contract between Henry McCarty and J.R. Anderson & Co., July 3, 1860, ibid.; *Daily Dispatch*, December 28, 1853.
178. Egbert G. Leigh Jr., *An Appreciation of Colonel Archer Anderson, Late President of the Tredegar Company, for the Records of the Tredegar Company* (Richmond, VA: Tredegar Company, 1918), 2.

179. Ibid., 2–3; Richmond, Fredericksburg and Potomac Railroad, *Seventy-Third Annual Meeting of the Stockholders of the Richmond, Fredericksburg & Potomac Railroad Company* (Richmond, VA: Wm. Ellis Jones, 1905), 10.
180. Leigh, *Appreciation*, 2–3.
181. J.R. Anderson speech, 1890, TBR.
182. Larry J. Daniel and Riley W. Gunter, *Confederate Cannon Foundries* (Union City, TN: Pioneer Press, 1977), 4; Steger, "United to Support," 212.
183. Dew, *Ironmaker to the Confederacy*, 44.
184. Ibid., 45.
185. Ibid., 47, 50.
186. Steger, "United to Support," 225.
187. Dew, *Ironmaker to the Confederacy*, 84.
188. Ibid.
189. *Nashville Union and American*, August 29, 1860.
190. Dew, *Ironmaker to the Confederacy*, 93.
191. Knowles, *Mastering Iron*, 193; William H. Richardson to Governor John Letcher, December 15, 1862, in Fred C. Ainsworth, Joseph W. Kirkley and Elihu Root, *The War of the Rebellion: A Compilation of the Official Records of the Union and Confederate Armies, Series IV, Volume II* (Washington, D.C.: Government Printing Office, 1900), 240.
192. Dew, *Ironmaker to the Confederacy*, 95.
193. Ibid., 96.
194. William S. Christian to Archer Anderson, December 1909, Administrative Records, TBR.
195. John N. Ingham, *Biographical Dictionary of American Business Leaders: A–G*, Vol. 1 (Westport, CT: Greenwood Press, 1983), 17.
196. Leigh, *Appreciation*, 4.
197. Steger, "United to Support," 230.
198. Slave receipts, Anderson Family Records, TBR.
199. Steger, "United to Support," 250.
200. Ibid.
201. Dew, *Ironmaker to the Confederacy*, 240.
202. Jeffery C. Turner, "Cloverdale Furnace: A Century of Iron Manufacture in Botetourt County Virginia, 1789–1889" (master's thesis, Virginia Polytechnic Institute and State University, 1984), 98; Dew, *Ironmaker to the Confederacy*, 257.
203. Dew, *Ironmaker to the Confederacy*, 108.
204. Anne Kelly Knowles, "Labor, Race, and Technology in the Confederate Iron Industry," *Technology and Culture* 42, no. 1 (January 2001), 1–26.
205. Raber, Malone and Gordon, *Historical and Archaeological Assessment*, 105.
206. R.E. Johnson, "The Tredegar Iron Works of Richmond, Virginia," in Michael L. Wayman, ed., *All That Glitters: Readings in Historical Metallurgy* (Montréal: Canadian Institute of Mining and Metallurgy, 1989), 57.
207. Daniel and Gunter, *Confederate Cannon Foundries*, 6.
208. Ibid., 10.
209. John V. Quarstein, *C.S.S. Virginia: Mistress of Hampton Roads* (Appomattox, VA: H.E. Howard, Inc., 2000), 196.

210. *New York Herald*, December 23, 1861.
211. Mark K. Ragan, *Submarine Warfare in the Civil War* (Cambridge, MA: De Capo Press, 2002), 19.
212. Ibid., 25–27.
213. Quarstein, *C.S.S. Virginia*, 28.
214. Ibid., 29.
215. Ibid., 30.
216. Maurice Melton, *The Confederate Ironclads* (New York: South Brunswick, 1968), 30.
217. Lieutenant Colonel Jerome A. Watrous, ed., *Memoirs of Milwaukie County: From the Earliest Historical Times Down to the Present, Including a Genealogical and Biographical Record of Representative Families in Milwaukie County*, Vol. 2 (Madison, WI: Western Historical Association, 1909), 77.
218. *Richmond Dispatch*, June 26, 1885.
219. Quarstein, *C.S.S. Virginia*, 36, 38.
220. Melton, *Confederate Ironclads*, 78–83.
221. Report on water tights, *C&O v. Tredegar* Suit Papers, TBR.
222. R.E. Johnson, "Tredegar Iron Works of Richmond, Virginia," 56.
223. E. Susan Barber, "Cartridge Makers and Myrmidon Viragos—White Working-Class Women in Confederate Richmond," in Janet L. Coryell, Thomas H. Appleton Jr., Anastatia Sims and Sandra Gioia Treadway, eds., *Negotiating Boundaries of Southern Womanhood: Dealing With the Powers That Be* (Columbia: University of Missouri Press, 2000), 201.
224. Ibid.
225. Ibid., 206.
226. Ibid.
227. R.E. Johnson, "Tredegar Iron Works of Richmond, Virginia," 57.

Chapter 3

228. Elizabeth Wright Weddell, *St. Paul's Church—Richmond, Virginia—Its Historic Years and Memorials—Volume I* (Richmond, VA: William Byrd Press, 1931), 246.
229. Dew, *Ironmaker to the Confederacy*, 285.
230. Letter from Jefferson Davis to Robert E. Lee, April 1, 1865, in George B. Davis, et al., *The War of the Rebellion: A Compilation of the Official Records of the Union and Confederate Armies, Part III: Correspondence, Etc.* (Washington, D.C.: Government Printing Office, 1894), 1370.
231. Dew, *Ironmaker to the Confederacy*, 291–92; Michael D. Gorman, "A Conqueror or a Peacemaker? Abraham Lincoln in Richmond," in *Virginia Magazine of History and Biography* 123, no. 1 (2015): 3-88.
232. Ibid., 294.
233. Ibid., 295.
234. Letter from Charles Ellis, Jonathan Fry, et al., to President Andrew Johnson, July 6, 1865, TBR.
235. Letter from D.W. Flagler to Brigadier General J.C. Kelton, April 29, 1865, TBR.
236. Dew, *Ironmaker to the Confederacy*, 301.

237. Pete Martin, "Century Plant," *Saturday Evening Post*, July 24, 1943, 88; Dennis Maher Hallerman, "The Tredegar Iron Works: 1865–1876," (master's thesis, University of Richmond, 1978), 15.
238. Dew, *Ironmaker to the Confederacy*, 149.
239. Ibid., 305; Hallerman, "Tredegar Iron Works," 14.
240. Hallerman, "Tredegar Iron Works," 19.
241. Ari Hoogenboom, *Gustavus Vasa Fox of the Union Navy—A Biography* (Baltimore, MD: Johns Hopkins University Press, 2008).
242. Hallerman, "Tredegar Iron Works," 23.
243. Ibid., 25; Ernest B. Fricke, "The Kelly Pneumatic Process Company and the Steel Patents Company," in *Encyclopedia of American Business History and Biography—Iron and Steel in the Nineteenth Century*, edited by Paul F. Paskoff (New York: Facts on File, 1989), 221.
244. Hallerman, "Tredegar Iron Works," 81.
245. Correspondence, Outgoing, 1841–1951, Letter book, July 5, 1867–September 10, 1867: 844. TBR.
246. Charles Minnigerode Jr. to James Nathaniel Dunlop, March 23, 1871, James Nathaniel Dunlop Papers, 1840-1888, VHS.
247. Joseph Reid Anderson to David Eynon, November 6, 1866, James Nathaniel Dunlop Papers, 1840–1888, VHS.
248. Hallerman, "Tredegar Iron Works," 82.
249. Ibid., 81.
250. Ibid., 58.
251. Ibid.
252. Michael B. Chesson, *Richmond After the War: 1865–1890* (Richmond: Virginia State Library, 1981), 164.
253. Ibid., 63.
254. Ibid., 82.
255. Ibid., 84.
256. Ibid., 93.
257. Ibid.
258. Ibid.
259. Ibid., 106.
260. Ibid., 110.
261. Hallerman, "Tredegar Iron Works," 104.
262. *C.O. v. Tredegar* Suit Files, TBR.
263. Comparative Statement of Sales of Finished Products, 1868–1872 Inclusive, *C&O v. Tredegar* Suit Files, TBR.
264. Hallerman, "Tredegar Iron Works," 113.
265. Sobel, *Panic on Wall Street*, 156.
266. Augustus J Veenendaal Jr., *Slow Train to Paradise: How Dutch Investment Helped Build American Railroads* (Stanford, CA: Stanford University Press, 1996), 111.
267. Joseph A. Schumpeter, *Business Cycles: A Theoretical, Historical, and Statistical Analysis of the Capitalist Process* (New York: McGraw-Hill Book Company, Inc., 1939), 335.
268. Sobel, *Panic on Wall Street*, 178.

269. Ibid., 192.
270. Hallerman, "Tredegar Iron Works," 126.
271. Ibid., 67.
272. Units Produced, Box Cars and Gondolas, 1872–1880, TBR.
273. Ibid.
274. J.R. Anderson to Colonel Algernon S. Buford, August 2, 1870, TBR.
275. Hallerman, "Tredegar Iron Works," 122.
276. Ibid., 119.
277. *Alexandria Gazette*, January 17–January 28, 1876; Hallerman, "Tredegar Iron Works," 118–19.
278. Tredegar Company to stockholders, July 8, 1876, TBR.
279. Richard Roberts, *Southeast Wales Industrial Ironworks Landscapes—Year 1: The Core Ironworks Areas* (Heathfield: The Glamorgan-Gwent Archaeological Trust Ltd., 2005), 66. http://www.ggat.org.uk/cadw/swi/pdfs/year_1/GGAT80%20Ironworks%20Year%201_Part1.pdf, accessed July 9, 2015.
280. Charles Wilkins, *The History of the Iron, Steel, Tinplate and Other Trades of Wales* (Merthyr Tydfil: Joseph Williams, 1903), 182.
281. Roberts, *Southeast Wales*, 66.
282. R.W. Wright, "Richmond Since the War," *Scribner's Monthly* 16 (May–October 1877), 304.
283. Foundry Sales Books, June 1876–August 1879; September 1879–December 1883, TBR.
284. Chesson, *Richmond After the War*, 47.
285. Ibid., 162.
286. Ibid., 34.
287. Offering circular, Tredegar Timber Company, Incorporated, February 6, 1957, Albemarle-Tredegar Merger, TBR.
288. Letter book, November 4, 1880–November 17, 1892, TBR.
289. *Alexandria Gazette*, April 23, 1887.
290. Sales and Shipping Records, Loadings, Railroads Freight Cars, 1892, TBR.
291. U.S. Association of Spike Manufacturers, minutes, 1885–89, TBR.
292. Reports of Spike Allotments, May 1899, U.S. Association of Spike Manufacturers, TBR.
293. James River Valley Immigration Society (Richmond, VA) Records, 1888–89, VHS.
294. Ibid.
295. *Richmond Dispatch*, June 15, 1889; Richard P. Rotewell, et al., "Industrial Notes," in *The Engineering and Mining Journal* (May 18, 1889), 461.
296. Foundry Sales Book, June 1, 1889–September 30, 1892.
297. *Poor's Manual of Railroads*, Vol. 55 (New York: Poor's Publishing Company, 1922), 1,192.
298. *Richmond Dispatch*, February 9, 1886.
299. Dabney, *Richmond*, 237.
300. Erwin H. Will, *The Past—Interesting; The Present—Intriguing; The Future—Bright: A Story of Virginia Electric and Power Company* (New York: Newcomen Society in North America, 1965), 11.

301. Geschwind, *Osterbind Family*, 43.
302. Henry Carter Osterbind/Ellen Jane Clarke, Chronological Notes, MLG.
303. F.T. Glasgow to J.R. Anderson and Archer Anderson, December 4, 1886, File: The Osterbind Connection to the Tredegar Iron Works, MLG.
304. The Tredegar Company, *Tredegar Iron Works: Manufacturers of Horse and Mule Shoes* (Richmond, VA: W.C. Hill Printing, 1913).
305. Patent no. 349,950, H.C. Osterbind, Machine for Rolling Horsehoe Blank Bars, September 28, 1886.
306. Geschwind, *Osterbind Family*, 48.
307. *Richmond Times*, September 8, 1892.
308. A.G. Osterbind, et al. to Joseph R. Anderson, December 25, 1879, Administrative Records, TBR.
309. Joseph Reid Anderson to A.G. Osterbind, et al., December 26, 1879, Administrative Records, TBR.
310. *Richmond Times*, September 10, 1892.
311. Ibid., September 9, 1892.
312. Ibid.
313. Ibid., September 11, 1892.
314. Bruce, *Virginia Iron Manufacture*, 258.

Chapter 4

315. Oliver Zunz, *Making America Corporate, 1870–1920* (Chicago: University of Chicago Press, 1990), 13, 21.
316. Ibid., 71–77.
317. Robert B. Gordon, *American Iron, 1607–1900* (Baltimore, MD: Johns Hopkins University Press, 1996), 173; Bradley Stoughton, *The Metallurgy of Iron and Steel*, 4th ed. (New York: McGraw-Hill Book Company, Inc., 1934), 38.
318. Stoughton, *Metallurgy*, 42; Gordon, *American Iron*, 223.
319. David Nasaw, *Andrew Carnegie* (New York: Penguin Press, 2006), 142.
320. Stoughton, *Metallurgy*, 46.
321. Paul F. Paskoff, ed., *Encyclopedia of American Business History and Biography—Iron and Steel in the Nineteenth Century* (New York: Facts on File, 1989), xxxv.
322. William T. Hogan, *Economic History of the Iron and Steel Industry in the United States, Volume I, Parts I and II* (Lexington, KY: Lexington Books, 1971), 92–93; United States Department of the Interior, *Report on the Manufactures of the United States at the Tenth Census, June 1, 1880, Part I: Statistics* (Washington, D.C.: Government Printing Office, 1883), 2.
323. John Chamberlain, *The Enterprising Americans: A Business History of the United States* (New York: Harper & Row, 1963), 144.
324. Department of the Interior, *Report on Manufacturing Industries of the United States at the Eleventh Census: 1890, Part III: Selected Industries* (Washington, D.C.: Government Printing Office, 1895), 412.
325. Stephen H. Cutliffe, "Cambria Iron Company," in *Encyclopedia of American Business History and Biography—The Iron and Steel Industry in the Nineteenth Century*,

edited by Paul F. Paskoff (New York: Facts on File, 1989), 41; Kenenth Warren, *Bethlehem Steel: Builder and Arsenal of America* (Pittsburgh: University of Pittsburgh Press, 2008), 22.
326. Nasaw, *Andrew Carnegie*, 141.
327. William Manchester, *The Arms of Krupp: 1587–1968* (Boston, MA: Little, Brown and Company, 1968), 118.
328. Hogan, *Economic History*, 37.
329. Tredegar Minute Book, 1867–1899, TBR.
330. Notice to the Bondholders of 4 Percent Mortgage Bonds of the Tredegar Company, May 31, 1898, TBR.
331. Paul F. Paskoff, "Open Hearth Process," in *Encyclopedia of American Business History and Biography—Iron and Steel in the Nineteenth Century*, edited by Paul F. Paskoff (New York: Facts on File, 1989), 266.
332. Estate of Edward R. Archer, private notebook, 1902–1906, TBR, 14.
333. Ibid., 19, 38, 88.
334. Raber, Malone and Gordon, *Historical and Archaeological Assessment*, 113–16.
335. *Richmond Times-Dispatch*, January 30, 1907.
336. Archer notebook, 50–68; Raber, Malone and Gordon, *Historical and Archaeological Assessment*, 113.
337. Tredegar Foundry, Rolling Mill and Horseshoe Mill Sales Books, 1890–1900, TBR
338. Peter J. Rachleff, *Black Labor in the South: Richmond, Virginia, 1865–1890* (Philadelphia: Temple University Press, 1984), 20.
339. Ibid., 101, 106.
340. George Talmage Starnes and John Edwin Hamm, *Some Phases of Labor Relations in Virginia* (New York: D. Appleton-Century Company, 1934), 85.
341. Ibid., 102–103.
342. Nathan Vernon Madison, "Joseph P. Devine (d. 1890)," *Dictionary of Virginia Biography*, Library of Virginia (1998–), http://www.lva.virginia.gov/public/dvb/bio.asp?b=Devine_Joseph_P, accessed May 1, 2015.
343. *The Machinist* 41, no. 1 (May 1986); "History of the IAM," http://www.goiam.org/index.php/headquarters/history-of-the-iam, accessed February 23, 2014.
344. *Richmond Dispatch*, September 20, 1887; ibid., September 22, 1887; *Alexandria Gazette*, August 26, 1905.
345. A.A. Jr. to August Krengel, April 30, 1925; J.R.J. Anderson to William Jonson, February 16, 1927, TBR; A.A. to Ellen Osterbind, August 5, 1914, MLG.
346. Statement of Mr. Charles E. Wade to James Wade Sr., October 27, 1925, Administrative Records, TBR.
347. A.A. Jr. to August Krengel, April 30, 1925, special letter book, 1918–44, TBR.
348. Archer notebook, 106.
349. Elwood Harris to Roy E. Johnson, June 7, 1985; Elwood O. Harris to Roy E. Johnson, December 18, 1986, Elwood and Harry Harris Collection, 1974–1993, VM.
350. Elwood Harris to Roy E. Johnson, June 7, 1985, VM.
351. *Richmond Times-Dispatch*, April 8, 1909.
352. Geschwind, *Osterbind Family*, 46.

353. Archer notebook, 140.
354. F.T. Glasgow to H.C. Osterbind, June 13, 1893, File: Osterbind Connection to the Tredegar Iron Works, MLG.
355. Victor J. Evans & Co. to H.C. Osterbind, March 13, 1912; Victor J. Evans & Co. to H.C. Osterbind, March 4, 1913, File: Osterbind Connection to the Tredegar Iron Works, MLG.
356. Mary Mason Anderson to Ellen Osterbind, January 1, 1912, Ibid.
357. Archer Anderson to H.C. Osterbind, January 11, 1900; Archer Anderson to H.C. Osterbind, April 29, 1902; Archer Anderson to H.C. Osterbind, January 8, 1910, File: H.C. Osterbind/ Ellen Jane Clarke, MLG.
358. H.C. Osterbind's diary, February 5–April 9, 1904, File: Osterbind Connection to the Tredegar Iron Works, MLG.
359. Geschwind, *Osterbind Family*, 52.
360. Archer Anderson to Ellen Osterbind, August 5, 1914, File: Osterbind Connection to the Tredegar Iron Works, MLG.
361. Production and Labor Records, Payroll Ledger, 1910–11, TBR.
362. Geschwind, *Osterbind Family*, 31.
363. Ibid.; Production and Labor Records, Payroll Ledger, July 1884–December 1887, TBR.
364. Production and Labor Records, Payroll Ledger, 1910–11, TBR.
365. *Richmond News Leader*, June 29, 1953.
366. Production and Labor Records, Payroll Ledger, 1918, TBR.
367. Geschwind, *Osterbind Family*, 46.
368. Carter Clarke Osterbind Notes, MLG.
369. Ibid.
370. Anton Guenther Osterbind Notes, MLG.
371. H.A. Gillis to H.C. Osterbind, August 18, 1905, A.G. Osterbind Notes, MLG.
372. *St. Luke's Herald*, November 20, 1915.
373. Joicey Haw Lindsay, "Henrico County, Virginia, Naturalizations, 1844–1858," *Magazine of Virginia Genealogy* 22, no. 4 (November 1984): 14; *Times Dispatch*, March 24, 1910.
374. *Times Dispatch*, March 24, 1910.
375. Angus Sinclair, et al., *Railway and Locomotive Engineering* 11 (November 1898): 512; P.M. Arthur, et al., *Brotherhood of Locomotive Engineer's Monthly Journal* 22 (December 1888), 1,099.
376. Angus Sinclair, et al., *Railway and Locomotive Engineering: A Practical Journal of Motive Power, Rolling Stock and Appliances* 25 (April 1912), 148.
377. E. Renee Ingram and Charles W. White Sr., *Buckingham County* (Charleston, SC: Arcadia Publishing, 2005), 39; Richmond Planet, February 16, 1895.
378. Registers of Signatures of Depositors in Branches of the Freedman's Savings and Trust Company, 1865–1874, Washington, D.C.: National Archives and Records Administration, Micropublication M816, 27 rolls; Virginia, Deaths, 1912–2014, Virginia Department of Health, Richmond, Virginia.
379. Don Browne, interview with author, August 5, 2015; *Richmond Planet*, February, 16, 1895; Ingram and White Sr., *Buckingham County*, 39.

380. War Department Contracts, 1907–9; 1910–12; 1913–15, TBR.
381. *Richmond Times-Dispatch*, November 7, 1915.
382. War Department Contracts, 1913–1915, TBR.
383. *Richmond Times Dispatch*, October 4, 1914.
384. Ibid., October 20, 1915.
385. *Greensboro Daily Records*, October 22, 1915.
386. John Harris, *Bloodless Victories: The Rise and Fall of the Open Shop in the Philadelphia Metal Trades, 1890–1940* (New York: Cambridge University Press, 2000), 205; L.W. Boody, et al., *Philadelphia in the World War, 1914–1919* (Philadelphia: Philadelphia War History Committee, 1922), 231.
387. War Department Contracts, 1915–1917, TBR.
388. K. Austin Kerr, "Decision for Federal Control: Wilson, McAdoo, and the Railroads, 1917," *Journal of American History* 54, no. 3 (December 1967), 550–60.
389. Archer Anderson to Office of the Chief of Ordnance, December 18, 1917, War Department Contracts, 1915–1917, TBR.
390. National Industrial Conference Board, Railroad Wages and Working Rules—Research Report Number 46—February, 1922 (New York: Century Company, 1922), 13–14.
391. A.A. Jr. to the Shop Committee, May 20, 1918, War Department Contracts, 1918–1919, TBR.
392. Thomas Savage to A.L. Clary, August 21, 1918, War Department Contracts, 1915–1917, TBR.
393. Captain C.C. Bloch to Tredegar, October 1919, War Department Contracts, 1915–1917, TBR.
394. St. George Mason Anderson to Ordnance Department, October 8, 1918, War Department Contracts, 1915–1917, TBR.
395. Description of the Tredegar Property, 1922, Administrative Records, TBR.
396. Elwood Harris to Roy E. Johnson, June 7, 1985, VM.
397. Jennings C. Wise, "The Board of Contract Adjustment of the War Department," *Virginia Law Review* 6, no. 3 (December 1919): 182–95.
398. George W. Baer, *One Hundred Years of Sea Power: The U.S. Navy, 1890–1990* (Stanford, CA: Stanford University Press, 1993), 59–60.
399. War Department contracts, 1918–19, TBR.
400. Income tax returns, TBR.
401. Ibid.
402. Ibid.

Chapter 5

403. *Richmond Times-Dispatch*, January 5, 1918.
404. Andrew D. Christian to E.H. Trigg, February 4, 1942, Administrative Records, Stock Correspondences, TBR.
405. Pete Martin, "Century Plant," *Saturday Evening Post*, July 24, 1943.
406. *Richmond Times-Dispatch*, January 14, 1918; Thomas McAdory Owen and Marie Bankhead Owen, *History of Alabama and Dictionary of Alabama Biography*,

Notes to Pages 133–146

Vol. 3 (Chicago: S.J. Clarke Publishing Company, 1921), 821; J.R. Anderson to Walter D. Leake, Esq., November 8, 1871, Anderson Family Papers, TBR.
407. *Richmond Times-Dispatch*, March 14, 1918; Tredegar Minutes Book, 1867–99, TBR.
408. Edward Archer's diary, VHS; Martin, "Century Plant," 88.
409. Tredegar Co. to Mrs. Frederick B. McBride, February 28, 1936, TBR.
410. *Moody's Manual of Railroads and Corporations Securities*, Vol. 2 (New York: Poor's Publishing Company, 1922), 505.
411. *Richmond Times-Dispatch*, September 4, 1920.
412. Description of Tredegar Property, 1922, Administrative Records, TBR.
413. Statement of Water Wheels and Their Estimated Power, May 2, 1920, TBR.
414. *Richmond Times-Dispatch*, April 25, 1926.
415. St. G.M. Anderson to Willard Brown, July 30, 1919, TBR.
416. St. G.M. Anderson to R.B. Schenck, September 19, 1919, TBR.
417. Archer Anderson Jr. to Julian Kennedy, May 3, 1921, TBR.
418. Humphreys & Glasgow, Ltd., to A.A. Jr., March 28, 1924; J.R. Cain to A.A. Jr., November 30, 1925, TBR.
419. Price, Waterhouse & Co. to Tredegar Co., April 5, 1924; A.A. Jr. to Price, Waterhouse & Co., May 29, 1924; A.A. Jr. to John A. Selph Jr., November 1, 1924, TBR.
420. St. G.M. Anderson to C.T. Bryant, December 23, 1920; St. G.M. Anderson to John J. Cosby Jr., December 23, 1920; A.A. Jr. to A.J. Beatty, July 12, 1921; St. G.M. Anderson to Tredegar (notice), July 18, 1921; St. G.M. Anderson to Tredegar (notice), September 21, 1921, TBR.
421. Description of Tredegar Property, 1922, TBR.
422. Kevin Hillstrom, "Iron and Steel in the Modern Era," in Kevin Hillstrom and Laurie Collier Hillstrom, eds., *Industrial Revolution in America: Iron and Steel* (Santa Barbara. CA: ABC-CLIO, 2005), 273.
423. Income tax returns, TBR; Report of Stockholders Committee, July 14, 1950, TBR.
424. Sales of Finished Products, *C&O v. Tredegar* Suit Papers, TBR.
425. Reports on Fire at Horseshoe Department, April 24, 1926, TBR.
426. *Richmond Times Dispatch*, February 7, 1927; September 10, 1931; December 28, 1933; July 28, 1934; January 22, 1935; War Department Contracts, TBR.
427. Virginia Trust Company to Archer Anderson Jr., October 25, 1932, TBR.
428. List of Tredegar Stockholders Between September 21 and November 1, 1932, TBR.
429. A.A. Jr. to Salaried Employees (notice), January 14, 1933, TBR.
430. Hobbs, *Canal on the James*, 49.
431. Raber, Malone and Gordon, *Historical and Archaeological Assessment*, 23, 44; Archer Anderson Jr. to commissioner of IRS, March 3, 1919, TBR.
432. "Consulting Engineers' News," *Steam* 25, no. 4 (April 1920), 118.
433. Raber, Malone and Gordon, *Historical and Archaeological Assessment*, 46.
434. Tredegar to Mr. Leon M. Fuquay, Federal Power Commission, Washington D.C., October 31, 1938; Paul Miller to Federal Power Commission, Atlanta, July 31, 1939, TBR.
435. Hillstrom, "Iron and Steel in the Modern Era," 275.

436. War Department Contracts, 1940, TBR; Ellett, "Report," 20.
437. Andrew D. Christian to E.H. Trigg, February 4, 1942, TBR.
438. Report of Stockholders Committee, July 14, 1950, TBR.
439. A.I. Findley, et al., "Personal," *Iron Age* 110 (November 23, 1922), 1395; A.O. Backert, *ABC of Iron and Steel*, Vol. 2, Part 4 (Cleveland: Penton Publishing Co., 1917), 280.
440. Miller to Admiral Bloch, February 6, 1943, Administrative Records, TBR.
441. Miller to Navy Board for Production Awards, April 18, 1945, TBR.
442. Martin, "Century Plant," 90.
443. Ibid., 26.
444. Irwin A. Goodman to Miller, June 13, 1945, TBR.
445. Labor Agreement between the Tredegar Company and Federal Labor Union #23004, April 4, 1944, WHS.
446. William Green to J.W. Gray, April 24, 1945. WHS.
447. *Richmond News Leader*, August 14, 1957.
448. Ibid., September 6, 1944.
449. Ibid., August 14, 1957; Elwood Harris to R.E. Johnson, December 18, 1986, VM.
450. *Richmond Times-Dispatch*, February 21, 1942.
451. Miller to Stockholders, March 10, 1944; Renewal of Nomination for Army-Navy Production Awards, 1944, Administrative Records, TBR.
452. Annual Report to Stockholders for the Year Ended December 31, 1947, TBR.
453. Income tax returns, TBR.
454. Ibid.
455. *Richmond Times-Dispatch*, June 20, 1946; Paul J. Smith to William Green, May 2, 1949, WHS.
456. Report of Stockholders Committee, July 14, 1950, TBR.
457. William Bradford Williams, *Munitions Manufacture in the Philadelphia Ordnance District* (Philadelphia: A. Pomerantz & Company, 1921), 526.
458. List of Stockholders of the Tredegar Company, 1957, Albemarle/Tredegar Merger, TBR; R.W. Krise to Paul E. Miller, 28 May 1948, TBR.
459. E.H. Trigg to Stockholders, November 29, 1949, TBR.
460. Charles Miller, interview with author, October 26, 2014.
461. Annual Report to Stockholders for the Year Ended December 31, 1947, TBR.
462. *Richmond Times-Dispatch*, November 5, 1951; Charles Miller, interview with author, October 26, 2014.
463. Annual Report to Stockholders for the Year Ended December 31, 1950, TBR.
464. R.E. Johnson, "The Tredegar Iron Works," 58.
465. Report of Stockholders Committee, July 14, 1950, TBR.
466. Charles Miller, interview with author, October 26, 2014.
467. Tax returns, TBR.
468. Chronological Notes, Henry Carter Osterbind/ Ellen Jane Clarke, MLG.
469. William F. Haase Papers, MLG; *Richmond Times Dispatch*, December 10, 1933; May 11, 1958.

470. Lucille Haase to Margaret Looper, October 11, 1940, William F. Haase Papers, "Aw Gee, Honey," Lucille W. Haase, unpublished memoir; Lucille Haase to Margaret Looper, September 7, 1945, MLG.
471. *Richmond News Leader*, June 29, 1953.
472. Martin, "Century Plant," 92.
473. Work Injuries Cooperative Survey, United States Department of Labor, Bureau of Labor Statistics, 1955, TBR.
474. Annual Report to Stockholders, for the Year Ended December 31, 1955, Albemarle-Tredegar Merger, TBR.
475. R.W. Krise to Herbert J Biel, February 23, 1953, TBR.
476. Summary of Plan of Merger, Claiborne Papers, 1803–1954, VHS.
477. Income tax returns, TBR.
478. Floyd Dewey Gottwald, *Albemarle: From Pines to Packaging—75 Years of Papermaking Progress, 1887–1962: An Address at Richmond to Newcomen Society in North America* (New York: Newcomen Society in North America, 1962), 8.
479. Lockwood Trade Journal Co., Inc., *1690–1940: 250 Years of Papermaking in America* (New York: Lockwood Trade Journal Co., Inc., 1940), 80.
480. Raymond W. Krise note from Meeting of Tredegar Stockholders, January 31, 1957, Albemarle-Tredegar Merger Correspondence, 1955–1957, TBR.
481. Notice to Stockholders of Albemarle Paper Manufacturing Corporation, January 4, 1957, Albemarle-Tredegar Merger Correspondence, 1955–1957, TBR.
482. Analytical Report, Dun & Bradford, Inc., February 4, 1957, Albemarle-Tredegar, TBR.
483. Francis B. Rapp to Tredegar, January 31, 1957, ibid.
484. Board of Directors Meeting Minutes, December 19, 1956; Correspondence, Alex W. Neal to Tredegar Company, November 7, 1956, ibid.
485. Meeting Minutes, December 29, 1956, ibid.
486. Ibid., December 19, 1956.
487. Ibid., February 19, 1957.

Epilogue

488. Department Shutdowns, Tredegar and Albemarle Merger, TBR.
489. Roy E. Johnson to Edward Harris, May 8, 1985, Elwood and Harry Harris Collection, 1974–93, VM; Bruce Gottwald, interview with author, January 8, 2015.
490. Johnson, "Tredegar Iron Works of Richmond, Virginia," 58.
491. Frank Williams Jr. to F.D. Gottwald Jr., March 15, 1957, Tredegar and Albemarle Merger, TBR.
492. Ibid.
493. Frank Williams Jr. to Stockholders, May 5, 1960, Claiborne Papers, 1803–1954, VHS.
494. Ibid.
495. R.E. Johnson to Edward Harris, July 22, 1985, VM.
496. Ibid.
497. Ibid.

498. R.E. Johnson, "Tredegar Iron Works of Richmond, Virginia," 59.
499. R.E. Johnson to Calder Loth, November 12, 1985; Johnson to Elwood Harris, May 14, 1986, VM.
500. James Oliver Horton and Lois E. Horton, eds., *Slavery and Public History: The Tough Stuff of American Memory* (New York: New Press, 2006), 158; Harry Kollatz Jr., "Valentine 2.1," *Richmond Magazine*, June 19, 2012, http://richmondmagazine.com/news/valentine-2-1-06-19-2012 (accessed July 1, 2015).

INDEX

A

Accokeek Furnace 26
Albemarle Paper Manufacturing
     Company 156, 157, 158, 159,
     161, 163, 180, 186, 187
American Federation of Labor (AFL)
     114, 150
Anderson, Archer 48, 59, 65, 69, 83,
     104, 110, 111, 119, 124, 126,
     131, 132, 135, 172, 176, 177,
     181, 183, 184, 185
  and steelmaking 110
  as president of Tredegar 104
  death 131
  education 65
  hired at Tredegar 65
  youth 65
Anderson, Archer, Jr. 102, 132, 133,
     134, 135, 138, 139, 143, 146, 147
  and "History of Tredegar" 137
  death 147
  youth 132
Anderson, Joseph Reid 15, 16, 17, 37,
     38, 40, 44, 48, 65, 68, 78, 86,
     93, 100, 108, 117, 126, 132,
     133, 174, 175, 179, 181

  as chairman of Association of Spike
       Manufacturers 95
  as receiver 92
  death 100
  education 38, 39, 45
  hired by Tredegar 38
  leases Tredegar 42
  military service in Civil War 68
  president of the Tredegar Company
       83
  purchases Tredegar 45
Archer, Dr. Robert 38, 62, 65, 83, 109,
     111, 133, 173
Archer, Edward 83, 133, 185
Armory Iron Company 44, 55, 173

B

Bellona Foundry 27, 71
Bessemer process 17, 85, 93, 106, 107,
     108, 109, 110, 139
Bethlehem Steel 108, 123, 124, 125,
     128, 138, 139, 141, 182
Black Heth Mines 36
Botetourt County 13, 14, 34, 37, 38,
     39, 43, 67, 71, 83, 94, 159, 162,
     170, 173, 177

Index

Brackens, William 70, 71
Brown's Island 76, 128, 157
Bryden Horse Shoe Works 148
Byrd family 30, 173, 178

C

Chesapeake and Ohio Railroad 144
   and lawsuit against Tredegar 143
Colburn, Zerah 61
CSS *Virginia*/USS *Merrimack* 72, 75, 115

D

David Ross. *See* Oxford Iron Works
Davies, Rhys 9, 10, 11, 24, 25, 32, 33, 34, 36, 57, 86, 157, 169
Davis, Jefferson 43, 69, 78, 165, 178
Deane, Francis Brown 12, 27, 28, 30, 32, 33, 34, 36, 37, 38, 41, 42, 43, 57, 104, 145, 157, 171, 172
Deane, Morton 121, 123
Delaney, Alexander 121, 122
Delaney, Chester Alexander 59, 122
Delaney, Matthew 23, 57, 58, 59, 121, 122, 135, 175
DuPont Chemical Company 105, 128

E

Edgar Thomson Steel Works 106
Ethyl. *See* Albemarle Paper Manufacturing Company
evacuation, of Richmond 78, 79, 111

F

Falling Creek 25, 170
Frankford Arsenal 125

G

Gallego Mills 27, 31
General Motors 156
Glasgow, Francis 58, 84, 100, 104, 117, 132, 135, 181, 183, 185

H

Harvie, John 30, 31, 32, 144, 171
Hecla Iron Works 49
Hunter, James 25, 36, 57

I

industrial slavery 52, 53, 54, 55, 56, 102
iron plantations 53

J

James River and Kanawha Canal 36, 37, 42, 48, 52, 75, 81, 88, 117, 143, 153, 157, 171, 173
James River Company. *See* James River and Kanawha Canal
Jamestown 25
J.R. Anderson & Co. 62

K

Krise, Raymond 153, 155, 156, 159, 186, 187
   past experience, and president of Tredegar 153
Krupp Gusstahlfabrik 108

L

Lincoln, Abraham 79, 80, 178

M

Merthyr Tydfill 25
Miller, Paul 147, 148, 149, 151, 152, 153, 154, 155, 185, 186
   appointed president of Tredegar 147
   resignation 152
Mills, Nicholas 41, 42

N

Neabsco Iron Works 53, 171, 175

O

Old Dominion Iron and Nail Works 98, 125

INDEX

open-hearth process 107, 108, 110, 139
ordnance, at Tredegar 16, 27, 34, 39, 42, 43, 54, 66, 70, 71, 72, 79, 123, 124, 125, 128, 129, 142, 147, 149, 151, 152, 153, 154, 155, 156, 159, 173, 184
Osterbind, Anton 52, 59, 60, 74, 99, 101, 102, 116, 118, 119, 120, 176, 183
Osterbind, Carter Clarke 100, 120, 154, 183
Osterbind, Henry Carter 99, 100, 101, 109, 113, 118, 119, 120, 170, 172, 174, 176, 181, 186
Oxford Iron Works 26, 53, 54, 175

P

Panic of 1873 90
pig iron 21, 22, 23, 26, 30, 34, 37, 39, 43, 51, 53, 55, 67, 91, 106, 107, 135, 146
puddling
  1847 puddler's strike at Tredegar 55
  end of puddling at Tredegar 94
  origins 22

Q

Quivers, Emmanuel 55

R

R. Archer & Company 44, 45
receivership (Tredegar) 92, 93, 97, 109, 110, 118
Richmond and Alleghany Railroad. *See* Chesapeake and Ohio Railroad
Richmond Arsenal 67, 76, 79
Richmond Coal Basin 28, 171
Richmond Locomotive and Machine Works 99, 122
Rutherfoord, Thomas 31, 34, 172

S

Saugus Iron Works 26
Sirhowy Iron Works 22

Sirhowy River 21, 25
Souther, John 61
strikes, at Tredegar 54, 57, 70, 87, 102, 113, 127, 150
submarines (built at Tredegar) 73

T

Tanner & Delaney Engine Company. *See* Richmond Locomotive and Machine Works
Tayloe family. *See* Neabsco Iron Works
Tredegar Battalion 67, 70, 78, 79, 122
Tredegar Forge and Rolling Mill 33
Tredegar Free School 48
Tredegar Iron and Coal Company (Wales) 92, 93
Tredegar Iron Works
  and the Great Depression 141
  during the Civil War 67
  during World War I 123
  during World War II 146
  founded 32
  New York office 87
  purchase, and closure 158
  reorganized as the Tredegar Company 83
  slavery at Tredegar 53
  united as J.R. Anderson & Co. 60
Tredegar Ironworks (Wales) 19, 23, 24, 34, 92
turbines, water 45, 71, 115, 135, 150

V

Virginia Foundry Company 32, 33, 42, 172
Virginia Manufactory of Arms 27, 44, 48, 62, 67, 70, 161

W

Wilson, Woodrow 126

ABOUT THE AUTHOR

Nathan Vernon Madison is a historian and author and a graduate of the University of Mary Washington (BA) and Virginia Commonwealth University (MA). This book being his first major work of local and industrial history, he also writes regarding the history of American popular culture. Two of his works, *Anti-Foreign Imagery in American Pulps and Comics, 1920–1960* (McFarland, 2013) and *Comics Through Time: A History of Icons, Idols, and Ideas* (ABC-CLIO/Greenwood Press, 2014, contributor), have been nominated for Will Eisner Comic Industry Awards. His other works include contributions to *The Dictionary of Virginia Biographies* and *Blood'n'Thunder* magazine. He also serves on the Editorial Board of the *Pulp Magazines Project*, a peer-reviewed, academic resource and database dedicated to the popular fiction of the late nineteenth and early twentieth centuries.

www.ingramcontent.com/pod-product-compliance
Lightning Source LLC
Chambersburg PA
CBHW042142160426
43201CB00022B/2373